NEW DIRECTIONS
IN PASTORAL CARE

NEW DIRECTIONS IN PASTORAL CARE

Edited by
Peter Lang and Michael Marland

Basil Blackwell
in association with the
National Association for Pastoral Care in Education
and the Economic and Social Research Council

© 1985 National Association for Pastoral Care in Education

First published 1985
Reprinted 1986

Published by
Basil Blackwell Limited
108 Cowley Road
Oxford OX4 3JF
England

British Library Cataloguing in Publication Data
New directions in pastoral care.
   1. Personnel service in education——Great Britain
   I. Lang, Peter   II. Marland, Michael
   III. National Association for Pastoral Care in Education
   371.4'0941   LB1027.5

   ISBN 0 631 14149 9
   ISBN 0 631 14151 0 Pbk

Typeset in 10/12pt Linotype Sabon
by Katerprint Co. Ltd, Oxford
Printed in Great Britain

Contents

Preface

The contents of this book have a range of interrelated origins. The introduction and conclusion have been written by Peter Lang. A number of papers are revised versions of papers first delivered at a research seminar, 'The future research needs of pastoral care', organised by NAPCE and Warwick University's Education Department. The seminar was sponsored by the Economic and Social Research Council, and held at Warwick University in February 1984. An edited version of the discussions that developed from some of these papers will be found in the appendix. The seminar was attended by some forty academic and other educational researchers, LEA representatives and teachers who were members of the NAPCE National Committee (see List of Participants, p. 231). This group as a result of considerable and detailed discussion produced a set of suggestions which, while not representing any sort of agreed consensus nor imperative recommendations, does represent the highly productive outcome of the bringing together of a group containing a wide range of expertise, perspectives and differing interests in the general area of pastoral care. These suggestions are included in a concluding section (p. 199) and are made above the editors' signatures.

There are some papers included here which were presented at the seminar which lack of time prevented being fully discussed. Finally there are a number of papers from those who had been invited to the seminar but were unable to attend. The papers in this book cover many of the areas which would be seen as central to any notion of pastoral care. They also offer a breadth of coverage which is in itself unique in that it is the first time that such a broad range of topics relating to pastoral care has been considered by such a wide group of participants from a research and analysis-based focus. The key thing uniting the contributors to this book is their acknowledgement that pastoral care has reached the stage where thought must be given to its future and that such thought must be based on a rigorous and systematic approach underpinned where appropriate by research and not, as so often in the past, on amorphous good intentions.

Acknowledgements

To NAPCE, without its support it is unlikely that the seminar would have taken place or this book published. All royalties from this book will be paid into NAPCE national funds.

To the ESRC which provided the financial support needed to run the seminar.

To Warwick University Institute of Education which also gave financial support.

To Rick Rogers who by acting as a rapporteur recording and writing up data from the seminar, and in assisting with the preparation of this book has given invaluable assistance.

Introduction

Peter Lang

New directions

The phrase 'New directions' included in the title of a book can often be very misleading. The directions can turn out to be along already well-worn paths, or lead to destinations only appearing worthwhile from the author's particular idiosyncratic perspective. However, in the case of this book the inclusion of 'New directions' in the title is entirely justified. Firstly, the directions are indeed 'new', and though more in terms of 'how to set off' than 'where to arrive', they represent the ideas of a range of experts in the field rather than of a single individual. What the book says is seen by this group of experts as of considerable significance. It is on these grounds that the editors have selected this title.

In terms of those who have written papers for it, those who attended the Warwick seminar (see List of Contributors, p. 231), and whose discussion has also contributed to the text, this book represents the widest range of individuals whose views, ideas and expertise have so far been brought together under the general title of pastoral care.

There are several dimensions to the notion of 'wide-ranging' in this case. One dimension was that of *specialist* interest. There were those whose interest is with the practice of pastoral care in schools. There were also those whose main interest is in a particular aspect of pastoral care or something closely related to it — multi-cultural issues, gender, health education, study skills, parental involvement and so on.

A second dimension was in terms of *perspective*. Here a key division was between those who are mainly concerned with a critical perspective on pastoral care seeking the formulation of a critique, and those whose main concern is with technique and practice, looking to ensure that the quality of the actual pastoral care undertaken is 'improved'. Equally, differences in perspectives can be related to the work situation of those involved. Those working in schools were often concerned with the specific problems of pastoral care within individual school settings, LEA advisers on the other hand brought a perspective which reflected the problems of working across a number of schools and in different regions of the country. Those involved in teacher education and national training projects contributed a particular perspective as did those whose specific concern was research. For example, the trainers and educators focussed on the problems of developing courses in an area which was so ill-defined, and often undervalued by their colleagues. They were also interested in considering how the effectiveness of different styles and strategies of training might be established. One point the researchers felt needed particular attention was the development of specific and clearly articulated research methodologies for working in the area.

The final dimension, closely allied to the previous two, was that of *special expertise* – in some cases this related to the problems of practice and administration and in others to a specific aspect such as health education or careers. Some of those involved brought a particular expertise in terms of training. Perhaps most importantly a considerable number of those involved had expertise in the area of educational research.

The second justification for the title is that the major approach promoted in this book, and which is one of its key unifying themes, is completely new in conception. This new approach stresses the need for increased rigour, analysis and systematic evaluation in relation to the understanding and development of pastoral care. A central argument is that these objectives can only be achieved through a significant increase in the amount of research undertaken. It is further argued that such approaches must be systematically applied to all facets of pastoral care not simply to those of special interest or fashionable at any particular moment in time. *Thus what this book proposes is a situation where rigour, analysis, systematic evaluation and research are understood as a central part of pastoral care and its process, not just as an occasional trimming. Such a proposal is certainly new.*

The third justification is that many of the ideas put forward, the perspectives that are used and the questions which are raised in the various papers are original and so take those involved in the field in new directions.

A final and most important point is that the book includes an attempt to review systematically the development of research into pastoral care to date. This is something that has never been attempted before and should be seen as a major conceptual breakthrough. Peter Ribbins and Ron Best's paper, which opens the book, represents an impressive and systematic review of research undertaken up to the present time and offers an approach to categorising and classifying this work. This is in itself an important contribution in terms of our perceptions of the new directions to be taken. Their paper also provides the first systematic and firm basis which researchers both in and out of schools can use to contextualise and orientate their own work.

Having discussed one part of our title at length it is now appropriate to comment briefly on the remaining element: the use of the term 'pastoral care'. The use of this term cannot be claimed to give any tight or clear conception of exactly what the book will be about, and recently the term has been regularly criticised at a number of levels both in the literature, for example, the papers by Dooley and Hughes in *Perspectives on Pastoral Care* (Best, R., Jarvis, C., Ribbins, P.), and in practice. For example in 1983 the national committee of NAPCE received a proposal from their Northamptonshire and Leicestershire branch that the words 'pastoral care' should be removed from the association's title, as they felt it to be confusing, misleading and inappropriate. Indeed there have been tentative proposals for some alternative usages – 'the welfare curriculum' is one suggestion and another current favourite is 'the affective curriculum'. However, the editors, while accepting these points and noting that there are problems about the usage, also recognise that the use of any other term could be even more confusing. The term 'pastoral care', however imprecise and weak an analytic concept, is at least a participant's concept – in that it does map for most teachers the area within which their work will lie. Equally, as used in the title of this book the term will arouse expectations in most teachers which will be broadly in line with the actual content. No other term could achieve this.

The current situation

In presenting these new directions it is not the intention of the contributors to this book to dismiss pastoral care as it currently is. Lang (1983a) has already made the distinction between the present literature of pastoral care in terms of technique and critique. Both areas have made a considerable contribution to the development of pastoral care. The major work of Best, Jarvis and Ribbins (1977, 1980, 1983), Lang (1977, 1980, 1982) and Williamson (1980) has laid the foundations of a critique of pastoral care – raising questions about its origins and the way it functions. The critique draws particular attention to the existence of a 'conventional wisdom' (Best, Jarvis and Ribbins 1977), 'official meanings' (Lang 1982) which conflict with the 'actual views of teachers', 'unofficial meanings' and the practice of pastoral care – also highlighting the hidden curriculum of much pastoral care and the related tension between the 'official meanings' of care, 'semi-official meanings' of discipline and administration, and the 'unofficial meanings' of containment and pastoralisation (Williamson 1980). For a full description of these different levels of meanings see Lang 1982; 1983b. The literature of technique, generally approaching the nature and practice of pastoral care as something quite unproblematic, has undoubtedly contributed a great deal to the development of pastoral care in terms of its basic practice. Writers such as Marland (1974), Blackburn (1975, 1983), Button (1981), Baldwin and Wells (1979–1981), and Hamblin (1978, 1981a, b) have put forward a range of strategies, programmes, approaches and techniques which have made a valuable contribution to the way teachers practice pastoral care.

At a practical level there have been a number of significant changes in the last few years in relation to pastoral care. First, as Lang's research reported in this book suggests, there have been important changes in approaches and attitudes connected with pastoral care even within its traditional form. By 'traditional' is meant schools whose thinking about pastoral care goes no further than setting up a house or year structure with its related house or year head and tutorial roles. Pupils' responses over the last few years indicate the development generally of a more caring and sensitive attitude among an increasing number of the teachers with pastoral roles in systems of the type described above. Second, the development and spread of active tutorial work and its related training programme to many parts of Britain is of major significance to pastoral care (Baldwin and Wells 1979–1981).

Finally, the development of the National Association of Pastoral Care in Education (NAPCE) from an idea put forward by Michael Marland to a small group of interested individuals meeting at Warwick University in the early months of 1982, to an association of over 2000 members with a well-established journal by the summer of 1984, is not only a major and unique development but one that has considerable implications for the future. NAPCE has provided a vehicle for the interest, enthusiasm and commitment of hundreds of teachers throughout the country who are involved in or simply interested in pastoral care. It has also provided a voice for some of their frustrations, and has indeed begun to investigate some of the inadequacies of the current situation. (See Best and Maher's report *ibid* on the NAPCE pilot training survey.)

However new a book is, it must be clear about the position it starts from. This volume endeavours to do rather more than that. It takes the view that problems, contradictions and inadequacies must be learnt from, and where there are firm foundations they should be built on. A book concerned with where we are going must attend to, and attach the greatest importance to, where we have been. This point is of particular significance to the area of pastoral care whose origins and development has been so characterised by problems and contradictions, many of which can be found reflected in current practice.

Who is this book for?

The editors hope that this book will be of interest to anyone involved in education, parents as well as teachers, and indeed any enquiring reader wishing to extend their general knowledge in the educational field. However it would be misleading to suggest that the book is not presented in the hope that it will be of value to a number of particular groups involved in education. In this sense this book is directed to those with an interest in and concern for pastoral care. It is directed to teachers, students and trainers, and also to all those involved in a practical way with pastoral care both in and out of school. It has something to say to LEAs and their advisers, and to HMI and academics with a general interest in education. It also has much to say to those involved in policy making at every level, and to all those involved in educational research.

The main intention is to promote thought, discussion and action. The book is prescriptive in that it stresses the need for rigour, analysis, systematic evaluation and research, and seeks to promote a higher level of debate than has previously been common. Also it argues that it is essential for all these factors to be considered in future. Nevertheless, the book's aim is to stimulate rather than legislate; to start people off in certain directions, not to specify in detail their destinations.

Rigour, analysis, systematic evaluation and research

The approach proposed by this book, which should also be seen as its central theme and one that contributes to the coherence of its contents, is the need for the greater application of rigour, analysis, and systematic evaluation through research to the area of pastoral care. How should these concepts be understood in relation to the book's contents?

Rigour

The essential quality of rigour is tough mindedness in relation to work undertaken: the insistence on spelling out everything, an insistence on clarification, and the elimination of ambivalence. Things must be thought through in detail, criticism actively sought, and a detached critical view of the work taken. Basically rigour means not letting oneself off the hook.

Analysis

The Oxford Shorter Dictionary defines analysis as 'The resolution of something complex into its simple elements'. This is in essence what this book means by analysis. It is to seek for clarity as to the total composition of any situation; to endeavour to uncover the underlying reasons for things; to distinguish patterns; to ask whether material gained is reliable and valid. In the editors' view it is not a particular style of analysis which is crucial, but rather the insistence on an approach that involves analysis.

Systematic evaluation

In the case of evaluation, the use of the term systematic implies that it will be clearly established why a particular approach is seen as appropriate, and that the approach adopted will be likely to reveal limitations as well as strengths.

Research

Lawrence Stenhouse has described research as 'systematic study that is subsequently made public' and this definition does encapsulate what the editors of this book see as research's essential characteristic. Research is not so much about the adherence to a particular method, as commitment to a set of guiding principles. Certainly it does provide a range of methodologies and is supported by a number of theories, it should be repeatable, and its data and processes should be accessible to others, but it is not a blueprint for a particular course to be taken. It offers a diversity of approaches. There is abundant evidence for the fact that in the field what happens is often rather different from the idealised notions presented in the textbooks. See, for example, Bell and Encel (1978), Bell and Newby (1977) and Burgess (1984). It has also been strongly argued that research cannot be neutral and value free (Sharman and Wood 1979). The emphasis in this book is on research as a general approach guided by a set of defined principles rather than a specific set of procedures; in each case the procedures adopted by researchers will depend on the problems under investigation.

Why research is important

Having briefly discussed the nature of the approaches proposed in this book, we shall now discuss the importance of the book's central theme. Research was the theme which brought the participants at the Warwick seminar together, it was taken up in every paper and was central to all the discussion that took place. The importance attached to research reflects the fact that broadly conceived it can offer those concerned with pastoral care a considerable amount, and it can offer things of central importance that nothing else can.

In relation to education and pastoral care, research can make key contributions in the areas of description, prescription, the answering of questions and the provision of theory. These will now be considered, starting with description and prescription. One analytic point to be stressed here is the importance of ensuring that description and prescription are adequately distinguished. In the past in commentaries on pastoral care the two have frequently been confused and what has been presented as description has in fact been prescription. This confusion is found on occasions in the literature of technique where what appears to be a neutral description of what is already happening in schools turns out to be the author's idealised view of what should be happening. This partly accounts for a view often found among those not directly concerned with pastoral care, that exaggerated claims are made about it.

Description in relation to research means something rather more than that found in school prospectuses and staff handouts, or given by senior staff in official pronouncements, or for that matter something more than the staff room comments of teachers; though all of these have a place within a full description of what is happening within a school. As has already been suggested the type of description which research can provide will be a great deal more rigorous and systematic. Though it may focus on only a small aspect of a school's total activities, it will always be concerned to go beyond the official version of what happens and why, to clarify the various components and distinguish the underlying patterns that go to make up a full description. This includes not only the various versions of what happens but also what can actually be observed and the various meanings and understandings involved. Clearly, exactly what a description includes will depend to some extent on the aims, scope and level of the research, the perspective of the researcher and the particular research methodology employed. For example, qualitative ethnographic research of the kind touched on by Burgess in his paper *ibid* is of particular value to teachers wishing to understand more clearly what goes on in schools.

There are many ways that research's descriptive role can increase our understanding of pastoral care. For example, at the most straightforward level it can help to make clear what those in pastoral roles actually do and the ways they use the time available to them in contrast to what it is thought they do and what they are supposed to do. At a more complex level descriptive research could assist with a critical assessment of the somewhat ambivalent concept of 'good practice'. Schools and teachers frequently claim that what they really need to improve and develop their own work, is a range of examples of good practice which other schools and individual teachers have used. As suggested above such a concept is in fact a great deal more problematic than is usually recognised. What should go to make up a model of 'good practice'? Should it simply be defined in terms of the commentaries and presentations of those who have invested a considerable amount of time and energy on the particular example of good practice's development or should accounts of good practice be in terms of the wider, more neutral perspective of descriptive research? The view of this book must be that it should be nearer the latter than the former. However in terms of current practice it is usually only the former which is available.

Equally, how should a school use and respond to a model of good practice? This is at present just as complex a problem. Often such models are totally rejected with the scepticism embodied in the often quoted remark 'you couldn't do it in my school' which dogs the teaching profession. Alternatively, the models may be taken on board without any reflection, preparation or modification. An example of this is the indiscriminate adoption of pupil profiles initially developed in particular schools or areas. Descriptive research can make an important initial contribution to the clarification of areas of this kind. But there comes a point where research must also play a prescriptive role.

In many ways the prescriptive role of research involves much of what has been outlined in relation to description, and in fact research which started as purely descriptive may well move into becoming prescriptive. The major difference between descriptive and prescriptive research is in terms of focus – the way the research is carried out may be very similar. In descriptive research the focus tends to be broader – a concern with understanding in a general way. In prescriptive research we are concerned with a narrower focus seeking answers to specific questions and the provision of guidance on future courses of action. Prescriptive research aims to highlight deficiencies and to suggest needs and identify priorities. The aim is also to examine the effectiveness of one approach as against another.

An example of the way that prescriptively-oriented research could contribute to the development of pastoral care relates to the notion of a 'pastoral curriculum'. In relation to developing such a curriculum Marland (1980) suggested that the first task for a school is to establish a shopping list of pupil needs. McLaughlin (1983) also suggested that the pastoral curriculum should deal with those sets of problems the largest number of pupils are likely to encounter. Neither the establishment of needs nor the identification of major problems can be adequately undertaken on the basis of general discussion founded on little more than intuition. It is clear that any discussion and planning should be underpinned by some form of fairly systematic and rigorous investigation and this would be in the form of some sort of prescriptive research.

Thus there is a close relationship between the descriptive and prescriptive roles of research and both are important to development, innovation and the continuation of effective practice. In the case of development and innovation the descriptive role of research can make a valuable contribution. Certainly most development and innovation needs to start from a basis of understanding the current situation (as described by research). Indeed, where an attempt is not made to understand the reality of the situation, innovation may be introduced on the basis of a fantasy notion of the situation in which case the possibility of failure is greatly increased. The notion of pastoral fantasy (Lang 1982) is characterised by the situation where a school begins to take statements which at best reflect ideals as reflections of reality. Case studies of schools could produce numerous examples where such a process has or is taking place. Examples of this fantasy can be found related to process centred experientially-based group work now common as the intended vehicle for tutorial work in schools. Such work is very different from most of what is at present covered in teacher education. It is also contrary to some of the prevailing teaching ideologies in schools and, indeed, to the still prevalent didactic teaching mode. Thus where schools are endeavouring to develop such programmes and where no attempt has been made to investigate the situation as it actually is, it is very easy to overestimate (fantasise) the amount of skill, commitment, and energy that exists as a basis for the development.

Research can also provide solid information as to the best types of approach and the likely outcomes. The approach supported by this book would regard as essential that claims about needs, priorities and effective approaches should be supported with empirical evidence.

Research as a central theme in this book has two further important roles. The first of these is in attempting to provide systematic answers to questions about both theory and practice. At present pastoral care is an area lacking in developed and articulated support from a range of appropriate theory. Thus a key task of research in relation to it will be the development of directly relevant theory. The types of questions that may be asked of research are manifest and of a range of orders, see for example Marland's paper *ibid*. How these questions emerge and by whom they are formulated is part of another debate, (see Young M. (Ed.) 1971). However, it should be noted that this is not a neutral area. Research needs to play a central part not only in attempting to answer questions but also in helping to ensure that the right ones are asked in the first place.

A popular but often misunderstood research approach is what is described as 'action research'. Following Cohen and Manion's (1980) excellent discussion, the major characteristics of action research are that it is a small-scale intervention in the functioning of the real world and a close examination of the effects of such intervention. Action research is concerned with diagnosing a problem in a specific context and attempting to solve it in that context. It is usually collaborative and those involved take part in both the implementation of the innovation and in researching the outcomes. It is self-evaluative in that modifications are constantly evaluated within the continuing situation, the ultimate objective being to improve practice in some way or other. The nature of action research is such that it is particularly appropriate to those introducing innovations in school. Clearly it could play a valuable part in the development of many ideas put forward in this book.

Finally, what is perhaps the most traditional role of research is also of significance to the book's themes: the generation and testing of theory. At present the amount of theory that relates to the areas covered in this book is very limited indeed and this must be seen as a major deficiency both in terms of the academic status of pastoral care and its effectiveness. Analysis and systematic evaluation ultimately require a body of theory to draw on. A central purpose of this book is to encourage educationalists at all levels to work in new directions and to undertake research which will begin to provide this body of theory.

Schools and teachers have tended to be suspicious of the contributions research can make to their work (see the comments in Marland's paper *ibid*). However, if its potential contribution is presented persuasively their perspective may well change. It must be clearly shown that the various levels of research and analysis can help to provide at least part of the answer to questions such as:

Where are we now?
How are we doing?
What do we mean by?
What have we achieved?
Where can we go?
Where ought we to go?
What is needed?
How can we understand this at a theoretical level?

In the case of pastoral care, or indeed any other facet of the school's activities, questions such as these need the clearest possible answers. The point must therefore be emphasised that research can make a major contribution by addressing these issues.

What kinds of research?

As has been noted above, teachers are often sceptical about research and, as a result, somewhat hesitant about embarking upon research themselves. Apart from scepticism, their caution is often partly due to an exaggerated view of the specialised, elaborate and mystical nature of research. In relation to this it is important to realise that research can be undertaken at a number of different levels. Research should be concerned with approaches, methods and attitudes along a continuum rather than an absolute position – a point made in a recent editorial of *Pastoral Care in Education* (1984, 2, 1). It can offer a range of methodologies appropriate to different situations and tasks. It is also important to recognise that there are various phases in the research process, and alternative levels and methods may be more appropriate to different points in the process – see for example Burgess, R. G. (Ed.) *The Research Process in Educational Settings: Ten Case Studies* (1984).

Though it is possible to order research in a notional hierarchy of levels, this is inevitably a fairly arbitrary exercise and the dividing lines between one level and another are at best hazy. Indeed the relationship between the levels, and the nature of the levels, is a subject which could merit a book in its own right. The outline that follows is very brief and intended only to give some preliminary guidance and insight.

Large-scale research

This type of research usually involves more than one school with conclusions tending to be based on comparisons. It is often based on the extensive use of questionnaires administered to a wide sample. There are few examples of this level of research being applied to pastoral care though B. M. Moore's (1970) *Guidance in Comprehensive Schools* could be seen as near to this model. The findings of this level of research are frequently popularised, for example, Bennett's *Teaching Styles and Pupil Progress* (1976) and Rutter's best-known work *Fifteen Thousand Hours* (1979).

Small-scale research (case studies)

This tends to have a narrower focus in terms of the area examined and the breadth of the sample. Such research often concentrates on one school. A central task of such research is usually that of description and analysis, and an endeavour to describe and understand what is going on in a specific school or a particular facet of its activities. Examples are presented in: Sharp and Green, *Education and Social Control* (1975), Best, Ribbins and Jarvis, *Education and Care* (1983), Burgess, R., *Experiencing Comprehensive Education* (1984).

Research projects/higher degrees

These projects are often undertaken on a part-time basis. The work may often be for a higher degree in the first instance. Examples are given in: Thorp, 'Evaluating Practice: pupils' views of transfer from the Primary to Secondary School' (1983), Lang, *Pastoral Care: Concern for Contradiction?* (1982).

Individual research

Individual teachers or groups of teachers may undertake house research projects in school. There is generally a specific practical objective and often no intention of writing up the research for an audience beyond the school itself, though this may well follow. Burgess (1983) and *ibid* describes the way teachers might approach research of this kind in their own school.

The point that teachers need to recognise is that all levels of research are equally valuable and valid and that teacher based research can be as possible (Burgess 1983) and as valuable as large scale funded projects. Further, as Burgess argues in his paper in this volume, the two types of work can complement each other.

The contents of the book

The editors do not propose to outline the content of this book in precise detail. However, they do feel it is useful to outline the ways in which the major themes – needs, approaches, and new directions – are reflected in the papers, recommendations and discussion. Before doing this one note of explanation is needed. The subjects covered by the papers and touched on in the discussion are not presented as a definitive coverage of all that should be included under the title of pastoral care. In fact the editors are conscious of a number of significant gaps, not least the problems of the 16–19 year-old age group, youth training schemes and aspects of pre-vocational education. In relation to this point and to the book's major themes, the editors suggest that the book's coherence is of a different order than that of exhaustive coverage. It is based rather on the wide range and varying expertise of its contributors and ultimately on its support for an approach which, it argues, should be applied to all aspects of pastoral care whether specifically covered in this book or not.

The three themes will be found reflected in one way or another in all the papers presented in this volume. An example of need is highlighted in this quotation from Patricia Broadfoot's paper *ibid*: 'As is so often the case with educational policy-making, the "bandwagon" phenomenon means that development and dissemination of activities are not supported by an equivalent volume of impartial evaluation and research. Whilst considerable effort is currently being expended by a variety of institutions and authorities up and down the country concerned to develop their own prototype "profiles" no equivalent effort is being put into testing out the assumptions on which such profiling is based.' Alastair MacBeth's paper 'Parents, Schools and Pastoral Care' stresses the central role of research and also implies new directions which might be taken as a result: 'My broad contention is that research should make assaults on ways to convert the well known correlation between home background and school attainment into practical steps for making the pastoral care forces of the home and the school mutually supportive.'

Examples similar to the two given above could have been found from all the papers in this book, but as we stated at the opening of this section the intention has been to draw attention to the specific features of the book's coherence and to highlight its major themes. Finally, an interesting dimension to the recent development of pastoral care has been the discovery that it is not confined to the UK. There is evidence of interest in this area from Eire, Canada, Israel, the West Indies, Australia and New Zealand. Of even greater interest is the fact that where pastoral care has developed in parallel to Britain, both the problems and needs may be very similar as this quotation from N. H. Hyde's paper, 'An Overview of Pastoral Care from Western Australia', tabled at the Warwick seminar clearly shows:

> There is a need to encourage and support 'action research' at the school level. It is apparent that many schools have devised and implemented pastoral care schemes without any form of documentation or evaluation. Burgess (1983) has considered very adequately a number of important questions which relate to teacher-based research on pastoral care, and these need not be repeated here. However the present author would emphasise the conclusions reached by Burgess (1983) that the crucial uses to which school level research must be put include:
>
> (i) the dissemination of information;
> (ii) the generation of concepts which can contribute at a sub-level of theory construction; and
> (iii) the informing of policy and decision-making within the school.
>
> In respect of the latter, the research must be of a form which allows for the monitoring and tailoring of school programmes and be consistent with overall attempts to improve schooling. (1984)

This book is certainly intended to influence the development of pastoral care at a national level. The thought of this influence extending to an international level is a challenging one.

Pastoral care: theory, practice and the growth of research

Peter Ribbins and Ron Best

The task

Our brief is by no means an easy one: to attempt to 'map' the territory of theory and practice in pastoral care, to locate the place (potential and actual) of educational research within it, and thus to provide a context within which the subsequent papers of this seminar may be located. Given the rudimentary stage of development of systematic thought and practice in pastoral care, we shall be lucky to achieve much more than a framework of grid-lines and the odd coast or two upon which subsequent writers may ink-in the topography as the research endeavour progresses.

First, a word about the nature of research, or rather, an attempt to define the concept of 'research' as it will be used in this paper. We suggest that 'research' is an activity which involves the intention to resolve some problem or puzzle (Kuhn 1962) which is posed for us by our lack of knowledge or the fact that our present knowledge is in some way inadequate, and to make good the deficiency through the discovery of new knowledge. This pursuit of knowledge is not a haphazard affair: that which is discovered will be the product of a systematic search for truth using distinctive methods (whether they be ethnographic/inductive, hypothetico-deductive, illuminative evaluation or whatever), and adding to an existing corpus of knowledge through the development of theories, typologies and models. To undertake research thus defined, is to adopt a particular perspective or frame of mind. The researcher does not see the world as a teacher or headteacher or anything else, but as a *researcher*. Whatever the context within which the puzzles emerge (and whatever the role he is playing at the time), it is within his conscious experience as a researcher that they are given expression and their solution sought through intentional involvement in rigorous and systematic study.

This attempt to provide a framework within which research in pastoral care can be located is, itself, a piece of research; that is to say it has the characteristics outlined above. It is guided by the desire to know more than we do at the moment, to add to the sum of knowledge by the collection of empirical data, and to order that knowledge by means of the development of theories, models and typologies. It will lack the finer points of some research, however, firstly because the corpus of publicly-recognised 'knowledge' in pastoral care in education is only now beginning to emerge, and secondly, because a thorough and systematic search for the ingredients of such a corpus would require more in time and resources than we have at our disposal. What follows must therefore necessarily be partial and schematic, with theoretical and empirical works cited more as *examples* of what might be done than as anything like an exhaustive catalogue of what has actually been achieved.

We shall undertake this task in a number of stages. Firstly, there is clearly some notion − however vague and contentious − of what constitutes 'knowledge' about pastoral care. We have ourselves (Best *et al* 1977) written of the 'conventional wisdom' which is expressed in schools' official statements about pastoral care and legitimised in the early books of Marland (1974), Blackburn (1975) and Haigh (1975). This 'knowledge' often seems to be based more upon thoughtful prescriptions and descriptions of idealised 'good practice' than on firmly established facts about 'how things really are'. Like all 'knowledge', the 'conventional wisdom' is an historical phenomenon: it has developed over time and it is possible to attempt to trace the course of its development. The first stage in our analysis will be to outline and discuss some attempts to describe this development, and from these to derive a refined and elaborated description of the history of pastoral care as thought and practice.

The second stage will involve a consideration of what it is about education that the theory and research of pastoral care might be concerned to tackle. From a simple model of the environment within which pastoral care is practised, six themes will be deduced which will provide the foci for the discussion of later sections. The third stage of the investigation will be a review of the literature of pastoral care in education. Our intention in this section is not to attempt an exhaustive review or provide a comprehensive annotated bibliography, but rather to convey something of the flavour and variety of the literature in which 'knowledge' about pastoral care is expressed and transmitted. In the process, we shall have something to say about the foci of the works, their relative accessibility, and the degree to which they are founded upon research. This last point is important, for it is true of education generally, and of pastoral care in education in particular, that much of what passes for 'knowledge' has never been subjected to the public tests of truth which distinguish between what is *known* from what is merely *believed*. This means that much of what passes for 'knowledge' has little or no foundation in systematic empirical enquiry.

A concentration upon that part of 'knowledge' which *is* research-based is the concern of the final phase of our venture. Using a tentative classification of research methodologies, we shall construct a typology of research in pastoral care in education, and illustrate its potential as a means of mapping the field by locating on it some of the published research referred to in earlier sections of the paper.

Historical context

Some attempts to map the knowledge of pastoral care in education have already been made. These attempts have more to do with the development, through time, of particular attitudes to education, and of the changing focus of thinking in this area, than with the location of contemporary features of the scene. We shall outline two such 'maps' and comment on a third, before moving on to develop our own.

The first 'map' is that of Peter Lang who has been evolving an historical account of pastoral care over a number of years. In a number of papers (1982, 1983a, 1983b and Ribbins and Lang 1984), he seeks to identify changing emphases in thought and prescription about pastoral care since the public school tradition of the nineteenth century. The picture which emerges is summed up in a review in the inaugural issue of 'Pastoral Care in Education':

> In my view the first stage was in the nineteenth century and related to some aspects of the public and elementary schools. In the public schools during that century ideas of a school- master's responsibility for his pupils' moral wellbeing and general welfare emerged. In the sphere of elementary schools the dialectic between care and control can be clearly discerned, a dialectic which still exists in pastoral care today. The second stage was immediately post-war when some authorities following an idealised public school model developed house systems within their newly-founded compre- hensives. Much of pastoral care as it is now understood was later tacked on to these systems in a somewhat piecemeal way. . . . . The following stage took place during the early seventies when structural pastoral systems spread until they became a virtually ubiquitous feature of comprehensive schools. The final stage which takes us to the present has been the emergence of two as yet mainly unrelated strands, one strand being that of technique, the other that of critique. Technique is represented by the emergence of a literature relating to how you do pastoral care. . . . The second strand, that of critique, is represented by a small number of papers and articles which have called into question many of

16

the basic assumptions made about pastoral care and suggested that the whole area is far more problematic than is normally recognised. (p. 61)

The second 'map' is to be found in Blackburn's analysis of the developing role of the pastoral middle-manager (Blackburn 1983a 'Chapter 1', 1983b) where four phases are identified over the last three decades. Through the '50s, the emphasis was upon providing some sort of structural framework of relationships and activities in which children would be 'known', kept 'informed', 'controlled' and 'organised' within the otherwise mystifying and complex context of the new and large comprehensives. The performance of these functions were typically to be executed by the house system. Towards the end of the '60s (he goes on), new concerns emerged, especially 'the increasing range of choices that were offered to pupils in school and in further and higher education' (1983b, p. 19). Arising from the need to inform and help children to cope with these choices came the awareness of the wide range which confronts the child: thus through the '70s attention became more and more focused upon the need for guidance and counselling of an academic, personal and vocational nature. Finally, the last five years have seen the emergence of thinking about, and planning for, the use of group work as a resource for children learning the coping skills necessary to survive in schools and in life in general – the common concern of (*inter alia*) Baldwin and Wells (1979), Hamblin (1978), Button (1981) and Marland (1980).

Clearly there is some common ground in these accounts. Both stress the move from a preoccupation with structures to a concern for technique. However, there are some notable differences. For instance, Blackburn says nothing of the place of research in all this, whereas in Lang's scheme research is presumed by the idea of 'critique', either as that upon which a critique is founded or that by which critical conjecture can be substantiated or otherwise by empirical methods. In effect, Blackburn's position has something of the earlier phases about it, focusing as it does exclusively on practitioner concerns: on structure, role and (latterly) 'technique' in Lang's sense.

A third commentary also deserves note, and this is Hamblin's entry on 'Counselling and Pastoral Care' in Cohen and Manion (1983). It is interesting for three reasons: firstly because it is specifically to do with *research and development*; secondly, because it demonstrates the uneasy relationship – and apparent separateness – of theory, practice and the traditions informing pastoral care on the one hand, and counselling on the other; and thirdly, because it makes no attempt to structure the writings and developments it discusses either historically or typologically, despite giving a thumbnail sketch of some of the ideas and practices which are clearly central to the developing 'knowledge' of pastoral care.

We suggest that all three offer something of value, but require development. Blackburn's account is too simple to do justice to the problem, having, in effect, only two dimensions: a historical or chronological dimension on the one hand, and a recognition of the shifting focus or object of attention on the other. It says nothing of how those objects are viewed or the functions which are served by one sort of 'knowledge' or another. The dimensions of Lang's model are uncertain. Clearly his is also a *history* of pastoral care, but the categories he uses for characterising the four stages are not consistent: they are not of the same order throughout. For whereas the first three stages are to do with a particular ideology and its expression in the philosophy and implementation of policy by education authorities, the emergence of 'technique' and 'critique' have a research base to them. (The first involves action research, the second what might be termed 'critical empiricism'.) Some further dimension is necessary to transpose this into a neat and consistent model. Hamblin's offering, by contrast, makes no real attempt to construct an analytical model at all.

An historical model of pastoral care 'knowledge'

We can build upon the base provided by Lang and Blackburn, by adding a further dimension, *viz*. that of the *functions and types of 'knowledge' or understanding* that are involved in thought and writing about pastoral care. Such a dimension permits the consideration of, for instance, the distinction we have already made between prescriptions based upon beliefs or ideals, and descriptions and explanations that are derived from research. The result is a three-dimensional model within which all that has passed for 'knowledge' – including that derived from research – may be located (see Figure 1).

In terms of these dimensions, it seems to us that the 'wisdom' of pastoral care can be seen to have developed through five phases, each characterised by particular types of 'knowledge', and each tending to focus upon a particular issue or theme. These phases are:

1 The pre-history of pastoral care, that is, the antecedants of pastoral care which pre-date the use of the term itself. Where one begins with such a pre-history is to some extent arbitrary – all events were, after all, preceded by yet others – but Lang (1982) suggests that the ideological roots of pastoral care can be found at least as early as the late eighteenth century in the work of reforming headmasters of public schools. Although by no means the first, let alone the only,

Figure 1   Dimensions for a 'map' of pastoral care 'knowledge'

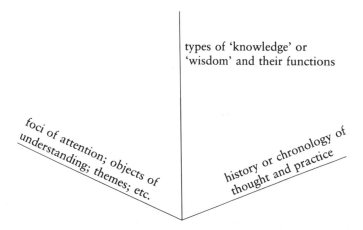

types of 'knowledge' or
'wisdom' and their functions

foci of attention;
understanding; objects of
themes; etc.

history or chronology of
thought and practice

reforming headmaster, it is of course Thomas Arnold of Rugby who is usually identified with the idea of the Christian ideal to be pursued, not primarily through academic learning but through an emphasis on first, religious and moral principles, second, gentlemanly conduct, third, intellectual ability' (p. 3). Later, the emphasis on competition and healthy living, games-playing and so on developed these theological and moral ideals into the dogma of the 'muscular Christian', echoed still in the competitive sporting ethos of the house systems of those comprehensive schools which, however unwittingly, have accepted the independent sector as the pattern to follow.

The development of state provision of elementary schools later in the century provided a different emphasis. As carefully documented by Simon (1960), this development was as much a response by the Establishment to its weakening control over the working classes as it had to do with a concern for their welfare. If it was the latter which was emphasised, this was often a retrospective legitimation of the strengthening of social control. Where genuinely felt, this added to a tradition which combined 'moral earnestness' with 'smug, condescending attitudes to the lower orders' which, with hindsight, can be 'clearly identified as self-righteous and patronising' (Hughes 1980, p. 26).

In effect, this pre-history was characterised by the dogma of the Christian 'ideal', only there were, it seems, *two* ideals: one, the man who would be fit to administer realm, Empire and industry; the other, the man who would obediently and diligently labour in and consume the products of that industry.

2   Beginning around the late 1940s, and doubtless connected with the statutory provision of secondary education for all, '"pastoral care"

19

began to be used in schools by teachers to categorise the multifarious activities they undertook on behalf of their pupils' (Lang and Ribbins, 1985), activities which were associated with certain institutional forms (houses, tutors). With comprehensive reorganisation, these structures became more and more complex, and more various in form, as horizontal systems of 'years' and 'schools-within-schools' appeared as alternatives to 'houses'. These developments appear to have followed a British tradition in educational provision, which can be summed up as 'first innovate, then work out the reasons later'! Thus, what was essentially a combination of inherited structure (from the houses of the public school tradition) and a pragmatic response to administrative and legal necessity (*in loco parentis*) only came to be 'reasoned' in a subsequent rationalisation. Rarely articulated in any degree, and then only in the rather pious terms of the paternalism of a previous age, this rationalisation was the fore-runner of what has since been termed the 'conventional wisdom'.

3 The 1970s saw the development of a 'conventional wisdom' of pastoral care, carrying an authority and respectability which was based on two factors: that it was reasoned and uttered by senior and prestigious practitioners (of whom Marland is the prime example), and that it was uttered in published works which carried all the hallmarks of scholarly enterprise. Such works as those of Marland (1974), Blackburn (1975) and Haigh (1975) were essentially prescriptions, based upon their authors' own experience, and advocating 'good practice' in a way which blurred the distinction between the reality of their schools and the ideal to which they hoped their schools aspired.[1] This 'conventional wisdom' appealed to commonsense and an assumed consensus about the 'goodness' and desirability of pastoral care conventionally conceived, and made little direct use of research though sometimes finding legitimisation in 'second-order' theories (see Craft and Lytton 1969). Its authors were neither concerned to test hypotheses nor to establish generalisations through description and induction, and where research was utilised it was often appropriated from peripheral (or even alien) sources to illustrate and support an argument. Where research was undertaken (for example, Moore 1970), this was usually descriptive rather than analytic and concerned to elaborate the commonsense notions of the conventional wisdom rather than to subject its propositions to a critical and rigorous test of truth.

As for the objects of this wisdom, the focus of attention was twofold: the problems and possibilities of institutionalised structures of roles as pastoral mechanisms, and the need to respond to children's actual or potential crisis of a personal, social and emotional nature.

4 The latter part of the 1970s saw the emergence of what Lang (1983a)

rightly identifies as the *critique* of pastoral care. This critique is of two kinds. On the one hand there is the emergence of some genuine (that is, explanatory) theorising which called into question the 'conventional wisdom' of the previous phase, and advanced hypotheses about the less palatable 'realities' of pastoral care. Thus, our own (1977) paper (recently echoed by Milner, 1983), was joined by historical (Hughes 1980), philosophical (Dooley 1980), and sociological (Corbishly and Evans 1980, Lang 1977) critiques of the 'conventional wisdom', displaying an emerging scepticism perhaps most graphically exemplified in Williamson's notion of 'pastoralisation' (Williamson 1980).

On the other hand, there has emerged a growing unease with the preoccupation of earlier phases with crisis counselling in the context of an organisational structure, and a gathering concern for prevention (rather than cure) through curriculum innovation. In some cases (Baldwin and Wells 1979, Button 1982) this has involved action-research in the research and development mould (Stenhouse 1975) to test, evaluate and refine curriculum materials. In others (Best, Ribbins and Ribbins 1984, Marland 1980, Hamblin 1978, Ribbins 1985) the concern has been to argue on both philosophical and pragmatic grounds for the merit of either a systematic tutorial programme or 'pastoral' or 'welfare' curriculum to be articulated with existing curriculum policies in such related areas as health education (Schools Council Health Education Project), careers education (Hopson and Hough 1973), personal and social development (Hopson and Scally 1981) and social education (APU 1981, HMI 1979).

5 Finally, we may consider the stage which we have now entered, and which is personified in this very seminar. In Kuhn's (1965) terms, we may consider our present concerns to be those of 'normal science'; that is to say, the intention is no longer to produce outspoken critiques of the 'conventional wisdom' or to achieve a revolution in thinking about pastoral care and the curriculum. Rather, the tasks before us are those of (a) researching systematically the various faccts of pastoral care in education, and (b) the development of technique through curriculum evaluation and the refinement of tutor-practice. A distinction between the two is somewhat misleading, of course, for the latter can (and some would argue must) involve some form of action-research in order to mount innovations upon a firmer basis than pious hopes or a capacity to swallow a publisher's 'blurb'.

Themes

Now it is clear that we have only just begun to tease out the variety of aspects of pastoral care about which 'knowledge' exists and others where there is more or less of a vacuum, it may be helpful to remind ourselves of the features of the environment in which pastoral care is to happen. The simplest of models will suffice:

> Pastoral care is something which happens/should happen between *teacher and student*, interacting in the context of an institution called a *school* or *college* which has *four inter-related dimensions* (disciplinary/order, welfare/pastoral, academic/curricular and administrative/organisational) and which is, itself, located in a wider *social, historical and cultural milieu.*

Each of the italicised words or phrases in this statement can be seen as a focus of attention about which 'knowledge' might be acquired. To these we might add:

> The conceptual analysis of 'pastoral care' and related ideas (e.g. 'welfare', 'guidance', 'counselling', 'concern'), and the associated ethical or moral issues which are entailed in any attempt to establish *justifications* for those activities and arrangements which are held to constitute or facilitate pastoral care.

From this model alone it is possible to list a considerable number of potential foci for research. They include:

1 The organisational and managerial structures, systems and processes of pastoral care in education.
2 The relationship between the pastoral and academic aspects of educational institutions, to include:
   (a)   pastoral care and the support of learning;
   (b)   'pastoralisation' and associated concepts;
   (c)   the 'pastoral curriculum';
   (d)   the separation of pastoral and academic structures.
3 The historical and philosophical underpinnings of pastoral care.
4 Pastoral care and the world outside the school/college, to include home-school relations and the interface between the welfare services and educational institutions.
5 The roles and perspectives of specialist pastoral-care agents, to include the school counsellor, school-based social-worker, etc.
6 The teacher and the student, to include:
   (a)   teacher roles, perspectives and attitudes;
   (b)   student roles, perspectives and attitudes;
   (c)   teacher-student interaction;
   (d)   the training of teachers for pastoral roles.

As we have already indicated, the establishment of a recognisable corpus of 'knowledge' about pastoral care in education is still rudimentary. Often, statements pertinent to our topic occur in bodies of 'knowledge' that have been established for a rather longer period of time. for example, the importance of home-school relations in respect of ideas about community education and compensatory programmes (Halsay 1972, Midwinter 1973) is clearly relevant to pastoral care without necessarily explicitly considering pastoral care as structure and process in schools. There is much which is equally relevant but no more 'visible' because generated in what is essentially a non-educationalist tradition, as in the case of the substantial body of knowledge produced within the mainstream of counselling theory and practice. (See, for example, the numerous articles in the *British Journal of Guidance and Counselling*.) Of course, the relevance of such work is sometimes made apparent as, for example, when focussed specifically on the pastoral nature of home-school relations (Craft 1980) or in writings specifically to do with counselling in schools (Jones 1977, Milner 1980, Hamblin, 1974).

Reviewing the literature

Writing about pastoral care less than a decade ago, we argued that:

> The general neglect of this concept amongst educationalists
> and social scientists is clearly demonstrated by the paucity
> of literature which deals explicitly with 'pastoral care' as its
> central concern. (Best *et al* 1977, p. 234)

This could hardly be said today, although it seems that little of the published literature in this area is unambiguously *research-based*. Certainly, there is very little *funded* research as a glance through the SSRC's research list or the DES's List No. 1 (1983) will quickly show. One of the most hopeful signs we encountered in the short time available was the great deal of evidence that 'pastoral care' topics have become quite popular amongst teachers undertaking research for professional and post-graduate courses. We shall have more to say shortly about the volume of dissertations and theses in this area and only wish to stress at this point that a considerable (and growing) *unpublished* literature of pastoral care already exists.

It is also true that over the last decade the literature of pastoral care which is *not* primarily research-based has also been growing and at an ever-increasing rate. Happily, it is now very difficult for even the most dedicated student to keep up with everything that is being published in books and journals. To take just one example, the journal *Pastoral Care in Education* is, this month (February 1983), in its fourth edition and in that brief time has published thirty-six articles on a wide variety of topics.

So numerous, in fact, has the literature of pastoral care and associated topics become, that since 1980 a number of annotated bibliographies and reading lists have begun to appear. We shall briefly deal with some of these. The first two were compiled by Blackburn (1980) and by Lang and Ribbins (1983) and are produced in conjunction with a touring exhibition available from the National Book League. Both are concerned only with *books*. Blackburn's (1980) list contains 175 references which are grouped 'to meet the interests of teachers who stand at different points of the spectrum covered by "pastoral care"' (p. 4). He does not suggest that all of the books necessarily fall neatly and exclusively into any one particular category, but seven groupings are used. These include an introductory group of basic and general books followed by a larger section dealing with organisational and leadership topics. The third and fourth sections consider texts dealing with aspects of the pastoral curriculum. Section Five is concerned with the ways in which schools can be organised and the relationships which can result from different patterns of organisation. Attention is also given to teacher- and pupil-roles, attitudes and interactions. The last two sections deal with contemporary thinking about 'childhood' and 'adolescence' and with a discussion of the kinds of problems which young people face.

Lang and Ribbins (1983) bibliography is essentially an expansion and updating of Blackburn's pamphlet. They adopt the same general categories with the addition of a group of ten texts dealing with various aspects of gender stereotyping and education. In their introduction the editors suggest that 'some areas have received a great deal more attention over the last two or three years than have others' (p. 1). Amongst the former are various aspects of personal and social education and the pastoral curriculum.

Both bibliographies discussed above focus mainly on books about pastoral care. The third, compiled by Alison McKay (1983) for the National Association of Young People's Counselling and Advisory Services (NAYPCAS) is described as a 'reading list for those interested in counselling and advisory work, particularly with young people'. It contains references to books, journals and audio-visual material, much of which has relevance to pastoral care in education. This bibliography is divided into fourteen groupings under such headings as 'Helping interventions', 'The skills and processes of counselling', 'Adolescence' and 'Group processes'. It contains some 120 annotated references to a variety of useful materials including a number of bibliographies and guides to available resources on such issues as *Sex Education* (Speight, undated), *Drugs and Alcohol* (Bell 1982), *Solvent Abuse* (Bell 1982) and *Training Opportunities in Counselling* (Ackroyd 1981), and a set of seven referral directories on themes ranging from counselling services in London to advisory agencies on psycho-sexual problems (pp. 22–23).

We have left till last an annotated bibliography and literature review recently published by the National Youth Bureau. This has been compiled and written by Alison Skinner with Hilary Platts and Brian Hill (1983) and deals with the topic of *Disaffection From School: Issues and interagency responses*. It offers an enormously comprehensive treatment of these and allied themes and contains over 450 references including books, journals, dissertations, government reports, local authority projects and unpublished papers. The literature in this bibliography is divided into three main sections and is then subdivided according to subject. The major divisions are between (a) individual or collective opinions on the causes of school-related problems (30 items); (b) research findings on the subject (118 items), and (c) accounts of policy, provision and practice (307 items). Finally, the bibliography is superbly *cross-indexed* by author, subject, and area/agency/project/source. Its authors modestly claim that 'The bibliography did not set out to be a comprehensive guide to the literature on disaffection from school. . . .' (p. 1) but it must be said that the study and practice of pastoral care would be very well served if annotated bibliographies of this quality were available on other key themes.

Taken together, these four publications offer over 700 references to books, journals, dissertations, audio-visual and other material dealing with, or relevant to, the practice of pastoral care in education broadly conceived. In our attempt to outline the material available, these references proved to be a useful starting point. We have also given attention to several books not contained in any of the bibliographies discussed above, and many articles located in a variety of journals. We have looked especially closely at the thirty-six papers published in the first four editions of *Pastoral Care in Education*, and two further papers to be published in the fifth edition. Finally, some attention will be given to the rapidly increasing number of dissertations and theses produced by students on a wide variety of long in-service courses leading to undergraduate and, especially, post-graduate qualifications. Given the paucity of funded research in pastoral care this growing corpus of student work represents a highly significant development. However, as is to be expected, much of it remains unpublished and therefore relatively unavailable. Some of this research is now beginning to find its way into the journals although much excellent work continues to gather dust on college and university shelves. One important function that *Pastoral Care in Education* can perform is to provide a forum for the wider dissemination of such research, and already six or seven of the papers it has printed have originated in such work. The part which student research can, and does, play in providing a research base for the literature of pastoral care in education is a theme to which we shall return shortly.

Some general points should first be made about the kinds of literature available. These vary in three significant ways:

1 in the degree to which they emphasise or are based in research;
2 in their relative availability to the reader in the sense of his actually being able to locate and read the work; and
3 in the audience to which they would be relevant and intelligible.

Obviously, the availability of a work depends on whether, and in what form, it is published. Books in print are probably the most accessible, with current journal articles next. Articles in back numbers or in unlikely journals, and books out of print are clearly less easy to consult, while dissertations and unpublished research reports are the most difficult to trace and use. The utility of even easily-acquired works is problematic, however, for this will depend very much upon both the needs and background of the reader and the character and concern of the work itself. Some works are simply useless to some readers because they deal with esoteric and highly specialised topics couched in language unintelligible to the layman, while others are more palatable though not necessarily erudite.

We found these variables helpful in shaping our own interrogation of the literature, and it will be useful to bear this diversity in mind in what follows.

Review of the literature

We shall now offer a partial summary of what is available in terms of the six themes or foci identified earlier. In doing this we shall make selective use of both published and unpublished work. In the main, the latter is made up of the growing number of student dissertations and theses but there are also a few quite useful reports of funded research which, for various reasons, remain unpublished. Since we intend to include reference to such unpublished research, it might be helpful if we say something more about it at this point.

Collecting information on what has and is being done proved a more taxing task than we had anticipated. Our preliminary trawls through the various registers, indexes and abstracts of dissertations proved less rewarding than we had hoped. However, we did come across enough evidence to substantiate our hunch that, in the last five years or so, students have become much more ready to take on 'pastoral' topics than they were ever in the 'seventies. Furthermore, all the evidence suggests that the popularity of 'pastoral care' as an area of student research is still waxing strong. Several points can be made about this.

Firstly, while the research seems to be concentrated primarily in those institutions of higher education which offer courses in some combination of pastoral care, guidance and counselling, it is by no means restricted to such places. On the contrary, wherever lecturers are to be found who have some interest in these topics, whether they be located in departments specialising in the curriculum, in professional training, in educational administration, in psychology, in special education or whatever, some of their students will be encouraged to research in pastoral care. Such a situation has the additional benefit that various pastoral topics are tackled from a healthy diversity of perspectives. Secondly, if we are correct in our assertation that most of the published contemporary literature of pastoral care is dominated by issues of 'technique', this is clearly much less true of student-based research. Our brief survey (and our own experience) suggests that whilst 'technique' is not ignored, greater emphasis is given to 'critique'. Thirdly, the topics which students choose are very various indeed as are the research methodologies employed. Finally, the research also varies very considerably in depth, in scope, and above all, in quality. The best is excellent, the worst is awful! Much the same judgement can be made of the literature of pastoral care taken as a whole, and to this we shall now turn.

Given that we considered over 800 items in the form of books, articles, reports, theses and the like, our account of the literature is necessarily *partial* and *schematic*. However, in so much as the sixfold classification of pastoral care issues outlined earlier in this paper is *comprehensive*, we hope to illustrate *synoptically* what is available. We shall also attempt to identify some of the key issues within each of the themes, and to keep in mind, when considering individual items, such factors as the type of 'knowledge' they deal with, the extent to which they have a research emphasis, their availability, and the audience to which they might appeal.

To recapitulate, the six main *themes* we have identified are:

1 the organisation and managerial structures, systems and processes of pastoral care in education;
2 the relationship between the pastoral and academic aspects of educational institutions;
3 the historical and philosophical underpinning of pastoral care;
4 pastoral care and the world outside the schools/colleges;
5 the teacher and the student;
6 the roles and perspectives of specialist pastoral-care agents.

While some of the texts we considered concentrate clearly on one of these themes, others deal with two or more. Attempts to classify the latter necessarily involve some distortion. For heuristic purposes, however, we believe such a classification to be worth attempting. Finally, there are a relatively small number of texts which cannot be readily fitted into even this group, usually because of their wide scope. These are normally more or less deliberately designed to serve as comprehensive introductions to discussions of pastoral care taken as a whole. Thus, for the most part, they deal with most or all the six themes. Rather than discuss these in each separate category, we shall deal with them as a group at the beginning of the analysis.

General texts

As we saw in our earlier discussion of the development of thought and practice in pastoral care, the term 'pastoral care' as applied to education can be traced back to the 1940s. However, it was not until the early seventies that the first book dealing explicitly with it was published. This was by Marland (1974), and was followed shortly afterwards by a number of other books dealing broadly with the place of pastoral care in schools (Haigh 1975, Hamblin 1978). In an article in 1977, Best, Jarvis and Ribbins coined the term 'conventional wisdom' for such accounts which, for whatever their merits, tended to adopt an unproblematic approach based on the view that 'pastoral care is pretty good, let's make it a little better' (Lang 1983, p. 61).Lang goes on to identify the emergence in the later 1970s of the two main strands which have dominated the literature. The first is concerned with *technique*, or 'how to do pastoral care', the second with *critique* which 'is represented by a small number of papers and articles which have called into question many of the basic assumptions made about pastoral care. . .' (p. 61). These comments are made in the context of a wide-ranging review of a collection of papers edited by Best, Jarvis and Ribbins (1980), *Perspectives on Pastoral Care*, which contains 'a number of telling theoretical critiques relating to pastoral care, alongside papers by all the well-known writers on pastoral technique' (Lang 1983, p. 61). Some of the papers contained in the book reported on-going research; others argued that not enough research had been or was being done and advocated more. Since then something at least has been achieved. However, it is also true that such research is only just beginning to find its way into the journals and, rather more slowly, into books.

However that may be, the growing interest amongst teachers and others has led to the publication of a number of quite useful and relatively short introductions to pastoral care in education. These include those of David and Cowley (1980), Galloway (1981), Hamblin (1981), McGuinness (1982) and Preedy (1981). All these studies make some reference to research but in none of them does the reporting of such research constitute a central intention. Given the paucity of research available in the late 'seventies,such an approach is understandable. It will be much less defensible in the 'eighties as the available research grows.

Much excellent material remains relatively inaccessible because it is contained in unpublished student dissertations. Amongst several that come to mind which take a general approach to the study of pastoral care, three excellent case-studies have been completed recently. The first is Woods' (1983, 1984) study of pastoral care over a twelve-year period at Oakfield School which identifies three phases in the evolution of a pastoral policy at the school and points up some significant discrepancies between 'official accounts' and what some of the staff saw as happening.

The second is Squire's (1982) fine study of 'Pastoral Care in the Urban School'. Mention here might also be made of another study of pastoral care in an inner-city comprehensive school, by Ayre (1982), although this piece of research is disappointing in some respects. Finally, a wide-ranging approach is taken by Lang (1982) in his study of Marshland Castle School, West Midlands. This research represents a major contribution to the 'critique' strand of the literature and it is in this text that Lang first suggested the relevance of the notions of 'critique' and 'technique'. A number of other useful concepts are developed of which those of 'pastoral fantasy' and 'pastoral incantation' are particularly suggestive. Furthermore, unlike much student work, Lang offers a sophisticated account of problems of research methodology and an interesting defence of a modified ethnographic approach.

There is also now available one major published case-study. In this study of Rivendell, a large comprehensive school in the south of England, Best *et al.* (1983) look at many aspects of pastoral care in a contemporary school using an *interpretive* methodology. This study was part of a six-year investigation and represents one of the few pieces of funded research to date. To an important extent, the report of this research (*Education and Care*), represents *both* an attempt to integrate 'technique' and 'critique' *and* an attempt to make a statement about the possibilities and problems of a particular research methodology.

Finally, it is sometimes argued that HMI have shown a disappointingly small interest in pastoral care in education. Whilst it is still true that the English HMI have yet to produce a survey of practice in pastoral care, they do now usually include comments on the pastoral aspects of provision in their published reports of school inspections. Furthermore, *Aspects of Secondary Education* (HMI 1979) does say something about what schools expect of their pastoral structures and a good deal about the contribution which such structures make to the provision of personal and social education programmes for pupils. If the English HMI have been a bit tardy this is not a criticism which could be made of their Scottish (HMI 1968, HMI 1975) or their Welsh (HMI 1982) counterparts.

The six themes

Structures, systems and processes

A prominent characteristic of many studies up to the mid-seventies was a tendency to emphasise problems of *structure* and to ignore *process* in thinking about pastoral care. This is particularly clear in the earliest accounts dating from the late 1950s (Howard 1958) and early 1960s (Pulbrook 1962), but remains substantially true of the writers of 'conventional wisdom' of the 1970s and 1980s. This is so even of some texts which are clearly research-based (as in Moore's, 1970, description of the structure of guidance systems in five schools), and of studies which make significant use of such research as was available (as in Halsall's, 1971, study of *The Comprehensive School*). Even such seminal texts as Marland's (1974) *Pastoral Care* give prominence to structural prescriptions in chapters dealing with 'Groups and Groupings', 'Roles and Responsibilities', 'Patterns of Care', and the like. Studies such as these tend to rely on *a priori* analysis of the advantages, for example, of vertical (house) as against horizontal (year) systems, rather than upon evidence provided by research into what actually happens in practice. In so far as evidence was offered it tended to be drawn either from the author's own experience or from the few accounts provided by other practitioners.

Such studies are often illuminating and many hard-pressed practitioners have attested to their usefulness. Our criticism is not just that they emphasise structure, but that they tend to adopt an uncritical stance, more or less ignore process, and make little reference or use of such research findings as do exist. This is also true of those studies which deal with various pastoral roles. A case in point are the two valuable studies by Blackburn in 1975 (*The Tutor*) and 1983 (*Head of House, Head of Year*); if the level of analysis contained in the latter study is more sophisticated, it is no less essentially structural in its concerns.

Like the earlier works of the 'conventional wisdom', the case-studies mentioned above give much attention to the structural characteristics of the institutions under investigation. However, they are different in that they do critically examine how such structures and roles actually operate. Such an approach is shared by the authors of several journal articles and dissertations of the last four or five years. These have dealt with the advantages and disadvantages of various pastoral systems (Grainger 1978, Young 1979), with horizontal versus vertical structures (Thompson 1982), and with the use of schools as pastoral centres for all the 16–19 age-group in the local community (Stephenson 1983). The last study has in part been written up (Stephenson 1982), but comparable studies remain unpublished. There are also some unpublished investigations of particular pastoral structures which have been undertaken by consultants. We came across a particularly interesting example recently of a case where a social worker and an educational psychologist were asked by the staff to look at the pastoral system of their school and offer advice (Curtis and Bartlett 1983).

Clearly, pastoral systems have to be organised and require management. No-one would suggest that there is not an important role for literature that shares experience of successful practice as several articles in the journal *Pastoral Care in Education* demonstrate (Blackburn 1983, Brackenbury 1983, Buzzard and Hamilton 1984, Hughes 1983, and Marland 1983). However, what is also needed is more research which systematically tests the kind of propositions practitioners offer about successful practice. Furthermore, we would contend that, where possible, researchers could make clear what the implications of their findings for practice actually are. Thus, in our own study (Best *et al* 1983) we somewhat rashly entitled the last chapter 'Getting it Right' and offered in it (a) a number of recommendations for the organisation of pastoral care within the secondary school, and (b) a set of suggestions as to how such recommendations might be implemented in practice.

The pastoral and the academic

The relationship between the pastoral and the academic work of the school has, until recently, been largely neglected. This can be seen in the paucity of literature and absence of theses dealing explicitly with this theme before 1979. Since then the situation has been dramatically reversed. So great is the volume of material that to manage it we have further sub-divided this category into four overlapping issues.

(i) Pastoral care and the support of learning

Some writers have stressed that the central function of schooling is the encouragement of worthwhile learning. Given this precept, the central purpose of institutionalised pastoral care must be to support the process of learning within the school. Perhaps the clearest and most widely-recognised exponent of this view is Hamblin, who makes the point in a number of his books (Hamblin 1978, 1981, 1982). The argument is most clearly spelled out in *The Teacher and Pastoral Care* and developed in his theory of 'critical incidents' in the career of the pupil. Each of the critical incidents he identifies (for example, 'induction', 'option choice', 'guidance for the fifth form') has received attention in the literature but it is the operation of the subject- or option-choice system within the school which best exemplifies this particular view of the pastoral facilitation of learning. This is one area in which there has been a good deal of published research although much of it does not deal centrally with the role of pastoral care (Hurman 1978, Weston 1980, Woods 1975). To a greater or lesser extent what all these studies share is a concern that option-choice systems may not work in the way that teachers intend. Much the same can be said of a number of interesting theses which have dealt with this theme (Batchelor 1976, Mowforth 1979, Myres 1980, Bland 1981, Eastgate 1982). This is a point taken up by some writers who argue against such systems and that pastoral care should play no part in such activities (Buzzard 1983).

(ii) 'Pastoralisation' and associated concepts

In one radical version of the relationship between pastoral care and learning, Williamson (1980) has argued that for some children at least, the function of pastoral care has been to deflect attention from the real inadequacies of the learning programmes and methods of the school. This process he has dubbed 'pastoralisation'. In a rather less extreme view, Buckley (1980) argues that 'the teacher who "cares" is the one who teaches effectively' (p. 183). Finally, in an account of some work in a large Midlands comprehensive, Roberts (1977) argues that some, at least, of the most serious of behavioural problems can be traced back to the organisation of the school's curriculum. All these, and similar studies, share the view that schools would need less pastoral care if only they got their teaching and the curriculum 'right'. The idea of getting the curriculum 'right' has been the inspiration of studies and papers dealing with a variety of more or less related issues, which we shall describe as a concern for a welfare dimension to the curriculum or, more succinctly, for the 'pastoral curriculum'.

(iii) The pastoral curriculum

The concept of the 'pastoral curriculum' has, itself, received considerable attention but for the present we shall use the words as an umbrella term for all those topics or subjects which have a 'pastoral' flavour and which are said (a) to have a claim on the curriculum and (b) which are regarded as having a learning or development as well as a caring dimension. If taken seriously such claims for a place in the curriculum would entail a substantial revolution in contemporary thought.

Some subjects with a welfare flavour have a surprisingly long history. The idea of a 'tutorial programme', for example, is very fashionable today but its antecedents are traceable to the middle of last centry. Lang (1982) quotes an example of the use of the term in the proceedings of the Clarendon Commission of 1861!

In the post-war era, a number of more-or-less distinct yet clearly overlapping subjects with a welfare flavour have received a good deal of attention and have always had their advocates. We have in mind here such subjects as health education, careers education, moral education and the like. It is not possible to do justice to them all in this paper but some examples of the kinds of things written on each might illustrate what is available. Very little of the research we could find dealt explicitly with the objectives or practice of health or sex education as an aspect of pastoral care as such, but this is not to say that it is all necessarily tangential to pastoral purposes. Thus the *Schools Council Health Education* projects, for 12–13 and 13–18 year-olds, contain a number of useful ideas although some reviewers (Healy 1983) have been critical of aspects of the programmes on offer. Examples of useful texts on sex education are the guides to available resources produced by Speight (1981), and by Went (1984). A handful of students have looked at aspects of the role of health education within the curriculum and at the ways in which it has been taught (Eldridge 1978, Scott 1979). Finally two dissertations consider aspects of sex education: Shaw (1980) discusses sex education as an example of curriculum integration, and in a particularly interesting study Fidge (1978) attempts to examine parental attitudes to sex education in a junior school.

Few studies in moral education deal directly with pastoral issues but that of McPhail *et al* (1972), although not recent, remains relevant. The link between careers education and pastoral care has received rather more attention from academics and practitioners. The work by Hayes and Hopson (1972) and the later book by Hopson and Hough (1979) have much to offer, as does the study of careers education in six schools by Law and Watts (1977). On an associated theme, the recent book by Watts (1983) provides much information on topics with special reference for the youth of today in looking at 'Education and Employment' and 'Education and the Future of Work'. There is also Willis' (1977) widely-respected study of how working-class kids learn to get working-class jobs and the contribution which schooling makes to this. This book was the product of SSRC-funded research and employs an ethnographic approach. Other research into aspects of careers education has been undertaken by students, a good example from the Welsh context being that of Grindle (1982). The topic of careers education, interpreted in a wide variety of ways, has also been tackled by several students of the Institute of Education of the University of London (Burke 1979, Bushin 1978, Watson 1979). The place of careers education in the curriculum, and of work as a focus for curriculum activities, is discussed in other dissertations (Abel 1978, Delves 1980, Goodall 1982). Some studies of work experience schemes have also been published including that by Watts (Ed) (1983) and Fitzgerald and Bodiley (1984). The latter study focusses on a Bedfordshire upper school and, amongst other things, demonstrates how time consuming for teachers the setting up of such schemes can be. They also conclude that the effort and burden of extra responsibility is well worthwhile. Finally, Best *et al* (1984) have published an article in *Pastoral Care in Education* which links the notion of 'careers education' with that of the 'welfare curriculum'.

In the 'seventies some shift in emphasis took place in the drive towards giving the curriculum a welfare dimension. This was less because health education and the rest went out of fashion, and more that they were, to an extent, superseded and, to an extent, supplemented by demands for a 'new' group of overlapping 'subjects'. These were (a) education for personal and social development; (b) tutorial group work programmes; and (c) education and training for social-, life-, study-skills.

The first of these has its roots in the kinds of subjects discussed above and in the kind of ideas that informed the Schools Council's *Humanities Curriculum Project*. In the last few years it has received powerful support from HMI (1979) and the APU (1981). The former study, *Aspects of Secondary Education*, focussed upon the provision made for the fourth and fifth forms in a sample of 384 secondary schools. Amongst other things HMI considered 'how far, and by what means, schools fostered the personal and social development of their pupils' (p. 2), and a chapter was devoted to this topic. We shall draw attention to two conclusions. Firstly, that 'in general, schools placed much greater emphasis on fostering the personal development of their pupils through pastoral care than through their curriculum. In only a seventh of schools of all types did HMI consider that sufficient detailed attention had been given to the ways in which the curriculum could serve the pupils' needs in this broader sense' (p. 208). Secondly, that 'both the concept and the assessment of "personal and social" development presented peculiar difficulties' (p. 2).

A couple of years later the APU (1981) were 'asked to produce a comprehensive survey of the whole area' (Foreword). Like HMI, they concluded that 'there was no satisfactory way round the difficulties inherent in proposals for assessment of this area (*ibid*), but were none the less able to produce a map of the territory 'expressed as a grid, representing in its vertical axes the general and specific aspects of personal and social development and its horizontal axes, knowledge, understanding, practical application and attitudes' (p. 7). Attention was then given to the parts of the curriculum to which different aspects of personal and social development can be allocated, implying, as with the HMI (1979) report, that any satisfactory provision must entail curriculum-wide considerations. Although HMI sometimes display a modest reluctance to claim that what they do is in any real sense 'research', it must be said that both the studies discussed in this section possess most of the characteristics of research. This is fortunate because few empirical studies which seek to explore the relationship between pastoral care and the curriculum in the context of particular educational institutions seem to have been attempted. Two honourable exceptions are the study by

Vousden (1983), and Joy's (1981) dissertation report of the characteristics of the relationship between pastoral care and the curriculum in two
schools.

A number of useful general studies of personal and social development have been published (David 1982). More recently, Purnell (1983)
describes and evaluates a personal and social development programme
for an open-access sixth-form with which he has been involved. Finally,
a number of students have researched various aspects of education for
personal and social development in the contemporary secondary school
including the development of the teacher's role (Cole 1982), and the
evaluation of particular programmes (Ribbins 1983).

A related, or perhaps alternative, approach has been adopted in the
provision of active tutorial programmes. In a recent paper in *Pastoral
Care in Education*, Baldwin and Smith (1983a) offer a rationale for this
approach:

> Our thesis is that changes in the school curriculum are being
> outpaced by changes in society. . . . The value system of
> schooling has been dominantly linguistically, cognitively, and
> intellectually based with little emphasis on the emotional,
> intuitive, practical and experimental aspects of human
> development . . . urgent requests, from teachers in Lancashire
> and elsewhere, for materials and help in working with young
> people on personal and social development programmes gave
> rise to the series of resource books known as *Active Tutorial
> Work* (p. 40). (See Baldwin and Wells 1979, Baldwin, Smith
> and Wells 1983.)

Baldwin and Smith (1983) acknowledge that 'the background and
rationale for the project . . . is founded on the research of Dr Leslie
Button' (p. 40). Button (1981) has produced his own active tutorial
programmes in *Group Tutoring for the Form Teacher*. Both Baldwin
et al and Button stress the care that has gone into field-testing their
programmes, but it is Button (1981) who stresses that 'the approaches in
these programmes, which I have called developmental groupwork, were
evolved through previous programmes of action research and experiment
. . .' (p. 2). He argues that action research includes an emphasis on *action*
in a variety of ways:

(a) the participants are actively involved in the study of
    situations that affect them personally;
(b) an enquiry about a situation may already begin to
    influence that situation . . .;
(c) the discoveries that they make may move the participants
    sufficiently for them to want to do something about what
    they have uncovered;

(d) in taking action, the same spirit of enquiry will be continued, and in this way it will be possible to monitor the impact of the action being taken. (p. 16)

Whatever else one might say about this approach, its most sophisticated theoretician clearly and explicitly acknowledges its research orientation.

A final approach or rather group of approaches, is broadly *skills*-based. Its concerns include life skills (Hopson and Scally 1981, 1982), study skills (Gibbs 1981, Hamblin 1982), information skills (Marland 1981), and social skills training (Ellis and Whittington 1981). Much of this work is carefully field-tested and Hopson and Scally (1980) offer a useful rationale for the programmes they were subsequently to publish. Some student research has taken place on aspects of these themes, and here particular mention might be made of research in progress at the University of Durham by Stakes (1984) on 'Life skills in a comprehensive school with special reference to pupils with special educational needs' and by Pyke (1984) on 'The development and evaluation of a life skills programme'.

The Further Education Curriculum and Development Unit (FEU) has translated many of these ideas into a form suitable for the FE context. In a series of publications which seem to take its seminal document *A Basis for Choice* (1979) as a base, the FEU has produced successively *Developing Social and Life Skills* (1980a), *Beyond Coping* (1980b) subtitled *Some approaches to social education, Towards a Guidance Base* (1981), and *Skills for Life* (1982).

As far as we know, Marland (1980) coined the term 'pastoral curriculum', arguing that 'every school should create a pastoral curriculum to establish the concepts, attitudes, facts and skills which are necessary to the individual' (p. 153). What Marland is stressing is that 'the art of the pastoral system is to help all individuals without always giving individual help' (*ibid*). That is, pastoral care has a learning dimension and, therefore, implications for the curriculum and for across-the-curriculum planning on a whole-school basis. Many of the issues which this proposal raises are *conceptual* and will be dealt with shortly. However, there are also practical and organisational problems and some of these are considered in an interesting dissertation by Vousden (1983) who seeks to determine empirically what level of agreement could be reached amongst a group of teachers on the content and method of distribution of such a pastoral curriculum in their school. He also considers the implications of a curriculum policy, based in part on the notion of the 'pastoral curriculum', for what has come to be known as the 'pastoral/academic split'. This issue also raises contentious philosophical problems but, for the moment, we wish to concentrate on the organisational implications of setting up separate pastoral and curricular structures within the school.

(iv) The separation of pastoral and academic structures

In his study of the consequences of setting up separate 'guidance' structures in Scottish secondary schools in the late 1960s and early 1970s, Bennett (1974) recognised that academic staff may see this as an innovation which deflects the attention of the school away from its central 'educational' purposes. Surprisingly little attention has been given to this issue although Burgess (1983) does include a discussion of 'House staff and departmental staff' in his study of Bishops McGregor School. This study is of additional interest because it is based on his PhD research: *An ethnographic study of a comprehensive school* (Burgess 1981) and because the author has published many useful papers culminating in a book on field research (Burgess 1984). Finally, Buckle (1984) is undertaking research into the relationship between the pastoral and the academic in secondary schools, perhaps appropriately entitled 'The Great Divide?'!

Pastoral care: historical and philosophical underpinnings

Until quite recently, neither professional nor, even, amateur historians or philosophers have given much attention to pastoral care. Professional historians continue to ignore it. Earlier in this paper we discussed some of the attempts which have been made to identify the main phases in the historical development of pastoral care and have even suggested one ourselves. Notwithstanding this, Hughes' (1980) paper and earlier book (Hughes 1971), and, especially, Lang's (1982) paper remain the only significant attempts to identify and document the antecedants and subsequent development of institutionalised pastoral care as such, although Daws (1976) does offer an interesting history of the development of school counselling. We shall be particularly pleased to learn of other examples of historical research into pastoral care as a whole or into any particular aspect of it.

Most students of pastoral care have shown some interest in conceptual and ethical problems, however in one early paper (Best *et al* 1977), we argued that 'The growth of pastoral care structures in secondary schools, and the popularity of the concept of "pastoral care" in the vocabularies of a variety of people involved in education, have occurred in the absence of . . . a clear and shared understanding of the concept . . .' (p. 128). In this paper and in others published subsequently, we have sought to clarify the concept of 'pastoral care' and its relationship with (a) such associated concepts as 'guidance' and 'counselling' (Best *et al* 1977) and (b) other dimensions of the work of the school, notably the 'academic' and 'disciplinary' (Best *et al* 1983, Best and Ribbins 1983).

The latter issue, particularly in the context of discussions about the 'pastoral curriculum', has received a good deal of attention recently and has even begun to interest a number of philosophers in 'pastoral care'. These include Hibberd (1984a) and McLaughlin (1984) who have subjected both Marland's (1980) and our own (Best and Ribbins 1983) ideas to a searching philosophical examination. McLaughlin (1982, 1983) has also been engaged in an interesting debate with Elliott (1982) on the idea of a pastoral curriculum.

For some years, Dooley's (1980) exploration of the relationship between the concepts of 'pastoral care' and 'authority' was the only paper by a professional philosopher expressly dealing with pastoral care. The growing interest of others including Wilson and Cowell (1983, 1984) as well as Hibberd and McLaughlin, is a development which is very welcome if long overdue. This development has coincided with a growing interest in conceptual problems amongst other writers. Some examples are Button's (1983) thoughts on the pastoral curriculum, Paul's (1983) paper on the need for consistency of aim rather than of treatment in our dealings with pupils, and Clark's (1983) attempt to explore the etymology and semantic development of pastoral care in terms of a series of semantic clusters. Special mention might also be made of Lord's (1983) attempt to tease out the interplay of three clusters or sources of principles and the development of thought and practice in pastoral care.

Students have also picked up this issue, and some of the best dissertations we have seen deal with philosophical problems. Explicitly so in the case of Chambers (1982) who attempts a 'philosophical appraisal', by no means always uncritically, of the ideas of Hamblin, Marland and ourselves. Grant's (1982) dissertation on 'Moral Objectivity: the preoccupations of pastoral care', is worth reading. Two other noteworthy studies are by French (1982) which involves an analysis of pastoral care in terms of 'the social construction of reality', 'the development of self' and 'the culture of the school', and by Rossborough (1982) which uses a framework derived from the concept of iatrogenics to examine the school experience of the educationally 'sick' and to relate this to aspects of school organisation, including the 'caring' aspect 'which provoke or exacerbate "problem behaviour"' (p. 2). Finally, there are some studies, which although not directly concerned with pastoral care, do have implications for the ways in which we might think about this concept. A good example of this is Weddon's (1979) analysis of the implications for education of the concept of the person.

Pastoral care and the 'world outside' the school or college

Schools and colleges are located within wider socio-political communities and are also a part of a network of welfare concerned with the needs and interests of children, adolescents and young adults. Developments outside the institution can have profound consequences for what happens inside them as the growth of youth unemployment over the last few years has so clearly demonstrated. The relationship between education, unemployment and the future of work has been subjected to a thorough analysis recently by Watts (1983). However, in thinking about pastoral care and the 'world outside', we shall concentrate on two rather different topics on which much has been published and some research carried out.

(i) Home-school relationships

The development of constructive links between the home and the school, and the teacher and the parent, has long been thought to be an important factor in determining what children make of their schooling. Many schools claim to foster links between the home and the school and there are a number of theses which deal with this theme. These tend to be based upon case-studies (Adams 1982, Harris 1976). Some deal with the primary sector (Smith 1981), and one interesting project, Farrell (1984), looks at 'parent involvement with children's problems in a school'. In another interesting dissertation, Eden (1978), considers the crucial issue of the nature of school-parent communication as this was perceived by the parents of a junior school. Given the importance sometimes claimed for home visits, there is remarkably little available on this theme although Llewelyn-Davies *et al* (1977) do describe a scheme in Birmingham in which two home-school liaison officers were appointed with both teaching responsibilities and a brief to develop closer contacts between schools and families. In another study, Raven (1980) offers an interesting evaluation of an educational home-visiting scheme set up in the Lothian Region for pre-school age children. Finally, perhaps the fullest discussion of home-school links continues to be that published in the new edition by Craft *et al* (1981).

(ii) Schools and the welfare network

The role of schools and other organisations in the welfare network and of the relationship between teachers and others concerned with the care of children has stimulated a body of writing. Brief descriptions of the network as a whole have been attempted by Craft (1980) and Welton (1983), the latter dealing explicitly with the place of school-based pastoral care within the wider picture. Another study by Fitzherbert (1977) describes the roles of various services (Health, Child Guidance, School Psychological Service, etc.) in the care of children and suggests how teachers can make best use of these services, whilst Macmillan (1977) focusses specificaly on the work of the Education Welfare Officer. In their section dealing with the Education Welfare Service (EWS) (p. 51)

Skinner *et al* (1983) include the study by Macmillan (1977) along with eleven others, amongst which are two reports by the Educational Studies Unit, Brunel University, of the EWS in the boroughs of Hillingdon (1976a) and Hounslow (1976b). This theme is also investigated by Parks (1983) in an unpublished dissertation which reports on some research in Warwickshire. Skinner *et al* (1983) also refer to fourteen publications which deal with aspects of the role of the School Psychological Service (SPS) (pp. 51–52), and to eleven more which consider the activities of the Child Guidance Service (CGS) (pp. 52–53). Several of these publications report on studies of individual local authorities. Examples of the SPS are of Hounslow (Educational Studies Unit 1976c) and Portsmouth (Wright and Payne 1979), and of the CGS are of the Central Regional Council of Scotland (Central Regional Council 1980), of Croydon (Gath 1977) and of Hounslow (Educational Studies Unit 1977). Reference might also be made to a useful early study conducted by the Hampshire Education Authority (1975) of its pastoral arrangements both internal and external to the school – in the wake of the suicide of Tina Wilson. (There had been allegations of bullying and truancy at the school she attended.) There are also a number of studies which explore the problem of interpersonal and interprofessional interactions between teachers and other welfare professionals. This is a topic which has received a good deal of attention. Skinner *et al* (1983) list twenty-two references and these include general studies of co-operation between education and the personal social services (Association of Directors of Social Services 1978), liaison between the Police, Education and the Social Services (Burton 1981), relations between social workers and teachers (Davies 1976, Social Work Services Group 1980), and case studies of a range of interagency co-operative exercises (Derrick and Watkins 1977). Problems of communication are often identified as a key factor in accounting for conflict between schools and the other welfare agencies. This issue is excellently explored by Dick (1983) in an unpublished dissertation which considers the extent to which ideas about confidentiality inhibit effective communication within the comprehensive school, between the school and the welfare services, and between the various agencies which collectively constitute the welfare service.

Finally, there have been at least two major pieces of funded research which have investigated the relationship between schools and the welfare network. The first, by Welton and Dwyer (1982), is available only in the form of an unpublished report. The study was located in Northern Ireland and set out to examine the organisation and operation of the welfare network for children attending three secondary schools. It was conducted as part of a wider programme of research at the New University of Ulster as part of the home-schools links project. As well as its substantive findings, it also has a number of useful things to say about

40

the advantages and problems of a case-study approach (pp. 2–7). The second study, published in Johnson *et al* (1980), reports some of the findings of a three-year DES-funded investigation and is divided into two parts. The first concentrates on the organisation and provision of pastoral care in four comprehensive schools in London, and the second on the welfare network beyond the school. Both the research methodology and theoretical content of this study have received some criticism (Best 1980).

The role of specialist pastoral care agents

Here we have in mind mainly specialists located in schools, such as school-based social workers and, especially, school counsellors. There is a very large literature and a good deal of research on a wide variety of aspects of the role of the school counsellor along with two journals (*British Journal of Guidance and Counselling* and *The Counsellor*) which publish many articles on this theme. Although we have ourselves researched and written about various aspects of the role of the school counsellor within the comprehensive school (Best *et al* 1983, Ch. 6; Ribbins and Nagra 1982) and have investigated teacher attitudes to the counsellor (Best *et al* 1982, Ribbins *et al* 1983) we do not feel that this is the place to attempt a review of either the literature or research on this theme and neither are we particularly well-qualified to undertake such a review. We hope somebody with a specialist knowledge of this area and an interest in pastoral care will attempt it.

The place of social work in schools and the role of the school-based social worker has attracted the attention of many writers. Bond (1981) offers a particularly interesting research report in which the relationship of the pastoral care staff with a school-based social worker in a Haringey comprehensive is explored. Other studies investigate the sources of tension between teachers and school-based social workers (Davies 1979, Packwood 1976), or consider possible roles for school-based social workers (Johnson 1977). In one early study it is suggested that the welfare work of schools may be better carried out by social workers than by teachers (Lyons 1973)! For further details of these and many other studies that address aspects of this theme, see Skinner *et al* (1983, pp. 59–63).

The teacher and the student

In our preparatory search through the literature we found more books, journal articles and dissertations dealing with this topic than with any other. Accordingly, our survey needs to be even more selective than usual and to give it shape we shall use the four sub-divisions of this theme as we identified them earlier in this paper.

(i) Teacher roles, perspectives and attitudes

Most general studies of pastoral care to some extent consider these subjects. Thus Marland's (1974) seminal book contains a chapter on 'Roles and Responsibilities' in which there are sections on 'the tutor', 'the intermediate pastoral head', and 'senior staff'. There are also books which deal specifically with *one* of these roles of which probably the best known are by Blackburn (1975, 1983). All these texts rely essentially on the experience and practical wisdom of their authors rather than on research. They also make assumptions about teacher perceptions and attitudes which might or might not be discredited if empirical investigation were carried out.

Other studies do rely much more heavily on empirical evidence than upon practical wisdom. Thus our own study of Rivendell (Best *et al* 1983) contains chapters on 'teacher perspectives', 'roles, styles and ideologies', 'identities' and the 'management of continuity and change'. There are also a number of journal articles which are research-based of which two by Pashley and Shepherd (1975, 1978) are particularly interesting because they explore how university staff see the pastoral role of the academic. The attitudes of teachers to pastoral care in schools has received a good deal of attention recently although little of this has as yet been published (Mace 1980, Ribbins *et al* 1982, Morgan 1984, Grace 1982). In this context, one early example of student research into the role of the teacher in pastoral care is interesting, not least because of its use of the term 'pupil guidance' (Ginifer 1972) for what would now be widely recognised, outside Scotland, as 'pastoral care'.

(ii) Pupil roles, perspectives and attitudes

If a good deal has been written on the roles and attitudes of teachers there is a great deal more which deals with students and pupils in similar terms. There are a number of texts which consider the perceptions which pupils and students have of various aspects of their experience of the school or college. For example, Thomson (1975) discusses the attitudes of secondary school pupils to their teachers and schools, Murgatroyd (1977) considers how pupils perceive counselling, and Lang (1983) offers a wide-ranging analysis of pupil attitudes to pastoral care based on some of his current research into this topic. Finally, White and Brockington (1983) depict the experience of seventy young people most of whom left school at sixteen. Their reflections upon their school experience, presented largely in their own words, make salutory reading, not least for teachers with pastoral responsibilities.

There are also a number of studies dealing with particular critical incidents within the career of every pupil. Curiously, although a growing number of studies deal with pupil perception of transfer from primary to secondary education, much less has been done on their perceptions of the process of choosing subject options in the third year. Thus there are a number of journal articles dealing, for example, with 'the structure of pupils' worries during transfer' (Brown and Armstrong 1982), 'pupils' views on transfer' (Thorpe 1983) and dissertations on similar themes (Henstock 1983, Mwale 1979, Thorpe 1980). Further studies consider how students entering or about to enter school sixth forms or colleges view transition (Ball 1983, Ball and Pumfrey 1984, Morgan 1984).

A third set of studies deal with the attitudes and perceptions of various groups of pupils to other aspects of their schooling. These include two dissertations considering student attitudes to pastoral care in sixth-forms and colleges (Kyte 1979, Morgan 1984), and a study by Bazalgette (1983) which looks, in part, at the way in which a group of eight underachieving disruptive girls see their own experience of school and of their role within it. Another dissertation, by Hutchinson (1979) deals with the 'attitudes of three ethnic groups of children towards school and discipline' and the fourth chapter of Tattum's (1982) book on disruptive pupils identifies five vocabularies of motive which his sample of 'deviant' pupils used to justify their behaviour.

Finally, there are many studies which deal with the attitudes of various categories of 'disaffected' pupils. Easily the most numerous of these are those which explore the views of truants and other school refusers (Buist 1980, Carroll 1977, Jackson 1978, Reid 1980). Skinner *et al* (1983) list many more such reports and also include references to several studies which deal with the attitudes of disorderly and disruptive pupils (Bird *et al* 1980, Marsh *et al* 1978, Sharp 1981).

(iii) Teacher–pupil interactions

Studies of this kind are enormously varied. Firstly, there are those which deal with particular critical incidents in the career of every pupil, for example, 'induction and management of transfer'. Horsfield and Shaw (1984) describe how one school manages this and Best *et al* (1983) critically examine what is taking place under the guise of 'induction' in another. A second set of studies consider a wide range of interactions between teachers and pupils, and pupils and pupils, concerned with the giving of help and the maintenance of control. Examples of the former include Friday's (1984) paper on 'Pastoral Care and the Academic Child', Rutter's (1975) study *Helping Troubled Children*, Murgatroyd and Wolfe's (1982) *Coping with Crisis* and Lago and Ball's ominously titled 'The almost impossible task: Helping in a multi-racial context' (1983). Examples of the latter include studies concerned explicitly with discipline and its maintenance such as Jennings' (1979) *Discipline in Primary and Secondary Schools Today* and the monograph by Coomber and Whitfield (1979) which arose out of some research sponsored by the NAS.

Numerous other studies consider the 'production' and the 'treatment' of the 'disaffected pupil'. Much of this rich literature deals with two broad classes of pupil – those who are difficult and disruptive in school and those who stay away from school. Skinner (1983) includes pages of references on both these themes.

Reports on children who stay away from school discuss a wide variety of related themes including studies of 'truancy', 'absenteeism' and 'school phobia'. Some consider the origins of such unjustified absence and include those which stress the role of the school (Carroll 1977, Reynolds and Murgatroyd 1977) or that of the home (Barker 1974) as a significant causal factor. Other studies either present and interrogate the complex facts about truants and other unlawful absentees (DES 1975, ILEA 1981) or they discuss and analyse some of the many factors claimed to be related to this phenomenon. Finally, several studies describe and evaluate the merits of existing methods and machinery designed to monitor, prevent and control all forms of unjustified absence (Avery 1978, Green 1980, Kahn, Nursten and Carroll 1981).

An even larger number of studies deal with all aspects of the difficult and disruptive pupil and many of these either report on research or make substantial use of it. This is true of the many studies which examine the extent and incidence of disruptive behaviour in schools either in the form of general surveys (DES 1975, Laslett 1977) or as field studies of particular schools (Lawrence 1981) or of specific LEAs (Bird *et al* 1980). A particularly good example of the latter is by Galloway *et al* (1982) in which they report on their two-year study of disruptive pupils in Sheffield. For a wider ranging, sociological study of the nature and meaning of disruptive behaviour in schools Tattum's (1982) study has much to offer although its treatment of off-site units has been questioned by some reviewers. As it happens the topic of 'off-site units' as a partial solution to the problem of disruptive (and truanting) pupils has received a great deal of attention (Skinner *et al* 1983, list fifty references). Much of what has been written reports on field research conducted in individual units (Ball, C. and M. 1980, Dain 1977) or in particular LEAs (Basini 1980). Conversely 'on-site units' within schools have excited less interest although some studies have been done (Jones and Forrest 1977, Leavold 1977). Yet other studies deal with the various aspects of the process and character of exclusion and suspension. Shoesmith (1982), in an unpublished dissertation, looks at suspension in two Midland LEAs and Ling (1983) does the same in another. Although Skinner *et al* (1983) do not quote any of these studies they do list eleven others which deal with this topic and also include twenty-six references to the activities and role of the courts (pp. 56–57). Finally a few studies consider the role of the 'delinquent school' (Power 1967, Reynolds 1976) in the production of delinquent, disruptive or truanting activities amongst its pupils and of the 'good school' in minimising such behaviour (HMI 1977, Rutter *et al* 1979).

Finally, there are a number of papers which deal with the characteristics of linguistic interactions between teachers and pupils in the pastoral context and some suggestions as to how these might be improved (Taylor 1980, Ribbins and Ribbins 1982).

(iv) The training of teachers for pastoral care

There is, as yet, very little written and very little research on this theme. The modest NAPCE pilot-study (Maher and Best 1984) reported *ibid* is therefore a welcome contribution. One or two studies suggest that the neglect of this area reflects the paucity of training available (HMI 1982, Jayne 1974). For those interested in 'preparing for promotion in pastoral care', there is only Marland's (1983) paper available.

The literature of pastoral care has made a late start but it is clear from this review that it is rapidly making up for lost time. We would predict that the kind of modest thematic review we have attempted here will have become quite impossible by the end of the decade. Only an extensive search using the facilities of modern information technology is likely to be able to gather anything like a representative sample, and it will then be impossible to do justice to the variety and the volume of work in the field in anything shorter than a full-length book.

Research in pastoral care

In various places in this paper, we have pointed out the distinction between what passes for 'knowledge' or 'wisdom' on the one hand, and established 'truths' which are founded on something more than beliefs or ideals (i.e. founded upon some systematic and rigorous enquiry). Of the 'knowledge' enshrined in the literature and described in the previous section, it is clear that much has no research foundation. In fact it is probably true to say that only recently has research contributed anything and then it is only a relatively small part of the total corpus of 'wisdom'. This might be illustrated in a development of the earlier model (see Figure 2), where the shaded area represents that part of all the 'knowledge' or 'wisdom' which is attributable to research. However, even within such a small area it is necessary to distinguish different types of knowledge. If we accept in some measure the phenomenological view that 'knowledge' is a social construct, and 'research' a social practice, then different research styles or methodologies will produce types of 'knowledge' which are in some way distinctive.

The epistemological and methodological problems of researching pastoral care have themselves been the subject of a number of articles. With a certain and acknowledged inconsistency, we have ourselves

Figure 2   A three-dimensional model for classifying pastoral care 'knowledge'

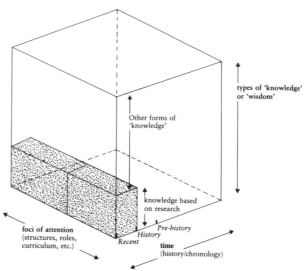

variously advocated a phenomenological approach (Ribbins *et al* 1977) and an eclecticism (Best *et al* 1979a, 1979b) in respect of our own research, and have given attention to the problems of data-collection and interpretation in researching this area (Ribbins *et al* 1981). These issues are re-addressed in our paper (Best and Ribbins 1985). Button (1981) has written of the strengths of action-research in the development of curriculum materials and tutorial programmes and more recently Delwyn Tattum (1982), in his work on disruptive pupils, argued in favour of a 'symbolic interactionist' approach which 'rests on the premise that human action takes place *always* in a situation that confronts the actor and that the actor acts on the basis of *defining this situation* that confronts him. Thus the study of violent behaviour would require that the student identify the way in which the actor sees and defines the situation in which he is placed and in which he acts violently' (p. x). Conversely 'Non-interactionist approaches view people as passively prompted to behave by compelling internal or external forces – a determinism the interactionist is distinctly wary of' (p. xi). In Hamblin's recent work (1981), two contributors (Jones and Doherty) discuss models of research which might be adopted respectively for the evaluation of pastoral care in schools and the in-service training of teachers for pastoral roles. Finally, *Pastoral Care in Education* has carried a number of articles concerned either directly or indirectly with the mechanics of research, notably those of Burgess (1983) and Winter (1983) who are concerned with the strengths and problems of teacher-based research and evaluation.

Of course, any attempt to classify research styles employed in this area to date will inevitably blur fine distinctions and no doubt offend some

Themes

Methodology	1 Teachers and students				2 Specialist roles/ perspectives	3 Institutions and the world 'outside'	4 Structures/ systems/ processes	5 The pastoral and the academic	6 Philosophical/ historical underpinnings
	Teacher-student interaction	Training for roles	Student roles/ perspectives/ attitudes	Teacher roles/ perspectives/ attitudes					
Philosophical								McLaughlin '82, '83 Hibberd '84 Marland '80	Dooley '80 Best et al '77, '83 Lord '83 Clark '83 Hughes '80 Lang '84 Lang and Ribbins '84
Historical									
Quantitative/ positivist	Galloway et al '82	NAPCE (Maher and Best '84)		Best et al '81 Antonouris '74, '76 Lytton et al '70 Best et al '83	Fulton '73		Monks et al '72 HMI '79 Ch. 9 HMI/SED '76		
Interpretive/ qualitative/ ethnographic/ case-study	Taylor '80 Ribbins and Ribbins '82 Tattum '82		HMI (Wales) '82 Lang '83			Johnson et al '80 Weston '80 Hurman '78	HMI (Wales) '82 Metcalf et al '82 Moore '70 Tattum '82 Best et al '83		
Action-research/ R and D			Bazalgette '83					ATW '79 to '83 Button '80 '81	
Teacher as researcher			Sadler '83 Tattum '82						

Figure 3   Typology of pastoral care research

researchers. However, models are necessarily simplifications which, while essential tools in understanding reality, inescapably distort that reality to a greater or lesser degree, so we trust that the purists of any methodological persuasion will at least bear with us long enough to consider the potential of one such classification. We suggest six broad types of research: philosophical, historical, quantitative/positivist, interpretive/qualitative/ethnographic/case-study, action-research/R and D, and teacher-as-researcher. If we apply these to the earlier list of potential foci for research, we have some sort of 'map' of the types of 'knowledge' which published research has so far illuminated (see Figure 3).

Obviously, in concentrating on the literature review, including as it does a glimpse of published and unpublished research, we have been unable at the same time to attempt to locate all such research on this map. The entries, which are restricted to published work, are therefore illustrative rather than exhaustive. The reader may like to test his or her awareness of such research by attempting to fill in the many gaps.

Summary and conclusions

We have attempted to provide a number of related theoretical frameworks within which all that passes for 'knowledge' or 'wisdom' about pastoral care in education might be located and analysed. This has entailed attempts to:

1   establish the distinction between knowledge based upon rigorous and systematic enquiry ('research-based'), and 'knowledge' derived either from thoughtful reflections upon commonsense experience or else from beliefs expressing nothing more than dogma and prejudice;
2   outline and critically examine previous attempts to describe the historical development of thought and practice in pastoral care;
3   derive from these descriptions a refined and coherent historical framework for the analysis of the growth and development of thought and practice in pastoral care;
4   deduce the set of themes with which the corpus of 'knowledge' about pastoral care in education must be concerned;
5   review, in the light of these themes, a representative sample of the literature which is concerned with pastoral care in education;
6   consider to what extent research has contributed to the corpus of knowledge contained within this literature;
7   note the variety of approaches to research which have been employed in investigating this area;
8   construct, from these approaches, in the light of the themes about which knowledge is concerned, a typology of pastoral care research;

and, finally,

9   illustrate the potential of this typology by locating some existing published research within its categories.

We have argued that, until quite recently, the developing wisdom of pastoral care has relied largely upon the prescriptions of practitioners derived from their own experience. We would not deny that this wisdom contained much of practical value, but such prescriptions have not commonly been based upon, nor sought confirmation in the fruits of systematic enquiry. This was perhaps easily justified when there was no alternative. What this review has established is that the recent development of research, published and unpublished, may already be sufficiently extensive as to render such a justification unacceptable.

Pragmatism and common sense are not unattractive qualities, but there is no virtue in the kind of philistinism which rejects the insights which research can bring simply because researchers are seen to be remote from practice. In regard to pastoral care, this is especially true for two reasons. Firstly, so much of the research now appearing is very much concerned with improving practice through both 'technique' and 'critique'; and secondly, because much of it is in fact being undertaken by the practitioners themselves.

Note

1. This practice is still adopted in some quarters. For two recent examples, see P. Dawson's self-congratulatory work entitled *Making a Comprehensive Work* (Basil Blackwell 1981), and D. John, *Leadership in Schools* (Heinemann 1981).

Preparation and support for pastoral care:
A survey of current provision

Peter Maher and Ron Best

This paper reports some findings from a small pilot-survey of initial and in-service training and local authority support for teachers involved in pastoral care activities. It represents a first attempt by NAPCE to establish the quality and extent of such provision, and to identify areas where improvements need to be made.

The study was undertaken in three parts: a survey of teachers and head-teachers in a sample of secondary schools (coordinated by Peter Maher); a survey of local authority provision (initiated by Peter Lang); and a study of colleges and departments of teacher-education (coordinated by Ron Best). The major part of the pilot-study was concerned with teachers' perceptions of the adequacy or otherwise of their initial and post-experience training as a preparation for their pastoral-care roles.

The survey samples

The eighteen schools from which the participants were drawn were spread nationwide. We cannot however claim they are representative of all types of areas. We can say that some were in large conurbations and others in rural areas; some were in heavily industrialised regions and some in a surburban setting. Together they represented a range of roll size from 418 to 1580. Seventeen of the schools were co-educational, the one exception was an all girls' school. The Burnham group sizes varied from group 8 through to group 13 (protected). Fifteen were single-site schools, two schools occupied two sites whilst one school was spread across three sites (Table 1). In our sample, there was a clear preference for pastoral structures which split the school in a horizontal fashion. Six schools operated a straightforward division into year groups, each with a year tutor. Some schools operated a two-tier system where the division was firstly into Lower and Upper or Lower, Middle and Upper schools in

Table 1 *Details of survey schools*

SUMMARY OF STRUCTURE

PASTORAL POSTS

Roll size	Est.	Group	Age range	Sites	DH	ST	4	3	2	SUMMARY OF STRUCTURE
418	43.2	10	11–16	1	1	–	1	4	–	Horizontal – Year Tutors
700	47	10	13–18	1	–	–	2	5	2	Horizontal – Year Tutors + Assistants
726	43	9	11–18	1	1	–	–	4	–	Vertical – DH (Pastoral) + 4 Houses
751	39.2	8	11–14	1	–	–	–	2	4	Horizontal – Upper and Lower School + Year Tutors + Assistants
760	45.2	10	11–18	1	1	1	–	–	5	Horizontal – Upper and Lower School + Year Tutors + Assistants
815	52.6	11	14–19	1	2	–	1	2	2	Headteacher declared 'No formal pastoral structure'
820	55	11	11–18	1	1	3	1	5	1	Horizontal – Upper and Lower School + Year Tutors (All girls school)
865	58.5	10	11–16	1	2	–	–	3	1	Horizontal – Lower (1, 2), Middle (3, 4), Upper (5) Schools
948	52	10	11–16	1	2	–	2	3	–	Horizontal – Year Tutors
1057	63.1	11	11–18	1	2	1	2	4	3	Horizontal – Lower School, Upper School + Sixth Form + Year Tutors
1070	65	11	11–18	1	1	1	2	3	3	Horizontal – Lower, Upper + Sixth Form + Tutors (Head of Lower = First Year Tutor)
1116	66.5	11	11–19	1	1	–	3	2	–	Horizontal – Year Tutors + Assistants (DH = Sixth Form Tutor)
1139	70	13	11–18	2	2	3	3	–	–	Horizontal – Year Tutors
1180	68.3	11	11–18	1	1	1	2	–	–	Horizontal – Lower (1, 2), Upper (3, 4, 5), Sixth Form
1210	88.5	12	11–18	2	1	3	1	8	10	Horizontal – Lower (1, 2, 3), Upper (4, 5, 6) + Year Tutors + Assistants. Split site
1376	80.3	12	11–18	3	1	2	2	4	5	Horizontal – D.H. (Pastoral), Lower (1, 2, 3), Upper (4, 5, 6), Head + Assistant + Year Tutors + Assistants
1550	90.2	12	11–18	1	1	2	5	4	1	Horizontal/Vertical-Lower (1, 2) Sixth Form, Years 3–5 split into 6 houses
1580	93.5	12	11–18	1	2	1	5	–	–	Horizontal – Lower (1–3) Upper (4, 5) Deputies, Sixth Form, Year Tutors

51

addition to a year tutor system. In both cases some heads of school and/or year tutors also had assistants.

Only one school had a distinct vertical structure with four houses. A second school had a strangely mixed system with horizontal groupings for first, second and sixth-form students while the remaining year groups (3–5) were divided into houses. The headteacher of the final school declared that he had 'no formal pastoral structure' but then went on to admit that two Deputies, one scale 4, two scale 3 and two scale 2 teachers had specific pastoral responsibility. This was an anomaly that we were unable to follow up.

The college survey set out to investigate the nature, extent and adequacy of training for teachers' pastoral roles provided by colleges and departments of teacher-education. For purposes of analysis, this training can be categorised as (a) initial professional training; (b) higher degrees and other post-graduate award-bearing courses; and (c) in-service training of various types. Fourteen institutions, selected entirely on the basis of personal contacts, were approached during September and October 1983. Twelve responded to the initial questionnaire by the closing date. Nine of the respondents were subsequently interviewed to explore the details of their initial responses, and their returns revised or supplemented where discussion showed this to be necessary.

The composition of the final sample was as follows:

Colleges of Education	1
University Departments/Schools of Education	4
University Institutes of Education	1
Polytechnic Departments/Schools of Education	2
Colleges of Higher Education	4
Total	12

While this is a relatively small number of responses, it does represent all of the five types of institutions offering teacher-education. It also contains institutions in very different settings and of various sizes. With caution, some generalisations may be permissible.

The survey of local authority provision was by questionnaire which was completed and returned by representatives of ten LEAs. These comprised one London Borough, two authorities in North-Eastern industrial areas, three Midlands authorities, three Southern (and relatively prosperous) Counties, and one authority serving a major conurbation. From such a small sample, it is clear that only very tentative comments can be made.

Initial training

Of the 91 schoolteacher respondents (other than the headteachers) surprisingly no fewer than 79 (87%) argued that their initial training contained either a negligible amount of work on pastoral care topics or nothing at all. This could not have been exclusively due to the lapse of time since training, as there were four probationers amongst this group, and we may anticipate that, having left college for less than a year, their memories would be reasonably fresh. We are assured too, of an increasing awareness of the need to train teachers for their pastoral role. the more recent experiences of these respondents could then be expected to reflect such a shift in emphasis. Three of the four probationers, however, described the pastoral care training content as 'very little', 'very small proportion', and 'practically nothing'. The fourth probationer recalled, as if to pierce the gloom with an optimistic light, 'there was an optional course in the last term, which was very popular'. Alas, our hopes are dashed when she concluded 'Unfortunately because of the numbers (of students choosing this option) I had to choose another option. Therefore I have no experience in this area.'

There were only six teachers in our sample who were able to talk in positive terms about their training for their pastoral role. One followed a very specific course tailored to her interests; of the other five, only one had the opportunity to follow a specific course in 'pastoral care' which was offered as an optional unit. Disappointingly, he describes the course as having had 'no direct relevance'. The remaining four followed courses where 'nothing was specifically labelled as "pastoral care"'. In one course it was possible to opt for modules entitled 'Adolescence, Peers and Parents', or 'Truancy and School Phobia'. Even having undertaken these specific modules, this teacher, after four years as a form tutor observed that 'no warning was given of how much administration was involved!'

The recollection of these teachers seemed to be supported by the information offered by the colleges. All but one of the institutions surveyed offered a post-graduate Certificate in Education (PGCE), and all seven of the public sector institutions (i.e. excluding the universities) also offered a BEd degree or range of degrees (i.e. Ordinary and Honours, age-band related). Four of these colleges also offered specialist Certificates in Education, two providing qualifications for FE lecturers and two for instructors in Craft, Design and Technology. One university school, formerly a free-standing college of education, is phasing out its BEd and replacing it with a BA in Education.

None of the various courses give much time to the consideration of pastoral care topics. Five of the twelve courses about which respondents attempted some quantification devoted 2% or less of the syllabus time to such topics, and in none of the twelve was more than 5% of the course allocated to them. Bearing in mind the very short duration of the PGCE course, especially after block teaching-practices are taken out, this often means a large group of students hearing a handful of lectures on a common 'foundations' course. One university department gauges this to be about five and a half hours, another two and a half hours, and a third half a day. Now of course this may underestimate the time actually spent on pastoral care issues, since they may also receive consideration under other headings. But it is arguable that the choice of labels does reflect the perspective and priorities of those who do the labelling. Certainly, *some* students receive *some* tuition in pastoral care as part of a component, but this means that it is not the main concern of the tutors and that the amount of coverage is both absolutely and relatively small.

Thus, while pastoral-care topics were said to be dealt with to varying extents, in the context of option courses in Pyschology, Youth and Community or Health Education, or else in the context of a Curriculum Studies course, only in *one* college was there a specific option in pastoral care. Of the many hundreds of student-teachers represented in this sample, only twenty pursue a pastoral care option. Nor is pastoral care especially in evidence in the more practical aspects of initial training. Although most, if not all, secondary teachers will be expected to be form tutors at some time – and many in their probationary year! – institutions are not always committed to training for such roles. While four of the institutions surveyed did require students to take on a pastoral-role on teaching practice (e.g. attachment to a tutor-group), another five did not. The remainder either had no clear policy or else 'encouraged' or 'recommended' such experience but left it to the placement schools to decide if and in what way such experience was to be gained.

When asked whether performance of such roles was assessed in teaching-practice grades, only two institutions responded positively. In no institution was there a formal statement of the criteria by which such a role would be assessed, although three institutions said that some informal consideration might be given as, for example, where a school's report on a student chose to make some comment in this area.

Of course it might be argued – and was, by some respondents – that such questions would have little point in respect of training for the primary sector where 'the pastoral' is held to be an integral part of much, if not all, of the teacher's role. It is less easy to sustain such an argument in respect of the secondary sector, however, and here it is interesting that half of the sample make little or no distinction between training for these two sectors in regard to what is offered on pastoral care. The picture, thus painted, looks gloomy. The vast majority to our teacher sample could not recall any training that was relevant to their pastoral role in school; those who could, for the most part found the experience of little practical value. This was confirmed by the survey of college provision which left the impression that this aspect of initial training is still much under-considered. However, not all teachers were confident that such training was even possible in the college context. Many simply could not see what training could have been given that would have made them more effective in their pastoral role. Such views were characterised by the teacher who told us: 'situations met in pastoral care are so different that I don't think you can train people for pastoral care; experience is more valuable than training.' Others are prepared to go further on this issue: 'Probably such training is not possible except on the shop floor.' It is certainly true that a whole range of teachers felt that their teaching-practice experience, their first appointments in school, and the help and guidance of colleagues was of far greater significance than anything offered by their college course. The comment from one that she had 'gained good experience on teaching practice' was echoed throughout the sample. Another was more specific and offered the praise: 'I was most fortunate to have an excellent guide and mentor in my head of year who saw me safely through my first year and fostered my interest in this area.' Some of those who found the degree of preparation 'woefully inadequate' were able to add that 'in a school with a more complete induction scheme, the lack is less noticeable.'

When we asked colleges to make their assessment of the adequacy of their institutions' provision for the development of teachers' pastoral roles the responses varied widely. To some extent this seems to be due to assumptions about *when* such training should take place. Thus, some respondents thought initial training to be adequate since pastoral care would, in any case, be a more appropriate focus for post-experience courses, while others (the majority) tended to compare initial provision unfavourably with their INSET programmes. Others pointed to recent developments in education (such as the Warnock Report and the 1981 Act) which they believe will entail greater involvement with pastoral issues than hitherto, but these challenges have not really yet been faced. A major problem mentioned by the university departments in particular, was the impossibility of providing adequate training for *any* aspect of the teacher's role in a course as short as the PGCE. As one respondent put it:

> Schools are becoming more and more difficult. All we can hope to do in the short time available is to give them (the students) a 'survival pack' as subject-teachers. Pastoral care has to have a low priority. We have to do what we can with the 'candy floss' informally.

Others pointed to institutional antagonisms of one sort or another which seriously hamper attempts to improve provision. Two respondents commented on schools' hostility to students being involved in form-tutor duties while on teaching practice, and another reported how the distribution of secondments by the LEA had effectively strangled at birth a DES-approved one-term course. A fourth described the failure of sccessive attempts to either expand provision in courses for FE lecturers, or gain some input into the secondary BEd and PGCE courses, commenting that:

> I view the present position as totally unsatisfactory. Staffing expertise is available immediately to significantly increase input in these course areas.

Overall, the responses indicate a general lack of confidence in the adequacy of this aspect of teacher-education.

In-service training opportunities

The next area of questioning sought to establish the extent to which in-service training had been used to compensate for what was perceived, by the majority, to be a poor preparation in their initial training. Of the 79 respondents who considered the adequacy of their initial training for pastoral care roles to be nil or very poor, only 44 had undertaken in-service courses which might have made good this deficiency. In all, only 49 teachers said they had been on any in-service training courses on pastoral care topics. (Of these, three offered courses which hardly seemed, to us, to relate to this topic, though in deference to their views we have included them.) The fact that only just over half had availed themselves of the benefit of any such course was significant in itself. A closer analysis of the length of service of the sample reveals a further, more disturbing aspect (see Table 2).

Table 2 *Percentage of respondents attending courses as analysed by length of service*

Length of service (years)	0–4	5–9	10–14	15–19	20–24	25–35
Total sample	16	12	28	16	9	10
% who had attended course*	25	42	57	69	78	60

* given to the nearest percentage point

Not surprisingly only 4 of the 16 teachers with less than 5 years experience had attended relevant courses. However, it might have been expected that the longer-serving teachers were more likely to have attended courses of this type. In fact, a considerable number of long serving teachers had not attended pastoral care courses. Of the 63 teachers in our survey who had more than 10 years experience, 37% of them had attended no courses on pastoral care topics.

How helpful had these courses proved to be for those 49 teachers who had attended? The courses were judged to have been extremely valuable and relevant by 20% of the teachers, while a further 43% found them beneficial. There was not one in our sample who had found such courses of no value at all. It would seem reasonable to conclude that such in-service provision had proved helpful to a significant proportion of the teachers questioned; however we are still left to wonder why there was such a substantial minority which had failed to improve its effectiveness in this way. One possible conclusion is that these teachers simply did not have the inclination to attend. Another might be that such courses were in short supply.

The institutions were asked to describe any courses (other than higher-degree and post-graduate awards) which offer specific components on pastoral care. The picture of provision is again patchy. One university department is planning a one-week DES-listed course in July (1984) but offers nothing at present, whereas another annually offers eight students half an in-service BEd programme on pastoral issues, and also offers six- and seven-day residential courses for some 70 teachers interested in group work and pastoral care. The university institute offers a one-year full-time Diploma in Pastoral Care and related concerns as well as occasional one-day DES teachers' centre courses, and gives minimal coverage (1½ days) to pastoral topics in its one term, full-time course in management for headteachers. Three of the public sector colleges and one university offer pastoral care options of some sort comprising anything from 10 to 50% of their in-service BEd programmes, and there is some 'pastoral content' in other schemes (e.g. the BEd in Special Educational Needs offered in one college). One polytechnic department offers sixteen places each year on a CNAA Diploma in Professional Studies in Curriculum and Pastoral Care, and one university offers a student-focussed Advance Certificate in Pastoral Care, although this attracts only a tiny number of secondments.

Local authorities were also asked to describe and assess what was offered by them in the way of in-service training. Their responses show clearly enough that *some* importance is given to pastoral care. Most respondents could point to some forms of in-service training provided within the authority (usually being a combination of teachers' centre and school-based courses), and six of the respondents indicated some intention by their authorities to further develop this provision. However, it would be easy to overestimate the adequacy of local provision. The in-service work that is mentioned does not suggest a systematic and comprehensive pattern of courses within any authority other than the large conurbation. Several authorities are described as having in-service activities which are of short duration (e.g. one-day seminars), others are specific to particular schemes (e.g. ATW), and one authority seems to rely on NAPCE conferences as a substantial part of its provision! Several respondents wrote of their intention to expand provision in this area, although these plans are either modest in scale (e.g. one authority hopes to further develop its already instituted ATW work, and another says it has demand for 'DWTG courses' which it will try to meet), or still at the stage of a desired but uncertain goal. Resource constraints are considerable, and as one respondent points out, little may be achieved if other curriculum areas have to suffer in order to release resources.

If provision of relevant courses by outside agencies is insufficient to meet demand, one option open to all schools is to run their own school-based courses. Such an in-serivce programme by the school can involve a more substantial proportion of staff than would be able to attend a similar course organised outside school. In addition, such a course can be made more directly relevant to the specific school's environment and therefore more attractive to the staff.

Of the sample, 36 teachers (40%), had attended school-based in-service courses. For 13 of these this was the only type of course they had attended on pastoral care topics; the remaining teachers had attended both outside and school-based in-service training courses. This still left a disturbing 29 teachers out of the total sample who had not attended any course on pastoral care. Put in another way, 37% of the 79 teachers who complained that their initial training contained insufficient training for pastoral care had made no attempt to remedy this deficiency by attending a course. The participants' response to these school-based in-service courses was good. Of the 36 teachers who attended such courses, 23 thought them to be useful or, in some cases, extremely useful; only 6 found them of little or no value at all. 59% of our sample of teachers had attended some course on a topic related to pastoral care.

The theme that ran throughout the comments on the courses was that much of the benefit was gained through contact with other teachers. One teacher offered a typical comment when he said that such courses '. . . provided opportunities to present problems and hear other peoples' approaches to resolving them. Common difficulties seemed to provoke a lot of discussion and useful ideas for approaches.' Another teacher listed four benefits to be gained from courses other than the direct experience of the course material. These were '(a) discussing common problems, (b) sharing experiences, (c) exchanging ideas and (d) planning ahead.'

Provision of courses

Were there any perceptible patterns in the provision of courses? When viewed on a regional basis, it is gratifying to note the uniformity of provision of pastoral care courses outside the school setting. One might argue that provision is inadequate and that some local authorities are apparently more generous than others. Otherwise the picture is very much as one might have imagined.

An apparent anomaly emerged, however, in regard to the provision of *school-based* courses. One region of the country which was represented by six schools in our sample, had no school-based provision whatsoever!

This is certainly a finding which needs clarification. Would a more representative sample show this apparent regional variation not to be valid? If it is so, what series of factors combined to produce such an extraordinary result? And might this be true of yet other regions not included in our sample?

Award-bearing courses were treated in the survey as a separate issue. In our sample, 28 teachers had undertaken an award-bearing course since qualifying. Ten of these teachers had attended courses which contained at least some elements on pastoral care topics and a further five found their courses had content which one participant referred to as 'of tangential relevance to pastoral care'. Of the ten, two had not completed the course (one an MA(Ed) and the other a BEd), because secondment for the full-time second year of the course was refused by their LEAs. Three, in fact, had done more than one such course: one had an Advanced Dip Ed and a Diploma in Counselling and Careers Guidance, a second had a Dip Ed and two MAs and the third had an Advanced Dip Ed and an MEd. Of these ten, six respondents found their course either worthwhile or extremely worthwhile, another one found some value in his course whilst the remaining three found only minimal relevance in the courses they had undertaken.

A number of the courses where some research was involved had been used by some of these teachers to do specific study in an aspect of pastoral care. Generally, taught courses were seen as being less relevant.

The institutions surveyed provide a variety of advanced courses including MEd, MPhil, PhD, Advanced Diploma, MA, MSc and BPhil awards. These are offered predominantly in the university sector although one college of higher education offers an MEd and an MSc, and the polytechnic an MEd in Curriculum Studies. All public-sector higher education institutions have the opportunity to sponsor MPhil and PhD applicants to the CNAA, although the number of such students in the field of education is known to be small. Respondents were asked to indicate the nature and extent of pastoral care content in such courses. The response was disappointing. Although one university department is about to introduce an option in pastoral care which will comprise half of the MA programme for those students who take it, this gain is more than balanced by the phasing out in 1982 of a long-standing provision for full-time MEd and Dip Ed courses in another university. In the remaining university departments, pastoral care features either as a topic for a small number of lectures only or is implied in other topics. It is covered in connection with Educational Psychology in the MA/MSc in one institution, with the MEd courses in two others (one of which includes a Guidance and Counselling option within the Educational Pyschology strand), and in the BPhil (Ed) programme in another. It also appears as a small part of some courses concerned with special education and behavioural and learning problems.

Two public-sector institutions admit that pastoral content in their Masters' programmes is nil while another reports that of the 30 or so students pursuing such programmes only one in any year would be concentrating on a pastoral care topic for their dissertation. It seems that the importance of pastoral care receives some recognition within provision at this level. However, it is invariably on the periphery of the main preoccupations of such courses. As one respondent writes:

> Some of the BPhil (Ed) courses do deal with topics that might be considered as 'pastoral'. . . . But there is no BPhil course dealing specifically with pastoral care. Much the same is true of the taught MEd. Thus 'pastoral' topics are included in a number of the courses (see Prospectus) including educational administration, educational psychology, special education, etc. There is no course as such which mentions pastoral care in the title (and I don't think the term is mentioned once in either prospectus!) Possibly the nearest equivalent is the professional training course for the MEd for educational psychologists – though even this does not mention 'pastoral care' as such!

Where options or more formal specialisms are present these are entirely due to the initiatives of particular individuals, and experience suggests that when the individual disappears, so does the provision.

However, there are some encouraging signs for the future when one looks at the research dimension of the institutions' provision. Although most of our sample report no major research at present, two of the public-sector institutions surveyed have recently completed SSRC-funded projects with a pastoral focus and one of the university departments is about to apply for external funding in this area. Two other public-sector institutions in the sample report LEA-backed consultancy on the use of tutorial time and related issues, and some lecturers are said to be researching pastoral care for their doctorates. While we have already noted the small scale of involvement of research students in pastoral care research, there are indications that this is growing.

There may be less grounds for concern about the adequacy of training, if new entrants to the profession are carefully and systematically introduced to the structure and processes of pastoral care in their schools. Over 70% of the schools surveyed claimed to have some sort of an induction programme. Some of these were very elaborate with lectures, seminars and visits for new teachers: in other schools the extent of the programme was confined to one pre-term meeting with the headteacher and what could be gleaned from the staff handbook. Of those schools running induction programmes only one was able to boast any extensive formal coverage of the role of the form tutor. Several schools however did operate an 'apprenticeship' scheme for probationers whereby they were offered joint responsibility for a form with an experienced tutor. This process of 'learning on the job' was seen as the most appropriate form of training that could be offered. Only one third of the schools had run a school-based course to do primarily with pastoral care during the previous three years. These were on a range of topics including 'personal and social education' and 'preparing tutorial material', sessions on the Warnock report, and 'the role of the form tutor'.

When LEA representatives were questioned, only three respondents thought their authorities made any special provision for the induction of probationary teachers into pastoral roles; one of these concentrated exclusively on using ATW, and the other two said it was only a part of a *general* induction and not pastorally-focussed. How satisfactory this would be depends on the length and quality of the course as a whole, and if the one respondent who writes of only a two-day general induction plus 'optional seminars' is at all typical, there is little basis for optimism.

Pastoral care and the local authority

Conceptions of 'pastoral care' within the local authorities surveyed were varied and sometimes idiosyncratic. While half saw pastoral care as stretching across the conventional continuum from narrow (conceived in terms of roles and structures) to broad (to include the idea of a pastoral curriculum, etc.), some perceptions are clearly a product of individual experience. For example, where a particular advisor has had an interest in Personal and Social Education, the Open University materials on this theme seem to have influenced the definition of 'pastoral care' used. One authority is actively fostering the development of an explicit pastoral curriculum in schools but this is in contrast with another where 'the Authority i.e. the Education Committee, has not discussed the matter'. Only one respondent thought pastoral care to be of little importance to his authority. The rest claimed that pastoral care is important, but what this means is again sometimes idiosyncratic. For example, the same authority referred to above says that 'great emphasis is placed on personal and social education'. The dominant view is that it is held to have 'substantial' or 'quite high' importance, comparable to that of any other area of the curriculum. The major conurbation had earmarked pastoral care as one of six or seven priorities for in-service work in 1983–5 and another authority was said to be currently experiencing an increase of interest in this area. Moreover, all but one of the authorities represented were described as having some representation of pastoral care in the designated duties of advisory staff.

These views were not supported by the teachers, however, and when asked about local authority support for pastoral care, the LEA advisers came in for some harsh criticism. Not one single teacher was aware of an LEA who had a specialist 'Pastoral care advisor'. Even so, only 38 (42%) of the sample thought that the appointment of such specialists was a good idea. One of these summarised the general feeling by suggesting that '. . . these staff would organise in-service training and be available and willing to give assistance on both policy and specific cases.' One Deputy Head suggested that the appointment of such specialists would serve to '. . . keep pressure on LEAs not to ignore pastoral care.'

Why was there such comparatively little support for additional advisory staff? To find an answer to this we must look at teachers' perceptions of advisors as illustrated by some of our respondents. Firstly, existing advisors were seen as very remote; one head of first year reported 'We last saw an advisor three years ago.' Another long-serving teacher in charge of an Upper School suggested that 'when advisors have such little impact on subject areas it seems unlikely that they will have much of a presence in this work.' For one teacher, a head of year with seventeen years' experience, his cynical conclusion was that 'most advisors are teachers who have had problems in the classroom.' It certainly was clear that many teachers felt that their LEA did not take pastoral care seriously, that it was a side issue, or an activity that merited little in terms of resources or time. One senior head of department summarised this feeling when he suggested that 'the LEA should be more involved (with pastoral care) and make its position clear.' Only three authorities surveyed seem to have offered any sort of published documentary guidance on pastoral care to secondary schools. Of these, one restricts advice to 'standard procedures related to exclusion/suspension/non-accidental injury/attendance regulations, etc.'; another has circulated a discussion document produced by a Teachers' Centre Pastoral Panel, while a third issues an elaborate paper entitled 'Aims and Objectives in the Secondary School'. In this document a significant section is given over to the 'pastoral needs of each pupil.'

Further, the designation of advisory staff with a responsibility exclusively for pastoral care is non-existent. All respondents wrote of staff having responsibility for a range of subjects – of the nine advisors in one authority, one has responsibility for pastoral care *and* PE, business studies, health education and outdoor education; and in another authority pastoral responsibility is combined with home economics, health education and textiles! – and/or a general advisory responsibility for a group of schools. As this array shows, combinations of subject responsibilities with pastoral care seem fairly arbitrary, although subjects which might be thought of as having a 'pastoral flavour' do feature – health education, careers education and RE were all mentioned.

Ways of improving teacher effectiveness in pastoral care

We asked teachers about changes they thought would improve their effectiveness in pastoral care. They were then asked to suggest ways in which these improvements might be achieved. A large majority (71) of our sample responded with at least one suggestion. Many of the suggestions touched on idiosyncratic school structures or weaknesses. One example was the school where the pastoral structure applied only to Band 2 and 3 pupils. There was no formal structure for Band 1 students: problems or enquiries with these students would be referred to the headteacher or deputies. Not surprisingly this structure came in for some criticism from teachers within the school.

There were, however, a number of significant themes that emerged. Frequent reference to the physical environment in which pastoral care was expected to take place illustrated a deep-rooted frustration. Clearly much of the counselling work with students, parents and colleagues took place in corridors, stock cupboards and classrooms. This poor physical environment signalled for many, a lack of appreciation on the part of school hierarchy and local authority, of the importance of this element of the pastoral task.

A major concern expressed by a considerable number of teachers related to the time available for pastoral work. This concern was focussed equally on two related issues. Firstly, there were those who felt that they did not have time to cope with the tasks expected of them as form tutors, and secondly, there were those who felt that the material they would like to include as part of the 'pastoral curriculum' could not be covered in the brief time allocated for tutor-group activity. When asked specifically if more 'free' periods would help, perhaps surprisingly, only 55 (60%) of our respondents thought they would. One head of year responded in typical fashion by suggesting that 'this would help eliminate the "crisis-counselling" that is too often the case. One could work more on the preventative aspect with more time.' One head of mathematics displayed an enlightened attitude when he explained: 'I feel I have a responsibility to encourage the development of pastoral "skills" of the teachers in my department, but I have little or no time to devote to this.' One somewhat surprising outcome was that a number of teachers, at all levels, advocated more free time for groups other than themselves. One head of year suggested: 'My timetable is quite adequate: however I feel tutors deserve more time.' A scale 1 English teacher stated that 'obviously heads of year need plenty of "free" time, whilst a head of fourth year pleaded that 'deputies need more free time.' No matter where they thought the extra time should be allocated there was general agreement that the time set aside for these activities was inadequate. One head of geography, who also acted as an assistant year tutor, observed that 'very few members of staff had purely pastoral responsibilities, and because of the demands of various duties, pastoral work is often just squeezed into very little "free" time'. Another year tutor summarised the argument by saying 'much pastoral work is too often rushed'.

There were many teachers who felt that there was a conflict between the espoused pastoral structure and their day-to-day experience of the pastoral care environment. There were statements made in schools about the role of the form tutor: 'this was the key person' 'at the hub of the pastoral wheel'; yet more often than not, as one teacher put it, 'form tutors were simply run down by the pastoral machine'. In the handling of critical issues they were simply ignored when their contribution could have been most significant: when the headteacher, deputies or pastoral team leaders dealt with one of their children the tutors were often neither consulted nor informed. There was a substantial call for greater understanding of the guidance structure and strategy within schools with a greater emphasis upon good communication and consultation with those who actually knew the children. Essentially the pastoral structure was seen to be too hierarchical whilst pretending to be something else.

Towards a policy for training

As the smallest of pilot studies, it would be inappropriate to say very much about the implications of these findings for policy, although it is obvious that our own notions of 'adequacy' have inevitably played a part in shaping this analysis. We can, however, note the respondents' own views on the subject. They were asked in what ways they thought training teachers for pastoral roles could be improved. Summarising the responses is not easy because they cover a very wide range of useful suggestions, but they can be seen as focussing on three issues: initial training; in-service programmes; and better teaching and researching.

Initial training

Most respondents made some suggestions under this heading. These included the following:

1   make pastoral care a compulsory component on all initial courses;
2   increase the length of the PGCE to make this possible;
3   emphasise the relationships between pastoral care and other issues, for example, multi-cultural education and special educational needs (SEN), in existing training courses;
4   increase integration in the currently fragmented curriculum for initial training;
5   make better use of teaching practice opportunities by, for example, attaching students to form-tutors, including this performance in

assessment, and requiring students to analyse critically provision of guidance and counselling in their placement schools.

In-service programmes

As well as a general advocacy of more and better courses (of all types) specialising in pastoral concerns, suggestions were also made for:

1 teacher exchanges to permit comparisons and cross-fertilisation of ideas between schools;
2 joint seminars with welfare services;
3 the setting up of discussion groups for teachers;
4 joint college-school staff development projects;
5 more opportunities for secondments.

Teaching and researching

Several respondents pointed to the need for more lecturers with specialist experience and qualifications in pastoral care and related areas. As one put it: 'Tutors on the PGCE should be trained in aspects of pastoral care: first train the trainers!' The same respondent thought that a move to more experiential teaching methods on such courses would enhance their quality. Another thought that a journal in the area (he did not know of *Pastoral Care in Education*!) would be of benefit.

Finally, one respondent commented on the desirability of further research funded by the DES or another body, for example, the ESRC. This pilot study had highlighted some of the areas in which such research would be very valuable indeed. Certainly a much fuller picture of regional, national and local training provision would help us in assessing existing needs in respect to enhancing the professional competence of pastoral agents, and such a picture could only be established through a research programme based on substantial funding of this type.

Local authority reaction

In the light of the results of this survey it is not surprising that the LEAs themselves are generally dissatisfied with present provision. Only one LEA registered unqualified satisfaction with present training opportunities, another said that, while one is 'never satisfied', at least the amount of provision was comparable to that in other curriculum areas. The remainder attributed their dissatisfaction to a situation in which there are inadequate numbers of advisory staff generally, and a lack of designated specialist responsibility for pastoral care in particular, and pointed to the serious resource constraints upon those improvements which they would like to bring about.

While it would be misleading to make any generalisations from a pilot study of a handful of local authorities, these results can be seen as giving cause for concern. Whether the unsystematic and generally inadequate provision of training and resources of all kinds (and especially of numbers of advisory staff) reported here is typical of the country as a whole one can only guess. Certainly these findings indicate a need for a thorough investigation of provision in this important area.

Conclusion and research implications

Since this has been a small and somewhat hurried pilot study, it would be unwise and inappropriate to make broad generalisations from the findings. However, a number of interesting issues have been raised. These have for the most part arisen directly from what the respondents themselves had to say, and on those grounds alone deserve further consideration. It is clear that there are some pressing problems and issues which require further exploration in order that authorities can have an accurate picture of present and future training and support needs. Some of the findings require confirmation by replicating sections of the survey with a larger and more representative sample of institutions, whereas others, to which the teachers themselves have pointed, probably need to be explored by case-study or action-research methods in particular schools and colleges. To do justice to these issues will require a research programme of such proportions as to necessitate substantial public funding. If it has done nothing else, this modest pilot-study has surely established a prima facie case for such a programme.

Acknowledgement
The authors wish to acknowledge the assistance of the Research Committee of the Chelmer Institute of Higher Education, which awarded a small but vital bursary towards the survey of teacher-education institutions.

Our needs in schools

Michael Marland

Introduction

Ten years ago I declared that 'the pastoral need' is 'the central task of the school' (Marland 1974, p. 12). Clearly most of the rest of the educational community have not thought so – at least if published and public manifestations are any indication. Pastoral care remains a desperately under-considered aspect of education, whether one is thinking of colleges and departments of education, the DES, the HMI, in-service courses, writers and educational journalism, or the research community. All are caught in a vicious spiral – so little is known that less is taught; few questions are thus formulated, and fewer researched.

True, some sharp researchers have thrown spotlights on a number of key questions. However, most of those have been concerned with the unusual pupil – the truant, the delinquent, the maladjusted, or deprived pupil. The central task of the school to give 'personal, educational and vocational guidance' to *all* has been put to one side by most of those who support schools by intellectual, procedural, philosophical, or research work.

In this paper, I consider the current state of research into pastoral care issues; the difficulties faced by teachers in making use of the research studies that do exist; and the potential value of research to the work of teachers in school. The paper looks in detail at four areas where we lack basic knowledge and research evidence which could help schools to improve the quality of their pastoral care provision: the needs of the child (as daughter or son, as pupil, as student and as information-user); the needs of the tutor; the structures of pastoral care systems; and key aspects of the pastoral curriculum. Finally, the implications for future research work are listed as a set of recommendations.

Research, pastoral care and the school

'Research' is often belittled by teachers, but little read. Even the most famous research is normally mediated by the press – often not even the specialist press. Neville Bennett and his colleagues at the University of Lancaster have checked this gap between opinions on research and the reading of it in a study of the impact of *Teaching Styles and Pupil Progress* (Bennett 1976). His research showed that of those teachers claiming knowledge of and expressing opinions on the work, the majority were basing their views on television references or the newspaper.

In many years of participating in discussion towards in-school decision-making I have come to distrust phrases such as 'Research shows . . .' or even worse 'Everyone knows research shows . . .' as being rhetoric to support prejudice with only rarely an actual reference to a research study. Similarly, in papers prepared for staff debate or as preparation for major decisions, it is very rare to find any use of the relevant research studies. I fear one must add that those with specific responsibility for pastoral care leadership appear to be amongst the least well-read professionally. Their colleague heads of departments are far more likely to have studied the relevant research literature.

Yet the UK has the most autonomous educational decision-making pattern in the world. Power is disseminated eccentrically and unpredictably from the Secretary of State to the class tutor or teacher. The node of power is in the teacher team (e.g. junior school staff, secondary school pastoral team or department), and most decision-making takes place there. If these local decisions are to be well made, the teachers must be able to draw on (and ideally commission) the research that will illuminate the matters on which they will be making decisions.

All aspects of the pastoral care of schools, primary and secondary especially, need research attention. In the teaching of reading, science, mathematics, language, and many aspects of the academic curriculum, research enquiries and even sometimes answers are available for schools to use for their consideration of in-school planning. In the pastoral aspects of schools far too much is hunch at its best, and habit more often. There has been some important work, but it is rare. Further, much of the relevant research work strikes me as excessively narrowly focussed (although that can have its values) and strikingly unrelated to how schools might deliver the pastoral care. Institutional and academic specialising almost inevitably leads to workers in one 'field' knowing little of the work done in adjacent areas. A citation analysis would probably show that only a few works appear in the references in research reports by workers in different fields. In a way 'pastoral care' can be thought of as a synthesising focus, needing to draw upon specialised research on psychology, sociology, curriculum, and management, and some very detailed aspects of these and other specialisms. Conversely, it would surely help if the researchers knew more of school pastoral care work, and considered more the implications of their research for actual pastoral care.

Looking back over twenty years of the important research journal *Child Psychology and Psychiatry*, the new editors say of their predecessors: 'They succeeded in integrating "psyche" with the social and educational worlds of the child, symbolised by the conventional team of psychiatrist, psychologist, social worker, and, if fortunate, teacher.' (Berger and Taylor 1984, p. ii). That difficulty of relating to the teacher is the fault of all of us, not merely the researcher 'out there', but I find it particularly strong in most research work that could be useful to pastoral care.

An excellent example of research which does focus on the relationship between specialist (in this case educational psychologist) and teacher is that of the North Paddington Primary School Project (Whitmore *et al* 1984). A joint study of the nursing, medical, and psychological services to fifteen primary schools in one Area Health Authority (as the NHS was then organised) was set up in 1977. Amongst the seven aims was a fascinating use of a physical and neuro-developmental examination of school entrants with the later learning and need for referral of the pupils. Of particular interest, however, were also the changes in the teachers' perception of the medical and psychological services, and the use of the psychologist as a consultant in individual pupil management by the teachers.

Part of the task, of course, is making more accessible the research that has been done. For those of us working from 8.30 to 5.30 inside a school without a moment to sit and read, the available research suffers from a number of problems:

1 most of it is into aspects which relate to our pastoral care work, but is from the specialised point of view of a particular discipline and needs re-focussing for in-school use;
2 the primary reporting is in a wide variety of journals, most schools cannot afford or do not organise access to this material;
3 a researcher often quite properly includes in a report a literature review, a description of method, and a great deal of supporting data. Not all of this is necessary for school use.

Just as 'pastoral care' is a synthesising concept, some synthesising of the relevant research is also required.

Some part of the research needed should be school-initiated and based. Although the difficulties of such work are great, many aspects of pastoral care research would lend themselves to such modes of research. The contributors to Jon Nixon's *Teachers Guide to Action Research* (Nixon *et al* 1981) have shown that the teacher-researcher has especial strengths drawn from the insider's perspective. My ambition is to see a family of schools or a large school on its own, supported by LEA advisers and local university staff, methodically analysing their needs and relating these to the research community. This would improve the quality of decision-making, help the career development of the teacher – and produce a more helpful feedback and stimulus to researchers. (I have described one modest contribution to this, which is a school 'journal club', in *Preparing for Promotion in Pastoral Care* (Marland 1982).)

The busy day of a tutor, junior school class teacher, secondary head of house/year, or deputy head leaves the teacher reeling from the buffets of the incidents. As teachers, we bring to each encounter and each decision an implicit 'theory', but rarely have we made ourselves conscious of the theories underlying our multifarious decisions and actions, and still more rarely are our theories and approaches supported by research findings. It is up to the pastoral care community, especially at this moment in its growing professionalism, to articulate some of its questions for the consideration of researchers.

The child

The child as daughter or son

The relationship between school influences and home ones has not to my knowledge been as carefully explored as one would think. The indicators of 'home' are usually the surely too crude ones of socio-economic class. Researchers considering school outcomes, whether overall such as Rutter or more specific such as Galloway, make statements about the similarity of areas that do not fully ring true. They often talk of school 'drawing from the same area'. However, as I walk to school in the morning I can see groups of secondary school children separating out, with some schools apparently attracting a noticeably more 'respectable' type of child. When schools in urban areas are fairly close together, the parental selection/rejection of certain schools produces an 'amplifying' effect – that is, once the proportion of difficult pupils reaches a certain threshold, certain parents fight against sending their children there and then the proportion becomes further exaggerated. When this happens, the peer-group pull changes the school and its effect on all pupils.

The need for a closer categorisation of families is not, however, primarily to understand better the relative effects of home and school, but to help schools consider their overall regime and their pastoral approach in particular. We know from, for instance, the fascinating research on the Lothian Region Educational Home Visiting Scheme (Raven 1982) of the changes in parenting priorities and attitudes that are possible. Families with difficulties in coping were given a methodical series of visits, and a range of changes were observed, including the attitudes of the schools to the families. This research also helps to illuminate differences in attitude that did not shift easily or at all. The families of lower socio-economic status, for instance, after the visiting were 'no less likely to want their children to be dependent on them' (*ibid*, p. 101). What we have not, as far as I know, looked into is the implications of the style of schooling that best interacts with styles of parenting, or how schools can work with parents.

I feel the need for a study of the relationship between parenting style and pastoral approaches. I find the analysis of families in Wilson and Herbert (1978) illuminating, and the later analysis by Harriett Wilson (1980) positively tantalising in what it offers to analysis. Wilson firstly studies parenting supervision, and develops the notion of 'chaperonage' to describe not so much the mere 'strictness' of the parents, but their concern for where their children are and what they are up to. She compares parenting and chaperonage styles with the 'delinquency' of the children. The correlation is staggering; and is *not* influenced by where they live or other social handicaps: 'The association of delinquency with laxness of parental supervision was confirmed.' (*ibid*, p. 231). I can see why funding for such detailed studies (in this case from the Home Office) is attracted by such obvious social problems as delinquency. However, I suggest that the questions raised are deeply significant to pastoral care for all. In the first place, what correlations are there between parenting style and school success, and, more importantly for action, what school 'chaperonage' and 'personal guidance' approaches best suit parenting backgrounds?

The child as pupil: 'Taking up the pupil side'

The Bazalgette/Grubb focus embodied in that title phrase of a recent article in *Pastoral Care in Education* (Bazalgette, 1983, 1, 3) is powerful, all the more so for putting a spotlight or a frame round a set of characteristics so obvious as to have gone virtually un-noticed. 'Of course' the child when at or related to school is 'a pupil', but the *pupilness* of that role has slipped between sociologists crudely correlating school success with class, and psychologists doing the same for intellectual ability. Meanwhile, the teacher has observed ruefully that some children, called 'pupils' without the implications being conceptualised, succeed and others do not, and teachers can usually forecast fairly well by external signs (such as being on time, having a pen, sitting still) the likely success or otherwise of the individual. School rules and day-by-day admonition have pinpointed these external signs, usually without consciously exploring their relationship with the *role* of pupil. Exhortations to school children have been vague ('Must concentrate more') or trivial ('Margins should be drawn with a ruler'). Educational and personal guidance (two-thirds of pastoral care responsibilities) has reactively helped individuals cope with difficulties, rather than helped them prepare for their future challenges as they go through school. (See Hamblin 1978, on 'critical incidents', for an alternative view.)

The power of the deceptively ordinary and simple phrase, 'the child as pupil', is that it helps us all to see that the child in school has a task, and that this task, like every other task in life needs learning – and thus teaching. Paradoxically, how to be a pupil is the hardest thing a child has to learn in school. (If she or he has learnt that, the school is a storehouse of riches.) Bitterly, it is amongst the rarest things teachers set about teaching. How much easier for the tutor to admonish or console the failed pupil than to prepare a course to avoid such failure!

One of the central pastoral tasks is to help pupils learn to be pupils. The whole school in all its aspects will have to be marshalled to help and the pastoral curriculum (Marland 1981) will be the articulation. Within that, there is little doubt that the pastoral programme will need to carry the major burden. The essence of 'being a pupil', or, rather, being able to 'fill the role of pupil', is undoubtedly, an attitudinal matter. To 'be a pupil' is to have expectations about what schools can offer, and optimism that one can draw on those offers. It is to believe that if the role is well played there will be gains for the role bearer. However, if a pastoral curriculum is to be planned to enable the child to fill the role and gain what is to be gained, some attempt to break down the broad role of pupil is necessary. Only then can the school help the pupil build up the model.

The pupil as student

Much of the school day takes place in classrooms and is ostensibly devoted to 'school work', and even the vaguest pupil has some idea that 'you go to school to learn'. Yet as one researcher put it: 'We have no direct studies of what this phenomenon "work" means to teachers and pupils' (Woods 1978). Certainly my impression is that the tutor, whose task of 'educational guidance' involves at the very least helping pupils cope with their work, has very few specific ideas of the most hopeful ways of inducting pupils into secondary school studies. Indeed in the masses of educational research in the last quarter of a century, so much of which has considered the pupil as a member of a social 'class' rather than a school 'class', there is little research I know that considers what ways pupils may be helped to come to grips with their schoolwork demands. The studies of the *difficulties* of subject matter and texts, for instance, have been deeply illuminating and influential to those who have studied them, e.g. the SSRC-funded 'Concepts in Secondary Mathematics and Science Programme' at Chelsea College from 1974 (Shayer and Adey 1981). The tutor needs to look at the process from the other direction, and across the subjects. She or he needs to know, more than instinct and the rushed feed-back of the tutor room will offer, what the obstacles are and what form of group and individual pastoral work will help convert the pupil into a student.

Peter Woods appears convinced that '"Work" has undergone a meta-morphosis, scarcely any longer involving the totality of the person. It is by and large a nagging necessity, to which people have adapted over the years, developing new meanings which are filtered through to their children direct from their first-hand objective experience of work and participation in work cultures, which help perpetuate "the cycle of inequality". No amount of teacher advice and persuasion can scratch the surface of this massive influence.' (Woods 1978, p. 325). This is not quite how it feels to me in school, but that last sentence rings true: some students come to school already able to understand schoolwork (and this is *not* simply an artefact of socio-economic class), but for those who do not, our pastoral care is vague and unfocussed.

It is generally agreed that induction into the school is an important pastoral task (e.g. Hamblin 1978, and Marland 1980b). Yet how well do we do it? How much do we know what is done? How much research has been carried out into possible ways? Some researchers have considered the start to secondary school, and the work I have seen is interesting: John Beck, in his unpublished PhD thesis, has found little of the trauma expected (Beck 1972), nor has a more recent study in the Camden/Westminster division of the ILEA (Division Two, 1984). However, this looks at the pupil and does not consider ways of effective induction.

'Induction', though, is not required simply 'to the school', but throughout schooling to new courses, aspects, stages. Narrowly-focussed but significant action research has been carried out by Jean Ruddock and her colleagues at the Centre for Applied Research in Education, at the University of East Anglia. The starting point was the observation that innovating programmes in schools are often inhibited by the ways in which 'the pupil group may act conservatively with regard to attempted change, or may misconstrue the aim of new approaches and so behave in ways which are conservative in their effect' (Hull *et al* 1981, p. 1). The team accordingly set up action research to test in practice the hypotheses:

1 That pupils' understanding of the form of an innovation would be increased if they were given access to concrete representations of it in practice (i.e. through video-tape recordings).
2 That such access would foster the development of a mutual commit-ment to the work sufficiently strong to counter the pull of existing conventions. (*ibid*, p. 4)

For the range of pastoral 'educational guidance' responsibilities their choice of examples (which was made for other purposes) was limited as they had to be innovations: (a) new sixth forms in these schools, (b) a new history project in a high school, and (c) a new humanities course using discussion-based learning in a middle school. However, the action research to some extent at least demonstrated their claim that:

> It seems that even children of middle-school age can develop an articulate critical awareness of classroom procedures which facilitates the explicit and collaborative management of learning in the classroom . . . . Pupils' achievement may be enhanced by their capacity to distinguish, understand, and be critical of the particular form of learning they are engaged in. Pupils' command of the structure and convention of the learning process is a topic we consider rich in research potential. (*ibid*, p. 129)

Here we are moving powerfully from the specific induction of a new subject or a new teaching style, to that pastoral task of educational guidance which is well-phrased in the title of another paper from the project: *Pupils' Grasp of Classroom Process* (Ruddock 1981).

A related aspect which has similarly been under-considered is the tutor's educational guidance task in relation to homework. In a review of the research Frank Coulter comments accurately: 'What teachers actually say or do to prepare their students for home study remains something of a mystery.' (Coulter 1979, p. 27). However, both he and the Mortimores in a thorough but brief survey (Mortimores 1981) consider the issue almost entirely from the point of view of the subject teacher – that is the setting of assignments, the briefer and the responder, and not at all from the pastoral viewpoint.

The student as 'information-user'

One aspect of the 'child as pupil' deserves special emphasis. We know from research into library-user education (Irving and Snape 1979), that there is very little effective groundwork done in what used to be called 'library use'. More recently, however, the concept has been deepened, and the student seen as someone who has processing information as one of her or his central activities – an activity which also has a key place in the adult working world. Ann Irving has reviewed all the research carried out so far in aspects of either 'library-user education' or 'study skills' in a study with a deeply significant title, *Educating Information Users* (Irving 1983). Her title has established a key phrase.

Extensive research consideration of undergraduate study-skill processes has led such writers as Ralph Tabarer to criticise the rigidity of most current study-skill approaches, even before they have been taken up by schools. Research in the USA, with typical thoroughness, has offered a controlled experiment with students (a) being given weekly instruction on 'information resources' (b) having library talks and lectures and (c) receiving no exposure to the library at all (Breivik 1977). The first group did best, but the last group did better than those given the traditional diet. Other USA writers have heavily criticised the effectiveness of current programmes (*cf* especially Nordling 1978).

In this country Douglas Hamblin has stressed 'how pastoral care can help make the processes through which pupils learn become part of a continuous dialogue between teacher and taught' (Hamblin 1981, p. 1), and he, properly in my view, brings the question of study skills into the focus of pastoral care. However, his view of study skills is not as wide or as related to information handling as it perhaps could be. A group of specialists, under the auspices of the Schools Council and the British Library, met in 1980 to try to pin down the essential skills, and to relate them to the pastoral curriculum in general, and the tutorial programme in particular (Marland 1981). However, even armed with Hamblin's *Teaching Study Skills*, the Schools Council/British Library's *Information Skills in the Secondary Curriculum*, Ann Irving's *Study and Information Skills across the Curriculum* (Irving 1985), and possibly the best students' text *Effective Learning Skills* (Healy and Goodhand 1983), the tutor or the pastoral team leader still seems to me to have been left uncertain about how best to divide the task of educating information users between contextual subject teaching and the tutorial programme. Research has hardly touched this central question.

Motivation

A key aspect of the pupil role is making use of the feedback from teachers. Thus a central part of the pastoral role of 'educational guidance' is helping pupils make the best of themselves by *using* the responses of teachers. I do not know much about the content of initial training psychology courses, but I doubt if they move very close to the tutor or primary classteacher's needs to understand motivation.

The typical tutor engages, I suspect, in a large amount of exhortation ('try harder') and encouragement ('you really can do it'). All of this is very unsystematic. I have found no UK equivalent of the fascinating US studies into achievement and motivation. Apart from its importance for the issues of equal opportunities, which I discuss later, the work of the American psychologist Carol Dweck, now Professor of Human Development at Harvard, seems to me to be of startling importance to our pastoral work in schools. Essentially she has shown that 'deterioration in quality of intellectual problem-solving performance is generally independent of proficiency at the task' (Dweck 1977, p. 44), and has developed in a series of papers the concept of 'learned helplessness' (e.g. Dweck 1977, Dweck and Bush 1976, Dweck, Davidson, Nelson and Enna 1978, Dweck and Goetz 1978, Dweck and Elliott 1983).

Years ago I remember it being said that 'a good form master is worth another couple of "O" levels a boy' (that was a boys' grammar school!), and we should all agree that part of the tutor's pastoral task is to help the pupil succeed to the best of her or his ability. We should also, I hope, agree that this helping is not solely for the sake of the successes thus gained within schooling, nor even entirely for the value in later life of the examination tickets thus achieved, but that the very process of learning how to succeed is one of the big lessons for all future life. It is this central pastoral task that has had, as far as I know, no research attention in this country, and we just do not know how to set about it.

Carol Dweck's studies point the way. She reports: 'Our research shows that the variable that consistently predicts response to failure is the child's interpretation of failure – what he thinks caused it and whether he views it as surmountable.' (Dweck 1977, p. 4) More recently, her research has focussed on the relationship between childrens' motivation and their theories of intelligence (Dweck 1984). From field research she has shown that children tend to polarise into those who have what she calls an 'incremental' theory of intelligence, and those who have an 'entity' theory. The former see tasks as manageable and failure as a useful lesson; the latter fear failure. A few sentences cannot do justice to what I find of immense power in pastoral care: a research-based theory of motivation that can be used for the pastoral curriculum (we should teach about learning), and for group and individual counselling (for she shows attitudes can be changed).

What we need to find out is whether this research is valid in this country and whether there are ways in which attribution research, understanding of motivation, and the theory of 'learned helplessness' can be researched to find pastoral procedures.

The structure of pastoral care systems

Best has criticised, to some extent, the concern of writers like myself with the 'structure' of pastoral care in schools (e.g. Best et al 1980), but he and his colleagues could have pointed to a flaw in the data we have used for our concern: we have been obliged to use anecdote and personal observation as remarkably little is known about the details of pastoral care structures. The DES surveys of teachers omit 'form period' and 'tutor period', and DES statistics are thus weak from the start (cf Secondary Schools Staffing Survey 1984). Amongst the plethora of facts displayed about secondary teachers, we just do not know about tutorial times. It is highly significant that the phrase 'contact ratio' is used as 'a measure of the assigned average load per teacher,' and the glossary defines this as 'teaching contact with pupils as distinct from administration, preparation, marking, etc.' (HMI 1979, p. 272). This does *not* include tutorial time!

Similarly, many national surveys have been concerned about training and qualifications, e.g. English teachers ('and so it would appear a third of those teaching English have no discernible qualification', Committee of Enquiry 1975) and Mathematics (the Cockcroft report). *Aspects of Secondary Education* analyses the qualifications of heads of departments (HMI 1979, p. 48) and their teaching experience (*ibid*, p. 49). Similarly, careful analyses were done of the staffing of Remedial, Religious Education, English, and French (*ibid*, pp. 41–56) and inadequacies commented on – but there is no consideration of the qualifications of pastoral care team leaders.

We know nothing of the basic statistics of allowance points to case loads, despite the huge national investment in pastoral care leadership. The range of Burnham points invested by LEAs, through schools, in formal pastoral care is amazing. The NAPCE survey (Maher and Best 1984, p. 1a) of a sample of eighteen secondary schools shows the staff invested into pastoral care leadership. If, for the sake of simplicity, deputy heads are omitted from the calculation, and the scale posts computed as the points used, it is possible to calculate the number of pupils per scale point. This I suggest is a rough-and-ready computation of the investment in pastoral care. The mean is 62, with a range from 32 to 131! Ten of the eighteen fall beneath the mid-point of 81. Some of the sample are schools with more than one site, and one might have expected a greater investment in these schools. The schools with more than one site include the highest investments.

Sites	Scores
2	63
2	32
3	55

Even that though does not explain the range. The remaining fifteen single-site schools range from 38 pupils per point to 131!

Very little research consideration has been given to the structure and responsibilities for pastoral care within the school. I and others have outlined our ideals, but they have not been put to the test of comparative research. Reynolds and Murgatroyd in the South Wales' absentee study (1977) have interesting comments on the tutor/middle management responsibility, and David Galloway, one of the rare research writers on pastoral care, discusses his and others' evidence on managing disruptive pupils in the light of responsibilities. He comments that although studies have emphasised the variables within the school, 'none, though, has focussed on much detail on the school's pastoral care systems' (Galloway 1983, p. 245). He goes on: 'Research on the relationship between pupils' behaviour and the organisation and practice of pastoral care is conspicuously lacking' (*ibid*, p. 246). His observations are very much from the point of view of the disruptive pupil, but I suspect it would be true of all pupils (Galloway *et al* 1982).

In the meantime, getting the team leader/tutor balance of responsibilities right in schools is hampered by this lack of research. *How* does the team leader lead an untrained group (HMI 1982, p. 33: 56% of probationers considered that they were not well prepared to undertake pastoral duties), who have little support (Maher and Best 1984), and for whom the main call on their time and loyalties, and therefore most career prospects, are elsewhere?

The tutor

Many writers in recent years have stressed the role of the tutor, perhaps first outlined in the chapter 'Roles and Responsibilities' of my own *Pastoral Care* (Marland 1974, pp. 74–80), and more fully developed by Douglas Hamblin (1978), Keith Blackburn (1975 and 1983), and Leslie Button (1981). I declared ten years ago:

> The role which is most often taken as read is that of the teacher in charge of the pastoral base-unit. The first-level pastoral figure is arguably the most important person in the school: the definition of his or her task is one of the school's most important planning tasks.' (Marland 1974, p. 74)

Best and his colleagues in their SSRC-funded case study research (Best *et al* 1983) and Peter Lang in his Warwick-based research (Lang 1983 and 1984) have shown that what is intended in those 'how to do it' accounts simply does not always happen. Indeed many pupils just did not realise what tutors were intended to be for (Lang 1983), and he comments:

> 'Individuals other than teachers, particularly parents, relatives, and peers were much more frequently mentioned than teachers, and teachers with specific pastoral roles were mentioned infrequently.' (1984, p. 7)

We need to discover the various elements of this partial failure: to what extent is it the result of, for instance:

1 lack of professional training of tutors?
2 lack of a school's definition of the role and briefing?
3 lack of leadership for tutors?
4 lack of induction and education of *pupils* into how to use the school?
5 lack of opportunity in terms of time and suitable selling in the school?

The fact is that we know very little about how tutors work at all! Compare, for instance, how much we know about the junior school-teacher of reading. Vera Southgate and her co-researchers have observed the teaching of reading, and compared their observations with the teachers' own logs (Southgate *et al* 1981, pp. 123–149). From this mismatch ('The teacher does not always do what she thinks she is doing, nor is the child always doing what the teacher thinks he is doing.' *ibid*, p. 134) it is possible to be fairly precise in recommendations to improve practice. In another example, the Bullock Committee (Committee of Enquiry 1975) produced a formidable body of hard data about the way teachers of English spent their week and the time within lessons. The breakdown of teaching and learning activities continues to be useful for in-school consideration of planning and the language curriculum. Similarly, we know precisely the incidence of writing and reading in the secondary classroom from observational research by the Schools Council's *The Effective Use of Reading Project* (Lunzer and Gardner 1979). When we know that, for instance, 'approximately half of all classroom reading occurs in bursts of less than fifteen seconds in any one minute' (*ibid*, p. 124) we are in a better position to take control of our in-school planning. Because of the long-agreed stress on the importance of reading, massive funds have been directed into such detailed research (and much other, of course), and this is continuing.

By contrast, the oft-quoted concern for social and personal development seems a sham: we simply do not know how often tutors talk to their tutees, for how long, or in what circumstances. We do not know what happens in tutor periods – indeed the ordinary observations of advisers, inspectors, team leaders, visitors, and senior staff seems much less frequent in tutor periods than subject lessons.

Even the important NFER study of *The Teacher's Day* (Hilsum 1971) does not appear to distinguish group pastoral time from other teaching. Indeed pastoral work is, typically, regarded as 'work with individual pupils' (*ibid*, p. 140). However, a detail in this study hints at what could be revealing, e.g. a mean time of 21.6 minutes per day (4.3% of working day) was computed to be devoted to 'pastoral tasks (*ibid*, p. 91), of course in their definition of 'pastoral': 'individual pupil, special occasions, extra-curricular activity' (*ibid*, p. 28). The 1978 follow-up specialising on secondary teachers (Hilsum and Strong 1978) is more precise, and has found a category 'Registration' – a phrase I hate as 'taking the register' indicates such a limited view of the tutorial role. This study looked at a sample of 201 teachers. It found that of the 35 minutes devoted to registration and assembly those teachers who carried out both duties spent 0.8 minutes mean time on 'pastoral' (2.2%) and 4.9 minutes (14.0%) on 'teaching' (*ibid*, p. 17). Those taking only registration had higher figures of 1.2 minutes (3.4%) and 7.9 minutes (23%). A closer look was taken at 38 teachers' 'registration' time. The researchers found that about five minutes was spent 'on clerical registration work', and they comment with surprising apparent ignorance of pastoral ambitions: 'As may be seen from the actual durations taken by registration procedures compared with the time set aside for this purpose, the allocated time was in general more than sufficient' (*ibid*, p. 173)!

A proper consideration of pastoral care is bound to involve enquiring how much time is currently available and how that time is spent. If the mis-match between 'the rhetoric of pastoral care' (Best's depressing but illuminating phrase, Best 1980) and the reality is to be removed, we need to know what is happening.

As well as the quantitative aspects outlined so far, we need to know about the apparently intangible questions of personal interaction. What has been researched and written on this agenda appears to be subject-lesson based (e.g. Hargreaves 1972, chapter 6). In most cases, the guidance we offer is to be given by tutor to tutee regardless of the personalities or feelings of the two. A few schools complement this by a more personality-based 'personal tutoring' system. For instance, at North Westminster Community School all potential HE students are given a 'personal tutor' halfway through their lower-sixth year, to complement the work of the 'group tutor'. This tutor is chosen by the person organising the scheme in an endeavour to match interests and to some extent personalities. The experience is that very happy personal relationships develop in these cases.

A colleague at North Westminster, Oliver Sterno, has suggested that we need to know more about the inter-relationships between tutor and tutee, and he argues for a research project on this:

1 The inter-relationship between tutor and tutee is fundamental to the tutorial system working effectively. What are the factors which affect this inter-relationship? This is a crucial consideration and yet it is either assumed that this concept is of little consequence, or it is set up fairly easily through institutionalisation.

2 This research thesis aims to analyse this inter-relationship of tutor/ tutees:
   (a) do tutees use their tutors as 'confidants' in similar ways regardless of individual differences between them? These differences could include gender, ethnic background, age, subject specialism and interests, social class, banding?
   (b) if there are anomalies, who do tutees go to as 'confidants' instead and for what kinds of matters?
   (c) are these anomalies due to family influences, e.g. is there only one parent present?
   (d) is the primary school experience influential?
   (e) do tutors perceive differences in their role which affects these inter-relationships?

3 The emergent issue here is one of trying to improve the effectiveness of pastoral care. This may be through attempting to reduce negative anomalies. Or it might be through devising a more specialist form of tutoring. The former might require more in-service education courses for tutors; the latter might require that tutors develop specialisms and

tutees would confide in particular tutors for specific reasons: in other words, the view that the tutor can have a holistic caring approach for their tutees could be misplaced.

Very little work that I can find relates to how the pastoral aspect of a teacher's role is seen in terms of maladjusted behaviour. We have a tendency to explain anti-social behaviour within a school by such broad categories as 'poor home background', 'unsuitable curriculum', or 'restrictive school rules' (the fashions change). Our repertoire of ways of helping these pupils is instinctive or traditional, rather than drawing on a methodology derived from research. The maladjusted child has always interested psychological researchers, but the relationship to possible strategies of help by the pastoral care of a school are rarely explored. For instance, one can see potential in studies such as that on 'Knowledge of Strategies for the Expression of Emotion among Normal and Maladjusted Boys' (Taylor and Harris 1984). Tests were given to 7–8 year-old and 10–11 year-old boys from normal and maladjusted schools 'to assess their knowledge of strategies of control for both facial and overt behavioural expression of a negative emotion' (*ibid*, p. 145). The main findings seemed to indicate that 'normal and maladjusted boys differ in the strategies they propose for reacting to provocation but not in the emotion that they expect to feel'. It is interesting from the point of view of those of us working with young people to note the researchers' caveat: 'It is tempting to conclude that maladjusted boys lack knowledge of control strategies. However, it could also be argued that while they know of such strategies, they find them difficult to apply in practice or choose to adopt counter-aggression instead' (*ibid*, p. 144). Why? And how can they be helped to deploy their knowledge of control strategies actually to use other responses? The 'personal guidance' of pastoral care work would be substantially helped by further research in this way. Even less research, that I know of, has been devoted to the ordinary pupil, that great under-researched species, and her or his needs from a tutor. It is said of students in USA high schools with separate 'guidance and counselling departments', 'if you haven't got a problem, then you've sure got a real problem' – because the student with no recognised problem tends to get overlooked. Is not the same true here? We do not know, but I fear that the personal and social growth of the undemanding pupil gets little help from tutorial work. In England and Wales the guidance and welfare of pupils is embedded not in specialist 'guidance and counselling departments' as in the United States, but in a system which is normally built round the tutor. Those of us organising pastoral care in schools, producing job descriptions, briefing, observing, and supporting just do not know enough about the actual or the possible.

Finally, one of my greatest problems in school is helping colleagues develop pastoral skills. The NAPCE pilot survey has shown the startling inadequacies of current in-service provision (Maher and Best 1984, pp. 4–12), and we know from NAPCE papers of the economical but effective programme of professional development in Clwyd (Weeks 1984). However, we have little knowledge of the best ways to produce effective in-service work in pastoral care, especially for the thousands of tutors. The standard, and in my view, very valuable book on *School-Focussed In-Service Training* (Bolam 1982) recognises the problem but is, yet again, far less full on school-focussed training for pastoral care than other aspects. A major national initiative is required.

The pastoral curriculum

From a time only a few years ago when to use the words 'pastoral' and 'curriculum' in the same session, never mind the same sentence, produced anger, the paired words are now in fairly common use. The most common meaning, to me regrettable, is merely to cover the activity of the tutor period. Indeed for some people the title of Jill Baldwin's and Harry Wells' *Active Tutorial Work* (Baldwin and Wells 1979, 80 and 81) is abbreviated, 'ATW', as the generic title for any tutorial work! I prefer to use the phrase 'pastoral curriculum' in the wider sense I defined in an essay of that title (Marland 1980), to mean 'the school curriculum looked at for the moment solely from the point of view of the personal needs of the pupil resolving his individual problems, making informed decisions, and taking his place in his personal world' (*ibid*, p. 157).

My argument is that the individual 'personal, educational and vocational guidance' of a school's pastoral work has to be prepared for by a 'pastoral curriculum' which is devised to teach the underlying facts, concepts, attitudes, and skills required by the individual for personal and social development, and also for any individual guidance. This whole-school pastoral curriculum is then divided amongst subject and pastoral teams. That which is reserved for the latter is called the 'pastoral', and within that is the scheme of work for tutors in their group sessions, and this is the 'tutorial programme'. Up and down the country many schools are struggling to produce this 'tutorial programme', usually without working out a whole-school pastoral curriculum first. Most schools are finding it very difficult indeed, and we all lack the external work which we can make use of in other aspects of the curriculum. With the exception of Button (1981), Baldwin and Wells (1979, 1980 and 1981), Bulman (1984), and Pring (1984) we are on our own.

Kenneth David in a Schools Council Study *Personal and Social Education in Secondary Schools* (David 1982) has considered 'the requirements within a school for such a coherent programme to be developed, and what can prevent the implementation of such work' (*ibid*, p. 29). He charts the stages of identification, review, and implementation, and, not surprisingly finds that 'the traditional school system of management through subject departments can be a major constraint' (*ibid*, p. 34). His ingredients for 'a co-ordinated approach' (*ibid*, p. 36) are sensible; however, the study, like others, is far from a research-based approach.

HMI considered in Chapter 9 of *Aspects of Secondary Education* (HMI 1979) 'the extent to which the curriculum, the content of learning, the teaching methods employed, the knowledge, ideas and skills made available and the intellectual frameworks provided as an aid to the ordering of experience, appeared to match the needs of all pupils' (*ibid*, p. 208). They add that 'it is clear that there are considerable intellectual and organisational difficulties in this approach' (*ibid*, p. 209), and certainly everything I have heard from colleagues in other schools as well as my own personal experience confirms that whole-school curriculum planning is extraordinarily difficult, and the whole-school planning of a pastoral curriculum the hardest part of that. (See also Bulman and Jenkin's forthcoming.) Where is the *research* on this aspect of the curriculum?

Occupations

Consider, for instance, the aspect of the pastoral curriculum concerned with 'careers', or as I prefer to call it, 'occupations', which is bound to be part of a pastoral curriculum, stretching far beyond tutorial periods to virtually all 'subjects'. Over ten years ago the DES expressed the view which is still unusual and over-ambitious in the reality of most schools that 'for all boys and girls careers education should be a continuous and important element in the curriculum' (DES 1973). By the 1979 secondary survey there appeared to have been little change: 'In general the potential for careers education within the subjects of the curriculum was not being exploited'. (HMI 1979, p. 232). I have myself argued that this is the way to plan curriculum, both as an understanding of the adult world and for specific 'careers guidance', much of which is too late, too little, and too narrow, trying to graft occupational counselling onto a tree of ignorance (Marland 1974, pp. 214–221; 1980, pp. 164–165). More recently, Cathrine Avent has argued the case in *Careers Across the Curriculum* (Avent, forthcoming). However, it is probably fair to say that the curriculum implications of this background to guidance have not been explored. We do not know the details of what is required, and our efforts in school are limited by the lack of research, despite the politicians' complaints about the need.

Sex education and health education

Take another element of the pastoral curriculum, sex education (itself a limiting phrase normally taken to mean education about reproduction and not about sexuality). Bridget Brophy (Brophy 1977) and Stevi Jackson (Jackson 1978) have made devastating criticisms of schools' education about sexuality, the first based on a survey of the texts and the second on field research amongst girls. Jackson's book on sexuality in childhood is also relevant (1982). However, it does not seem that we have done the research-based groundwork of what could and should be taught and learnt about sexuality to inform adequately our curriculum planning of this aspect of the 'personal' part of the pastoral curriculum.

One might have thought that 'health education' had been better covered, with Schools Council projects and a national Health Education Council. However, the publications from that combination (Schools Council 1983) have a gross gap between aspiration and the majority of the teaching/learning material. Community Service Volunteers have produced a teachers' pack, *Health*, which is good on the organisational side of health services, but still does not relate sufficiently to young people's needs (CSV 1982).

Option choice

A special facet of the pastoral curriculum which I should like to highlight is option choice. This process both serves the rest of the curriculum, by helping pupils make wise choices, and is part of the key content of the pastoral curriculum, by helping pupils choose wisely.

The United States school pupil faces 'electives' yearly from at least what we should call first-year secondary (grade 6). The professional help is typically given by 'guidance and counselling' *departments*, specialists with no teaching timetable. In this country it is usual to face the first 'option' choices at fourteen, leading to a two-year examination course. In both countries the choosing of subjects has a double importance: on the one hand the choices affect the student's future, both by encouraging or inhibiting success at school and by keeping later study and occupation possibilities open or not. On the other hand, these are also the most important choices an adolescent makes largely within the school's influences and teaching. Choosing options is a paradigm for all choices. As part of the pastoral curriculum the teaching of 'choosing' is central. Choosing options is thus a *real* experience to be used by the school to help the pupil learn about choice.

There has clearly been recognition of this importance and a continuing debate about the so-called 'compulsory core' since Jim Callaghan's 'Ruskin speech' in 1976, and in particular the agonised curriculum arguments in, e.g. *A view of the curriculum* (HMI 1980, especially Propositions 13 and 14) and the ILEA's *Consultation Paper on Curriculum in Schools* (ILEA 1980), which has as its first 'suggested principle': 'Children must have freedom to play a major part in determining their own lives.' (p. 15). It is therefore surprising that there has not been a major series of research studies on pastoral care and curriculum choice. In the USA the professional separation of the guidance task and its annual requirement has encouraged specific research. In this country, however, there have been only narrowly-directed and limited studies. In the last ten years, the first study was in 1974 (Reid *et al* 1974) and the next substantial one was based on questionnaires to 117 West Midland schools and a detailed study of two schools, funded by the SSRC (Hurman 1978). The bibliography to the latter lists three unpublished PhD theses and five journal articles, of which that by Peter Woods provocatively called 'The Myth of Subject Choice' is the best known (Woods 1976). In it he studies one secondary modern school and concludes 'there is an illusion of a range of choice, of selections of personnel delayed to the last moment, . . . of a common starting line . . ., and of common fare. . . . In fact, the range of choice is variable among the pupils, non-existent for some' (*ibid*, p. 46). Woods is convinced that 'pupils' subject choice is socially structured' (*ibid*, p. 147).

In 1982, the Schools Council published *Options for the Fourth* (Schools Council 1982), the result of a 'low-cost, exploratory study involving staff in schools, LEAs, and the Council in an extension of their normal work' (*ibid*, p. 7). There is some information about a small exercise on 'How pupils reach decisions'. It rated the influence of 'Parents' as first, 'School Option Information' as second, and 'Teachers' as third (*ibid*, p. 15), and rated 'Subject Teachers' as vastly more important than 'Form Teachers' (*ibid*, p. 16). However, the study is essentially taking a *curriculum* viewpoint, and, indeed, the Foreword puts the study firmly in 'the continuing process of curriculum review' (*ibid*, p. 6). Apart from a passing reference to 'poor guidance and counselling' (*ibid*, p. 35), the whole study has the usual Schools Council silence on pastoral care.

Finally, the SSRC funded a little-known project from 1980 to 1983 on 'Curriculum Guidance and Differentiation at 14+' (Smith 1984, which includes a good bibliography). His findings highlight 'cues which pupils have acquired about their own levels of ability', that 'through processes of guidance and counselling from teachers (formal or informal), pupils' choice are moved more in line with what teachers believe about their real level of ability', and, very significantly, that pupil ambitions are a 'relatively stronger' effect 'in schools where the options are less stratified' (*ibid*, p. 8). The research does not support Woods' 'social structure' model. Once again, the study does not focus on the process of guidance itself.

There have also been a number of small scale studies considering the relationship between choice and specific subjects, especially in relation to the sciences and girls. For instance, Keys and Ormerod (1976) have shown that girls rating physics high in their preference scale are less likely to be able to study it than boys with the same level of preference. (See also Ormerod and Duckworth 1975, and Ormerod *et al* 1979.) These all have implications for the educational guidance given by tutors and house or year heads, but this dimension is rarely if ever recognised. As I have stated elsewhere 'the corollary of choice is counselling' (Marland 1980 a, XV.1), and for the huge majority of pupils that means pastoral care via the tutor.

Thus those of us in schools have a very limited range of research (though much of it of good quality and interesting) to help us with the educational guidance aspect of pastoral care and options for the fourth year – and still less for post-sixteen! The research that has been done has usually been based on a very few schools, often pre-comprehensive reorganisation (e.g. Wood 1976) and almost all the time has been severely limited in terms of pastoral care application by having one of two focusses:

1   A sociological correlation model, in which the prime aim has been to correlate pupil choices with social class, ability, or earlier schooling.
2   A curriculum-planning model, in which the prime aim has been to map what subject range pupils have ended up with.

Almost nowhere in the literature of the research into choosing options is the pastoral process focussed upon. Unless we are to abandon choice, and that is both undesirable and unlikely, this research gap needs filling.

I have dealt with aspects of study skills in the previous section on the student as 'information-user', but it would be possible to take each aspect of the pastoral curriculum and demonstrate the lack both of a specific research focus into the topic, and how to weave it into the whole-school curriculum and pastoral programme. Indeed the absence of curriculum theorists and researchers from key focuses such as this is lamentable (e.g. Zeldin 1983, and Lee and Zeldin 1982, to name two recent Open University texts otherwise characterised by breadth and thoughtfulness). This is yet another aspect in which the curriculum demands of the aims of pastoral care have not been adequately researched or developed for those of us in schools to respond adequately to the exhortations. No wonder do HMI declare: 'Greater care in planning the time given to tutor periods and help and advice to tutors on how best to use this time would allow better use to be made of tutor periods.' (HMI 1979, p. 222). The new School Curriculum Development Committee's first six 'key themes' significantly include 'personal and social development' (TES 10.2.84.) and perhaps we can at last hope for a coherent and usable research approach.

There is also a depressing separatism when the profession addresses itself to new issues: the enthusiasts overlook pastoral care. I find that two of the major thrusts of this decade, each of which has generated valuable research, have almost entirely overlooked the pastoral aspects of schooling: equal opportunities and multi-cultural education.

Equal opportunities

The mass of valuable research and discussion on aspects of equal opportunities and education has focussed heavily on the academic curriculum. Indeed there is hardly a word about pastoral care in the entire UK literature of equal opportunities and schooling. Conversely, there is little or nothing on the literature of pastoral care that addresses itself to equal opportunities. (In my own symposium, *Sex Differentiation and Schooling* (Marland 1983), I managed only five pages!) Of course some of the work of NISEC and some of the work on counselling relates to gender.

However, some researchers have focussed powerfully on aspects of sex differentiation and motivation and anxiety. The research of Carol Dweck (both in her contribution to Marland 1983, and her other papers) and Margaret B. Sutherland (in 'Anxiety, Aspirations, and the Curriculum' in Marland 1983) show the need for a different approach to girls' anxiety. Carol Dweck can even demonstrate the different ways in which girls and boys react to 'peer' as opposed to 'adult' criticism. All these points have crucial implications for tutoring, but we have not yet begun to work them out. If equal opportunities is to be a real educational issue, it must be located in the central guidance processes of the school: pastoral care. At the moment we know, for instance, that science curriculum and methods alienate many girls, but we have not a single study of what happens to them in tutor periods.

Multi-cultural education

If the literature of feminism is reticent on pastoral care, that on the intensely urgent issue of multi-cultural education is positively empty. I intend by 'multi-cultural education' the twin complementary considerations of the Swann Committee, that is the educational needs of the children of ethnic minority families to ensure that they obtain their full rights to a good education, and also the educational needs of all pupils to be prepared for a multi-cultural world.

A standard and, in its way, admirable book *Teaching in the Multi-Cultural School* (Lynch 1981), covers many aspects of the curriculum and has chapters on most 'subjects'. However, the pastoral programme is *never* mentioned, and 'tutor', 'form teacher', or 'pastoral' do not appear once in the index! I may have missed some work, but as far as I know, the entire range of research studies and educational discussion texts on aspects of anti-racism in the UK has been blind to the pastoral perspective. The important research by David Milner (Milner 1983) has endeavoured to establish how young people develop their attitudes to race identity. The essential point is that these matters are 'taught', and therefore are amenable to school actions. Lawrence Stenhouse, before his sad death, did more than any other single person in this country to assist the research and intellectual consideration of *how* pupils develop attitudes, and how these could be influenced by teaching (e.g. Stenhouse *et al* 1982).

Despite the rapid growth of the number of bilingual pupils in certain parts of the country (18.6 per cent of the school population in the ILEA, for instance) and the fact that 'linguistic diversity . . . is so much a feature of everyday life in England today' (Linguistic Minorities Project, 1985, p. 1), there has been very little speculation, and still less research, about the pastoral needs of bilingual learners whose English is currently very limited. *How* is 'personal, educational, and vocational guidance' to be offered by a tutor or junior school class teacher who has no competence in the pupil's strongest language if the pupil does not sensitively and clearly understand the teacher's English? A recent report by a group of teachers and community workers in the ILEA, 'Educating Bilingual Learners' (Working Party 1985), recommends special 'complementary tutoring', but as yet we have no research on the results of pastoral care or into possible variations.

I have tried as a practitioner in a school to keep abreast of the research and writing on aspects of multi-cultural education. However, I have to stress that in the wide-ranging number of studies of aspects of ethnicity, immigration, and ethnic minorities in schools, I have rarely or never come across either an explicit or implicit understanding of the pastoral contribution. We know attitudes are amplified or created by schools; we know racial attitudes are an artefact of society. But we have not found a way of studying what actually happens and how it can be changed.

The report by the Committee of Enquiry, chaired by Lord Swann, might have been expected to have changed this, especially as throughout it emphasises the need for more research. However, the relationship between one of its major themes, underachievement and achievement, and pastoral care is not even touched upon (Committee of Enquiry into the Education of Children from Ethnic Minority Groups 1985, Chapter 3), and 'what can broadly be termed pastoral matters' appears to be seen (though no definition is attempted) as 'facilities for meals and dress . . . "rules and regulations" and . . . religious "rights and duties"' (*ibid.*, p. 203). At one point one sees a glimmer coming into the Committee's mind of the centrality of the pastoral task when it requires 'the school to be able to cater for any "pastoral" needs which an ethnic minority pupil may experience, for example in relation to intergenerational conflicts or educational aspiration' (*ibid.*, p. 326). However, the limited view of 'pastoral' (almost always with those nervous quotations marks of disbelief in its meaning) is assumed to be 'rules' about 'such matters as school uniforms, showers and changing, physical education and swimming' (*ibid.*, p. 513).

The relationship between pastoral care and the educational needs of ethnic minority children and of the whole population of pupils in regard to their perception of a multi-ethnic society is a major and urgent focus for educational research.

Conclusion

The common fallacies of pastoral care include an over-emphasis on individual work, an under-emphasis on content, and a belief that there is no theory but rather that it all depends on experience and getting to know the pupil. These fallacies combine with the unfortunate effects of promotion policies and the dearth of people with experience and interest in pastoral care in the advisory service and in colleges and departments of education to leave pastoral care without the research base it requires.

In this chapter, I have highlighted those aspects of pastoral care where properly focussed and effective research studies need to be carried out and their results disseminated to the teaching profession. For example, one of the central pastoral tasks is to help children to be pupils. But if tutorial work, tutorial team leadership, and middle-management case-work are to develop as fully professional tasks, the presently available research bearing on aspects of the pupil role must be drawn together, and fresh research initiated into being a pupil and the help required.

We need to study the relationship between parenting style and pastoral approaches and the correlations between parenting style and school success. We have to find ways of inducting pupils into secondary school studies throughout their schooling, and of teaching them how to handle and make best use of information. We need pastoral procedures which enable tutors and classteachers to understand motivation and to know how to ensure pupils learn how to succeed.

There is little research on the structure and responsibilities for pastoral care within the school, including how teachers use their tutorial time. We simply do not know enough about pastoral care structures to adapt, service or rebuild them. We also know very little about how tutors work, with no research available on the quality of the tutoring that goes on and of the inter-relationships between tutor and tutee. Although the inadequacy of in-service provision for tutors is widely acknowledged, we have yet to find out the best ways of producing effective in-service work in pastoral care.

The development of tutorial programmes within a whole-school pastoral curriculum is hampered by a lack of adequate research into essential elements of that pastoral curriculum, including education for careers, education about sexuality and health, and option choice. In addition, research into contemporary social developments, such as equal opportunities and multi-cultural education, has ignored the pastoral care aspects and applications of such developments. The last few years have seen a major growth of work specifically directed to pastoral care. One can say that the work of Best *et al*, Galloway, Welton, MacBeth, Johnson and others has provided the basis for a new professionalism, and the foundation of NAPCE and its rapid growth is a recognition of that. However, the level of knowledge at all levels and in all sectors of the system of what we mean by 'personal, educational, and vocational guidance' and how to deliver effective pastoral care for all is depressingly low. We hope there will be an upsurge of research to help the next generation of pupils more than their predecessors.

Research implications

Research, pastoral care and the school
A pastoral care abstracting service should be set up by the ESRC and/or NAPCE, possibly through the journal *Pastoral Care in Education*.

The structure of pastoral care systems
Team leadership of tutors in the secondary school and the division of responsibilities need analysing with a view to establishing criteria for school decision-making.

The child
Research should assess what pastoral care approaches best suit different parenting styles and backgrounds.

Research is needed to attempt to isolate more precisely aspects of the role of the child as pupil, and how children may be more effectively inducted into it.

Action research is needed into pupils' perceptions of the requirements and purposes of learning methods, including change of stages of schooling, varieties of classroom styles and homework, with a view to identifying pastoral procedures to enable pupils to be more effective as students.

Existing library-user education and information-handling research should be built upon to study the most profitable likely division between tuition and pastoral support. Guidelines should be established for the appropriate pastoral function.

The motivation research of Carol Dweck and her associates should be considered from a UK standpoint, and both replicated in a UK context and explored for tutorial action.

The tutor

Detailed studies of time devoted to both individual and group pastoral care should be set up, endeavouring to analyse the sub-uses of time and how this is spread amongst the pupils.

What is happening to tutors and tutees both in and out of tutor periods, and the interpersonal relations of tutors and tutees need to be researched by:

1 classroom observation and tutor logs of tutor periods;
2 observation and logs of one-to-one encounters of tutors and tutees outside the tutor period;
3 investigation into the effect of a tutor's personal characteristics on her or his relationship with different tutees.

Given the need to offer tutors, middle management and senior management rapid in-service development in pastoral care work, pilot research with proper monitoring and evaluation is required to help establish models of in-service work (school-based and LEA-based), and to cost them.

The pastoral curriculum

Research is required to clarify the underlying knowledge needed for a proper understanding of occupations, their relationship to life, and the factors in later selection. This research should then be directed to finding appropriate syllabus forms for this learning.

Curriculum research is needed into what young people need to learn for their personal and social development, and how schools can locate the components in a whole-school curriculum plan.

A programme for action research into current option-guidance methods, and possible ways of intensifying the value to the pupil of the tutor is required, with an examination of the possible tutorial repertoire.

Specifically pastoral research is needed into the relationship between schooling and ethnicity.

How do we help children learn from their experience in the school organisation?

David Armstrong

A problem about 'pastoral care'

I wish to start from an issue about 'pastoral care' in schools that has received considerable attention over the past five years[1]. This is that a good deal of what comes under the general rubric of 'pastoral care' is compensatory. The pastoral system gets used to cope with the fact that some children are not able to relate themselves as persons to the school, its aims, tasks, values and organisation. Consequently they have difficulty in managing themselves in relation to the educational opportunities which the school provides. Much of the activity of tutors, heads of year/house is then directed to dealing with the ensuing feelings and behaviour: disruptiveness, disorientation, loss of control, underachievement, boredom, absenteeism, uncertainty about the future, etc. This activity may have a 'welfare' focus: counselling, school-based social work, problem-oriented case-work with individuals, or simply getting to know the children, establishing 'good' personal relationships or making children 'feel at home' in school. It may also have a shadow side concerned with control and discipline,[2] these two aspects sometimes being distributed between different members of the pastoral team. Between these two aspects lie the more administrative functions of 'pastoral care': registration, reports, liaison with parents, sorting out timetable problems, and generally ensuring, in the words of one of the children interviewed in Peter Lang's study of pupils' perceptions of pastoral care, that 'we know what we should be doing'.[3]

All these aspects have a strong reactive element, in that they represent a response on the part of the school to children's actual or potential feelings of dislocation in or alienation from the institution of schooling. The greater the sense of dislocation or alienation, the more weight a pastoral system is likely to carry. Recently it has been argued that the pastoral activity of schools should be seen as preventive rather than merely reactive. The idea of the 'pastoral curriculum' has been introduced to provide a focus for this shift of emphasis.[4] The themes proposed for such a curriculum: personal relationships, learning about learning, the study of school as an organisation, preparation for life after school and the like, continue to reflect assumptions about what it is that may be dislocating or alienating about schools. The difference is that these themes are now to be brought directly into the educational context of the school, to be studied alongside or in advance of their actual experience by pupils. The danger remains that the experience of children in school is taken for granted, rather than leading to a consideration of what that experience has to say about the child's relatedness to school as an institution, which may have implications for general school policies, practices and structures. In both cases, reactive or preventive, what a pastoral system is *actually* doing as contrasted with what its intentions are, may just be to socialise the children into the particular educational and institutional regime of the school and/or to compensate those children who are unable readily to fit in with that regime for themselves. Children thereby become objects for processing by schools as organisations, rather than seen as active, intelligent participants in their own education.

Taking up the pupil role

The work carried out by The Grubb Institute, both with young people in and out of school and with headteachers and staff, suggests that many of the real concerns underlying the pastoral activity of schools can be brought into clearer focus if they are seen in relation to one basic concept: that of *taking up a role* – in the case of children the role of *pupil*. Thus we would argue that the pastoral system of the school is often brought into play to manage the consequences of children, or some children, not being able to bring into view or get a purchase on the role of pupil which the school is offering. The way children may be responded to within the pastoral system however, through the mobilisation of care or control, can exacerbate the problem these children face, even if it seems quite successful in bringing about some 'better' adjustment to the day to day experience of the school.

By 'taking up the pupil role' I am not referring to knowing the ropes: the rules of the system, what behaviour is expected, who is supposed to do what and when. A child can do all that, willingly or reluctantly, and still not be able to take up a role as pupil. I am rather referring to what happens when one is able to form some idea of the aim and task of the institution, what it stands for, what it seeks to do, to which I can relate my behaviour as a member from my own particular position. A role in this sense is an organising principle in my mind, which may need continual revision in the light of my experience, through which I can manage my own behaviour to make a contribution to the task of the system of which the role is a part.

Unlike teachers, children come to school under compulsion. Moreover teachers legally stand *in loco parentis* with all the temptations this offers to see oneself as responsible for everything that happens to a child. There may be a natural tendency to construe what takes place in school as something that is done *by* teachers *for* and *to* children. They are recipients of a process rather than contributors to it. The client is society, parents, educational values or whatever. But if the output from the school system is children learning something, the child must be able to take part in that system as a member, identify with it and contribute to his or her own learning in relation to a wider context than just his or her immediate needs, inclinations and wishes. It is learning that is the throughput of the organisation, not the child; and the child contributes to that throughput with or under the leadership of the teacher.

A child then in my terms joins the school as a member, in the role of pupil, when he or she is able to give some assent to aim and task, both of the school as a whole and of the various sub-systems: classes, forms, tutor periods, different years, etc. This is not a once-for-all event or decision but a constantly renewed process. Every year, day, lesson, represents a new act of joining or not joining. A child may take up the pupil role in one lesson and not in the next, one day and not the next. However, it is only insofar as a child does take up the role in this way that the rules, codes of behaviour and values represented by the school can begin to be given meaning and be tested rather than experienced simply as the more or less arbitrary expectations of adults in charge.

This idea of taking up the pupil role may appear somewhat simplistic and remote from the actual practice of teachers and schools. In fact, however, in any school there are likely to be children who understand the pupil role naturally and will take it up, even in cases where the quality or environment of teaching is not particularly supportive or enabling. In this regard too little attention is often paid to the fact that, for example, some children are able to learn from 'poor' teaching or teachers, no less than from the gifted, and of course vice versa. (This is not unlike the question which has perplexed some psychologists, how it comes about that some children grow up, mature and develop despite what appears to an outsider as the most unfavourable social and emotional environment.) A child can have a clearer sense of aim and task than a teacher, or perhaps as a result of experiences with some teachers, a particular child can bring a concept of the pupil role to bear in situations where otherwise he or she might be at a loss. On the other side there are clearly schools in which this idea of the pupil role implicitly informs the practice of the school as a whole.

Two examples

It may be helpful to give two examples of ways in which, in different contexts, a teacher may either promote or inhibit the process I am trying to describe. One example would be the ways in which a subject teacher tries to deal with questions about 'Why do we have to learn this?' Possible responses could be 'Because it's part of the curriculum', 'Because you're going to be examined on it.' Or the teacher may respond by mentally making a note to try and make the subject more interesting or easier and try to find out what lies behind the question on the basis of that assumption.

However the pupil may be trying to work out and test through this question what value learning, say French, represents, what it stands for in the curriculum of the school and the vision of education which informs that curriculum. If the question can be interpreted and honestly answered at this level the pupil will have been given information, 'something that makes a difference', which brings into view the opportunities that school is offering. He will have something to bite on, to compare with other observations, to frame the choices he is making about opting in or opting out. In my terms, by treating the question as an enquiry about the nature of school, the teacher focusses the role of being a pupil in the school, even if the pupil remains unsure whether he wishes to take up that role or not.

A different example, more directly related to the pastoral function, would be how a form tutor manages what children may communicate at registration. John Bazalgette has drawn attention to the significance of registration and its psychological importance as

> ... the point in the day at which (children) cross the boundary of the school and take up the pupil role in a formal sense. . . .[5]

How a form tutor regards this act and handles it, how seriously he takes it, the way he responds to personal information which may be offered about why someone is absent/not in uniform/looking miserable, how he relays information from other staff, how he manages the time boundary, will convey implicit messages about the way he construes both his own role and that of the pupils. If a tutor is relating to children as pupils he will seek to treat children primarily in the context of the school and the classroom, to bracket out what is conveyed about home or social life, rather than feeling responsible for the whole child, interpreting *in loco parentis* as being the substitute parent. This does not mean being blind to what a child brings into school from the outside world, but enabling the child to disengage from other important dimensions of his life so as to engage in school. It may be more supportive to a child who shows signs of obvious distress because of something happening at home, to help her contain that distress sufficiently to take part as a pupil in the lessons and activities of the day, rather than to address the distress head on by talking it over or mobilising welfare provision. One problem about the emphasis on personal relationships and caring which may be encouraged, particularly within the pastoral activities of a school, is that it can blur boundaries and distinctions which need to be held and worked at if the child is to manage himself or herself in the different contexts of the school. To take up a role implies being able to achieve some distance from oneself and others, to differentiate between adult and teacher, child and pupil, personal relationships and working relationships. A form tutor who believes in getting 'close' to children may make it more difficult for them to work as pupils in ordinary lessons.

Roles and context

I have suggested that many of the concerns which the pastoral system of a school addresses have to do, at least partly, with difficulties experienced by children in taking up the pupil role in the school and that some features of the pastoral systems may themselves exacerbate this. I have implied that whether or not children are able to take up the pupil role will depend, to an extent which may vary from individual to individual, on the detailed ways in which staff manage their relationships and interactions with pupils in various contexts, and how staff conceive and take up *their* role as teachers and tutors. Staff and pupils do not work in a vacuum, however. Whether or not a work or task role can be taken up and effectively worked with will depend in part on what is happening in the institution as a whole. In particular, the kind and quality of the leadership given by a head and senior staff in defining, communicating, and representing aims and tasks and reviewing these in the light of experience is likely to be crucial to both teachers' and pupils' sense of role. Aims and tasks are not just a datum to be taken as read: they are necessarily subject to negotiation and change in the light of changes in the community and societal context in which the school exists. Pupils, particularly older pupils, are as likely to be as alert to this as anyone else. If a school simply fails to respond to such changes, it may well forfeit whatever commitment pupils have hitherto been able to make to it. This is why the emergence of a much more hostile social and economic climate for young people has been rightly seen to pose a major challenge for schools.

Enabling children to take up the pupil role

I wish to propose that this represents a much neglected area in thinking about the practice of schools which would not only repay further research but without which decisions about school practices, policies and structures, particularly in the pastoral field may lack a valuable dimension. The aim of such research would be to understand the processes through which children learn to take up the pupil role and own it for themselves. The underlying hypothesis is that children who can do this are better able to manage themselves in school, to take responsibility for their own learning, to make choices, and to maintain working relationships with adults as teachers or tutors. An important corollary is that these young people will be better able to manage themselves outside school, even under far from favourable circumstances.

The questions research in this area needs to address include the following:

1   *How do children conceive the role of pupil in secondary school?* What range of meanings do they give to it? What variations exist both between schools, and within the same school between different age groups (compare Peter Lang's study cited earlier of the variations in how the pastoral system of a school is construed)?

1.1   *How do children relate themselves to the role or roles which they see the school as offering?* Do they experience the pupil role mainly in terms of the expectations and rules of others: teachers, tutors, parents, fellow pupils, standing over and against their own wishes and intentions? Or do they relate those expectations to some vision of school as an educational system which they are able to take ownership of for themselves? How far do these different ways of relating to role vary between different parts of the school system: academic or pastoral, one department or subject and another? Is there an underlying pattern to such variation?

To answer these questions means taking children's experience seriously, talking to them, either individually or in groups, not only about their views of school and what it means to them, but also about how they handle the different situations they meet: when they are being told something or given instructions, left to work on their own, taking part in an assembly, relating to a form teacher, a head of house, answering questions, being registered, moving between lessons, entering and leaving school at the beginning and end of the day, doing homework, representing the school in a team. Our experience at The Grubb Institute is that, whatever the well rehearsed risks of such a research approach may be, children and young people are far more resourceful in describing the quality of their experience than they are sometimes given credit for. Equally the approach is implied by the terms of the enquiry itself: to relate to a role is to acknowledge and work with, directly or indirectly, one's own experience of and in it.

2 *What are the individual variables which affect the child's or young person's perception of the pupil role in the same or similar schools?* These variables may include chronological or developmental age, gender, social class, race, ability, interests. They may also include the child's experience in other social and institutional settings, most obviously the family, but also in clubs, youth groups, religious or cultural institutions, and for some older children in work places. In all these settings children also have experience of relating themselves to a role and that experience is likely to bear on how they understand and relate to the role of pupil, both directly and indirectly, through the expectations adults themselves in those settings have of school.

3 *What characteristics of schools influence pupils' perceptions of role?* From the point of view of policy and practice in schools this is the central question to be asked. One aspect of it concerns teachers' behaviour and the assumptions both about being a pupil in the school and about being a teacher which underline that behaviour. How teachers manage their own day to day working relations with pupils, both in the classroom and outside, how they observe boundaries of time, territory and task, how they take up their own roles as subject teachers, form tutors, heads of year/house, how they relate to other members of staff, will all shape the way pupils see the regime of school and the rationale and consistency underlying its rules and regulations, both formal and informal. We need to know more about what is critical here and how it may vary with the type of school, its size and social composition, the organisational structures and patterns within which staff and pupils work.

A second aspect, which I have already touched on earlier, concerns the institutional context of the school as a whole: the way leadership and management are exercised by the head and senior staff, how aims and tasks are formulated, agreed, communicated and reviewed, the 'organisational ethos', to use Michael Rutter's term, underpinning the activities both of staff and of pupils, the relations established between the school and its wider community.

To begin to answer such questions may seem a tall order, calling for in-depth research over a wide sample of schools, research which by its very nature requires a significant commitment of staff's and pupils' time and energy and which, if insensitively handled, may be seen as intrusive and disrupting. A more hopeful and realistic approach would be to seek to work with a small number of particular schools whose heads and staff themselves are interested to explore how their pupils see and relate to their role(s) in the school and the ways in which the school does and can influence this. Without such collaboration any research programme of the kind I am envisaging will either fail to get off the ground or remain a largely academic exercise. In the long run its value will more than anything else depend on how far it contributes to enabling pupils and staff to become a learning community, not only in relation to external areas of knowledge, but also in relation to their own shared experience as members of that community, day after day.

Notes

1 As exemplified for example, in the articles collected in Best, Jarvis and Ribbins (Eds) *Perspectives on Pastoral Care*, especially those by Derek Williamson on 'Pastoral care or pastoralization?' and John Buckley on 'The care of learning: Some implications for school organisation.'

2 The inter-relations of 'care' and 'control' aspects of the pastoral function in schools is discussed by Best, Jarvis and Ribbins in the introductory chapter to *Perspectives on Pastoral Care*, and also in their more recent study, *Education and Care*. Peter Lang's study of pupils' perceptions of pastoral care provides a fascinating glimpse of the two aspects as seen by secondary school children, *cf* Peter Lang, 'How pupils see it: Looking at how pupils perceive pastoral care', *Pastoral Care in Education*, in 1, 3, 1983.

3 Peter Lang, 'How pupils see it: Looking at how pupils perceive pastoral care', *op cit*, p. 169.

4 *Cf* Michael Marland's magisterial article on 'The Pastoral Curriculum', in Best, Jarvis and Ribbins, *Perspectives on Pastoral Care*, Chapter 11.

5 John Bazalgette, 'Taking up the pupil role', *Pastoral Care in Education*, Volume 1, Number 3, November 1983.

Pastoral care and welfare networks

Daphne Johnson

Pastoral care as a boundary issue

The metaphor of pastoral care conjures up a picture of work done for the flock by the shepherd, within the fold. The so-called pastoral care of schoolchildren is indeed frequently conceived of and organised as an activity taking place within a school, of little concern to those outside it. But pastoral care can also be seen as a 'boundary' issue for schools, involving the school with various external agencies and entailing the crossing of the school boundary, in both directions, by teachers, counsellors and agency professionals.

During the 1970s, research by the writer and others into the perceived scope of pastoral work in schools identified seven principal aspects to pastoral care

1 to provide a secure base to which the pupil can relate within a large school;
2 to identify and respond to any problems the pupil is experiencing as an individual;
3 to monitor and regulate the attendance, punctuality, behaviour and progress of each pupil;
4 to systematise the recording and communication of information relevant to the welfare of individual pupils;
5 to make recommendations about special educational needs of individual pupils;
6 to interact with the pupil's home regarding all aspects of pupil performance;
7 to collaborate with the education welfare service and other agencies, so that pastoral care within the school and welfare provision and support outside the school complement one another. (See Craft *et al* 1980, pp. 314–5.)

Despite repeated attempts by those interested in the organisation and substance of pastoral care to stress its relevance for *all* pupils, the tendency to equate pastoral care with problems is by no means rare.[1] By examining pastoral care as a boundary issue, this paper may to some extent seem to reinforce the notion that pastoral care is of particular relevance for *problem* pupils, those who are already the clients of local clinics or social work teams, or whose families may be well-known to education welfare officers or the police. However, the boundary task of relating to other agencies of welfare and control is a continuing requirement for schools, and there is much scope for further research into the question of schools as part of a welfare network.

Existing sources of information about how schools interact with agencies are not numerous. Mention has already been made of research during the 1970s which examined the concept of the secondary school as part of a network of welfare agencies.[2] This project focussed on four secondary schools. The pastoral work of the schools was analysed, and a study also made of the work of the education welfare service, the social services (including intermediate treatment), the school psychological service, the child guidance clinic, the school health service, health visitors and health education officers, the youth and community service and the juvenile bureau of the police. The work of general advisers within the education departments of the relevant local authorities was also examined. A general picture emerged of many practitioners working hard on behalf of often overlapping groups of clients, but with little awareness or understanding of the efforts being made in adjacent services.

Much of the literature which discusses the practice and possibility of cooperation between schools and agencies concentrates its attention on the role of the social worker, and the various attempts which have been made to enable teachers and social workers to work together.[3] Fitzherbert (1977) was optimistic that the school might prove an acceptable and feasible route through to the family for social workers and other agency practitioners, avoiding the stigmatising effect of a direct agency approach to the home. Our own research, however, provided no evidence that agencies found it convenient or practical to work through the school. Usually they made direct contact with the home, and it was frequently only a chance remark by a pupil which made teachers aware that other professionals were working with the family (see Johnson *et al* 1980, p. 96).

Several writers have tried to educe, from the untidy reality of services with a concern for children of school age, a clear pattern. One such attempt is described in Craft's 'School welfare roles and networks' (see Craft *et al* 1980, pp. 327–348) which draws on several sources including Bolger (1975). Craft came to the conclusion that the wide range of welfare agencies which existed, together with what he described as the 'bizarre variety' in the forms of British schooling, meant that no single blueprint for school welfare provision could meet the varied circumstances of more than a proportion of schools. Nevertheless, he advocated that there should be:

> an internal convenor of welfare efforts within each school;
> the elements of a team of welfare specialists within each school;
> a clear channel out of the school to neighbourhood welfare agencies.[4]

These recommendations, whilst unexceptionable, seem to beg many of the questions raised by the earlier Brunel research (see Johnson *et al* 1980). In deciding what further research is needed, or what new helpful developments might be suggested with regard to pastoral care as a boundary-crossing activity, consideration should first be given to the key issues identified during the schools, parents and social services project which are briefly discussed below.

Factors which complicate school/agency cooperation
Differences in areas of jurisdiction

Here the term 'areas' is used in a strictly geographical rather than a figurative sense. It is an important factor in school and agency cooperation – though one rarely mentioned – that the areas from which the various institutions draw their client populations are not always coterminous. There are no geographical boundary problems at local authority level between the education department and the social services department of the same local authority. However, if a pupil moves from a primary school to a secondary school at a little distance, though still within the same LEA, the new school may well fall within the 'patch' of a different social work team from the previous school. Problems of continuity of knowledge of family background immediately arise.[5]

So far as health authority boundaries are concerned, following the 1974 reorganisation some area health authorities were coterminous with local authorities but others were not. So the boundaries of a school health service might or might not match the area within which all the schools of one local education authority stand. Subsequent *re* organisation of the National Health Service with the abolition of the area health authority level, and the consequent provision of some specialised agencies at regional and others at district authority level, has further complicated this question.

With regard to police authority boundaries, the schools within one local authority are conceivably covered by more than one police division. Any one *school*, however, is likely to have dealings with only one police division – unless some of the pupils come from outside the local authority boundary. The provisions of the 1980 Education Act make it more feasible, if not necessarily more likely, for parents to send their children to schools outside the local authority in which they reside. Any school, such as for example a denominational school, which regularly draws a proportion of pupils from across the LEA boundary, may find itself having to relate to juvenile bureau officers from more than one division, as well as to education welfare officers or social workers from several teams.

Differences in range of client population

The pupil population of any maintained school is chiefly made up of children of compulsory school age.[6] So also is the clientele of the Child Guidance Clinic, the School Psychological Service and the Education Welfare Service, though each of these services may have some functions to perform with under-fives, and also with the families of school children who come to the attention of these agencies. For a social work team, however, school-age children are only one of many categories of potential client. Many social work clients are elderly, and their needs may well appear more urgent than those of the young. The juvenile bureau of the police handles only offenders aged 10 to 17. This cohort does not neatly match the years of compulsory schooling, and certainly bridges the primary and secondary school years (whatever the local age of transfer), so that police officers from such a bureau have to know something about both the primary and the secondary schools of their area. But in any case the juvenile bureau is only a small sub-section of police activity, specialised in clientele but not in trained skills. The division as a whole is concerned with the whole local population, regardless of age.

The kind of complication for working together created by the two key issues so far referred to – differences in areas of jurisdiction and differences in range of client population – is chiefly one of having to relate to a large number of individual fellow-workers. The third key issue, however, is concerned with the working conditions, as well as the standing and experience, of the individuals with whom teachers or agency workers may have to relate, if they are operating as part of a welfare network.

Differences in seniority and status, and in terms and conditions of work

One of the most noticeable problems experienced in working together between schools and agencies is created by the differing hours of work and the holiday arrangements of the various professionals and other workers concerned. Although, to the teacher, the flexi-time arrangements which prevail in many agencies and local authority departments may cause inconvenience, it is undoubtedly the working hours and the availability of the school teacher which stand out as unusual from the point of view of agency practitioners. Many teachers pursue work-related activities of preparation and marking outside actual school hours, but the teacher is not usually contactable and available at the place of work outside those hours, nor during the school holidays which, unlike the leave periods of other workers, are always concentrated into consecutive periods of several weeks. Meetings between teachers and agency workers are ruled out for weeks at a time and even correspondence is difficult to maintain because of these differing conditions of work.

Another difficulty which presents itself when teachers and agencies try to work together concerns the use of the telephone. For some agency practitioners the telephone is an important and readily available working tool. For teachers, however, access to the telephone is limited both by the nature of their work and also the amenities of the workplace. Most ordinary teachers do not have offices or any private workplace in the school, and can only be contacted on the staffroom telephone at specific times of the day.

Space will not permit the detailed discussion of the recruitment, training and relative status of teachers and agency workers, but these are of course important points of comparison between professionally-staffed institutions. In the case of teachers and social workers, although there may in fact be little real difference in the populations from which teachers and social workers are recruited, the calibre of the training they receive, and their general standing in the public eye, there is in fact quite a mismatch between the levels of the teaching and social work hierarchies that are likely to make contact with one another in a professional capacity. The basic grade of social worker has a considerable degree of autonomy in his work. He may cross boundaries, entering the school, the home, and setting up inter-relationships with other agencies, acting as an individual practitioner. This is quite different from the situation of the junior teacher who is the nearest equivalent in the teaching profession. The teacher has a much more concentrated geographical location, a closely-defined timetable of work responsibilities, and an established place in a complex organisation which protects as well as constrains. The visiting social worker will almost certainly be required to conduct his business with a senior member of the teaching staff, and this may place the social worker at a disadvantage, especially since the senior teacher is operating on 'home ground'. Schools can be daunting institutional settings, even to visiting professionals.

In the authorities studied by the Brunel research team,[2] some professionals declined to visit the schools at all, preferring to operate exclusively from their own territory. Examples here were child psychiatrists in child guidance teams. They insisted that all liaison with the schools by way of visits or, in some cases, even of telephone calls, should be handled by the educational psychologists in the team, seconded from the School Psychological Service. While this could have been in order to avoid possible confusion arising from several channels of contact between school and clinic, in the cases examined it appeared rather that psychiatrists saw their own remoteness from the context of the school as a prerequisite for their clinical diagnosis of the problems of the schoolchildren.

One of the most noticeable and problem-creating examples of differences both of status and working conditions between teachers and agency practitioners was the case of the education welfare officer (now known at least in some areas as education social workers). EWOs, as they were formerly called, had apparent freedom to move about their 'patch', and to order their own working day. Nevertheless they were subject to considerable bureaucratic control by their own seniors in the service, and were at a relative disadvantage compared with teachers and all other agency practitioners so far as training, salary and general professional standing were concerned. Despite attempts to place education welfare on a par with social work, EWOs were undoubtedly at the bottom of the agency pecking order at the time of the Brunel research, and this is probably still the case in the majority of areas. The relative disadvantage of the EWO who was required to interact with a senior teacher, when visiting the school, was even greater than that of the junior social worker. At the same time, however, the class teacher, concerned about a particular child and wanting to arrange a welfare visit, might feel frustrated by his inability to speak directly to the EWO (who was rarely known by sight to more than a handful of teachers in a large secondary school). Instead the senior teacher, who evaluated priorities in the context of requests put forward by upwards of fifty class teachers, prepared the list of calls for the EWO and instructed him accordingly.

The practice of giving particular individuals on a school staff responsibility for liaison with welfare agencies will be further discussed later in this paper.

Differences in modes of work

We have noted that a social worker visiting a school in connection with the problems of a pupil/client may have to discuss the case with a teacher considerably senior in rank to the social worker, and one who does not necessarily know the child in question very well. The potential difficulties of such an encounter might easily be overstressed. It would however be difficult to overstate the difficulties likely to ensue if the social worker wishes to pursue collaborative work on the case *outside* the school, with the teacher closest to the child, perhaps through the medium of a case conference. It is almost impossible for a junior class teacher to undertake such work outside the school during school hours. Even were it possible, the class teacher might be in two minds about the desirability of handing over a whole class to someone else for the best part of a morning or afternoon, to dwell on the problem of one child.

The case conference is a social work mode. It has now been adopted as a mode of work by some teachers with a particular interest in the pastoral aspects of schooling, but such conferences are usually in-house affairs, bringing together a range of teachers who handle a particular child, rather than drawing together agency workers with different bases of expertise, as in the original social work mode. Moreover, the case conference does not come naturally to teachers. The whole tradition of institutionalised schooling is to bring together numbers of children so that they can share the skills of a restricted number of teachers, whereas in a case conference a number of professionals come together to consider the case of an individual child, a family, or at the most a small group of children.

While collaborative work with other agency professionals may take the teacher away from his class, and the exercise of his specific skills, it is also the case that some treatments recommended by agencies for school pupils take these pupil/clients away from their lessons, a practice which may not have the full approval of teachers.

Differences in values and priorities of teachers and agency workers

We cannot assume that institutions like education and social work have each been promoting consistent and unchanging values over the whole period of their existence. It would be helpful to our understanding of the way institutions work if we could painstakingly uncover the layers of social and professional thinking which have accumulated and superseded one another over time. One of the reasons that institutions are able to survive, over decades, and sometimes over centuries, is their adaptability and the fact that the values they incorporate and promote change subtly, if not dramatically, in tune with the times. But without delving into the past history of social work and education, at the time of the Brunel research in the 1970s teachers and social workers seemed to *share* many values. They were both concerned with, and committed to, the development of the individual, the promotion of effective and fruitful interpersonal relations, arousing a sense of community, and with taking a part in processes of socialisation and social control.

However, although different professionals may share the same underlying values, they may put them into practice in different ways. The teacher, for instance, who is concerned for the development of the individual pupil, is usually willing and eager to assess and judge that development, and to place his assessments on record. It is part of the teacher's job to assess pupils, in any number of ways, over the time of their working relationship in the school and to adjure them to catch up, or conform, or try harder. Social workers, on the other hand may be extremely reluctant to appear in any way judgemental of their clients. Social work aims to establish a relationship with a client which accords him respect as an individual and this inhibits any overt assessment or judgement of client capacity or achievement. Nevertheless the socialising task of social workers, which they share with teachers, is inescapable. However radical the social work approach, one aim is always to help the client cope with society as it is. But an important difference between the socialising that teachers and social workers do, is that social workers are socialising to general societal values – getting along with the world at large – while teachers may be socialising to particular institutional requirements – indicating the specific role of a good pupil and, even more specifically, the role of a good pupil in a particular school. Not surprisingly, given the geographical location and concentration of teaching in a particular physical setting, values to which teachers give high priority in their institutional arrangements are values of orderliness and predictability. Social work, because of its peripatetic nature, and because of its important element of crisis response, may try to retain orderliness and predictability as *professional* characteristics, but does not stress them as first-order requirements for *clients*.

Suggestions for future research into the interconnections between pastoral care in schools, and the welfare network of agencies

Research in the 1970s made it plain that the various welfare agencies with a concern for children of school age by no means comprised an interconnected *system*. Even as a *network*, their connections were tenuous, and working relations were complicated by the diversity of employing authorities to whom agency workers were accountable, and the differences in objectives, training and professional standing of the various agency practitioners concerned. A decade later, some replication of this research might be desirable. In particular it would be of interest to investigate whether the broadly-noted attitudes of agency workers towards one another and to teachers, and of teachers to agency workers, appear to have substantially changed. Are child psychiatrists now more willing to draw close to the schools? Do education welfare officers now have parity of standing with fellow workers in the welfare network? Are teachers less cautious or apprehensive about the notion of working together with other professionals? John Welton has suggested that in new research it would be desirable to focus on child need and child care as a conceptual framework within which the various interventions of school and agencies could be examined.[7] All the education and care services could be seen as supplementary to the care provided by the family, and an analysis of the differing values held by each service with regard to child and family would go far to explain dysfunctions in working together.

There is also a need to update our knowledge about organisational aspects of agency work. A number of changes affecting the agencies have taken place during the last decade and there is certainly a case for new research to examine and clarify changing network structures. In particular, changes in health service organisation will have affected the administration of child guidance, formerly provided at area health authority level, and the school health service generally will have undergone administrative change.[8]

Earlier research into the network of agencies has tended to focus on professionalised care. Yet, in addition to the local authority and health authority-based organisations, many voluntary groups and agencies make a contribution to the care of school age children.[9] The church is one such source of care. It has not hitherto been the practice specifically to identify the spiritual welfare of young people as a concern of pastoral care in schools. Nevertheless in the denominational schools, the local priest, vicar or a school chaplain, may play an important part both in the internal pastoral work of the school and also as a boundary-crossing member of the welfare network. Any future study of pastoral care as a boundary issue would do well to look beyond the more prominent and formally-organised agencies of care and control, and examine additional ways in which resources in the local community contribute to pastoral care.

The assumption must not however be made that all sectors of a local community are at one in their perception of the qualities and contribution of particular agencies, or agency workers. For example, some informal evidence exists that educational psychologists are held in mistrust by black and coloured parents. The possible ethno-centricity of agency workers is a question meriting research. Is it the case that the analysis and treatments available through established agencies are better adapted to the needs of the white indigenous population than to the ethnic minority families who become agency clients? Some research has already been carried out into the capacity of schools to meet the needs of a multi-cultural population but the role of, for example, the school psychological service or the child guidance clinic in this connection does not appear to have been similarly studied.

Educational guidance and careers counselling has not typically been seen in the United Kingdom as unequivocally a part of pastoral work.[10] Yet, like spiritual welfare, what might broadly be termed the 'vocational welfare' of pupils could well be defined as a pastoral concern. This is an area whose inter-institutional aspects are of increasing interest in the 1980s, and eminently worthy of the research which they will undoubtedly attract. In times of low employment, what feelers do schools put out in the direction of Job Centres and employment agencies? The work of the Manpower Services Commission, the Youth Training Schemes, the Technical and Vocational Educational Initiatives are all ramifications of the network to which schools must relate, and which are as yet virtually unexplored.

The agencies with which schools relate include agencies of control as well as care. The Brunel research, in the 1970s, examined contacts between juvenile bureau police officers and the schools, and the aspects of social work and education welfare which linked schools and agency workers with the Courts and Assessment Centres (see Johnson *et al* 1980). More recently, the use made in juvenile courts of reports supplied by schools has been studied by a NACRO working group, and reported in *School Reports in Juvenile Courts*, 1984. Further research could well be undertaken into the checks and balances which exist between the various agencies of welfare, education and control, not least into the implications for schools and agencies of the Police and Criminal Evidence Bill.

The two major Education Acts, in the early 1980s, raised or renewed a number of research questions with relevance for this paper's topic of pastoral care and welfare networks. The provisions of the 1980 Education Act and its attendant regulations, concerning the expression of parental preferences for schools and arrangements about admissions, have implications for all those who take part in the recording and dissemination of information about pupils. Agency workers as well as teachers have contributed to the compilation of hitherto confidential pupil records, on which recommendations for pupil transfer (from primary to secondary school, or from high school to sixth-form college) have chiefly been based. Appeals against admission decisions now bring such recommendations under public scrutiny, and revive the question of how teachers and agency workers can responsibly share the privileged information available to them about a child's capacities and background. Issues of confidentiality proved important facets of school/agency cooperation in the 1970s and the 1980 Education Act has added new dimensions to the topic which require to be researched.

The 1981 Special Education Act caused wide-ranging changes which superseded former arrangements for the assessment of special educational need. While those who took part in the previous procedure – educational psychologist, clinical medical officer, etc. – still have a part to play, the new legislation envisages a role for parents. Research is now needed into the extent to which parents are experiencing any genuine sense of participation in the assessment of their child's needs.[11] Many attempts have been made, over past years, to strengthen the position of the parent in the various transactions which come under the broad heading of 'home-school relations'.[12] Parents for the most part have however continued to feel at a disadvantage in their exchanges with teachers, and it seems likely that parents' interaction with the more rarely encountered agency professionals, during the assessment of a child's special needs, will not be without its problems.

Parents may not be the only ones to whom agency workers are still an unknown quantity. In the 1970s, teachers in fairly senior pastoral posts – heads of house or heads of year – often had only scanty knowledge of the range and work of outside agencies. No formal training on the subject had been available to them either in preparatory or in-service teacher training. Some short courses and seminars were beginning to be organised at the time of the Brunel research (which was itself funded in recognition of the gap in school-agency contact and understanding demonstrated by the Maria Colwell case (DHSS 1976)). An enquiry into the developments in teacher-knowledge of agencies, over the past decade, would be worth carrying out and this might in part be pursued by a study of the teacher training programmes and in-service courses now available.

In the 1970s it was a sore point with some teachers with pastoral responsibilities that they were actually prevented from getting closer to the agencies by their school's policy of having only one liaison figure authorised to contact the agencies and negotiate with them regarding particular pupils.[13] This policy, encountered in several large schools, was in line with Craft's recommendation of a 'clear channel out of the school to neighbourhood welfare services.' (Craft *et al* 1980, pp. 341–2.) For many teachers, ambitious to increase the range of their pastoral experience and introduce some element of professional specialisation into their role, the 'channel' available did not seem sufficiently broad. Many of these teachers had accepted pastoral posts at a time of secondary reorganisation, in default of the academic advancement which they might have looked for under other circumstances. By now, many of these fairly senior teachers will have retired, and the idea of making a career of pastoral care may have become obsolete.

New research into the organisation of pastoral work in schools, in the 1980s, might reveal whether teachers still resent having school contact with the agencies monopolised by a single liaison figure or whether, indeed, these specialist roles – school counsellor, deputy head (pastoral care) or head of careers – are still to be found. Two attempts to read the future were made by the present writer, on the basis of research into pastoral work carried out in the 1970s. One was concerned with school counsellors. These specialists, it was suggested, might become unfashionable anachronisms, whose place would not be filled when natural wastage removed them from the educational scene. (See Johnson *et al* 1980, p. 70.)

The other attempt at crystal-ball gazing concerned the whole future of pastoral work in schools, and here two alternative prospects were sketched out (Craft *et al* 1980, pp. 324–5). One prospect was for the reversal of the then current policy of taking problem pupils out of the mainstream school into specific units.[14] Along with these pupils, re-absorbed onto and boosting the shrinking mainstream pupil roll, might come some pupils at present on the roll of more long-established special schools. Agency workers might become more visible in the mainstream schools. Teachers' experience would be widened by dealing with a wider range of pupil handicaps. Their sense of being part of the welfare network, with a perhaps more urgent need for the network's support, might increase. The pastoral teacher, with or without specialised training, might have to meet the challenge of an increasingly satisfying and rewarding role in the school.

The alternative prospect had a different political resonance, and could be summarised as 'the decline and fall of the pastoral empire.' The development envisaged was in line with the notion of school counsellors and other non-teaching teachers becoming unfashionable anachronisms. It was based on the premise that pastoral systems and the tenuous links which schools had made with the welfare network had been a temporary expedient, becoming obsolete as comprehensive schools settled down to a more confidently formulated role. The fantasy of an alternative career ladder for a teacher via the pastoral system would be abandoned, since so much of pastoral work had proved to be unremunerated, and in any case did not call on the trained professional skills of the teacher. The only reputable professional specialisation would once again be subject teaching, and pastoral tasks would, as in the past, be a regular but unlabelled part of every teacher's repertoire. Smaller pupil rolls would be taught by smaller staffs, and the competition for teacher posts would ensure more effective teacher performance. The definition and treatment of pupil problems would be in school terms, without recourse to agency interpretation. In any case, difficulties with pupils would decline as the school became more effective in its teaching task.

In the mid 1980s, a number of factors do seem likely to bring about some diminution of the scope of pastoral care, and of the numbers of staff presently concerned in it. Smaller schools, falling rolls, the elimination of some specifically pastoral posts, the gradual retirement of those supernumerary teachers with 'protected' salaries who have been transferred to pastoral duties – all these factors tend towards a reduction in identifiable pastoral systems within schools. The creation of NAPCE, and the wide support which it has engendered, seems however to give the lie to the notion of pastoral decline and fall. A continuing sense of vulnerability may well be part of the motivation to maintain the special interest group, but whether or not those specifically engaged on pastoral tasks in schools are an endangered species, there is no doubt that pastoral work remains to be done and the permeability or otherwise of a school to those who seek to cross its boundary, or work in cooperation with teachers, is of increasing interest and research import.

Notes

1 For example, Marshall points out that '(school) social workers were regarded by potential clients not as a service but as persons one had to deal with if unfortunate enough to be in trouble.' Marshall, T. 'Ethical and political aspects of counselling and social work in schools' in Craft *et al* 1980, p. 302.

2 Schools, Parents and Social Services Project (1974–1977): a study of the relationships between secondary schools and welfare agencies, carried out by the Educational Studies Unit, Brunel University. See Johnson *et al* 1980.

3 For example, Lyons, K. 'School social work' in Craft *et al* 1980, pp. 233–243; Rose, G. and Marshall, T. 1975; Robinson, M. 1978. Robinson's description and analysis demonstrated the continuing separateness of the services intended to provide care for children, and recognised the rivalry which some bland accounts of a 'continuum of care' had tended to ignore.

4 Craft, M. 'School welfare roles and networks' in Craft *et al* 1980, pp. 341–2.

5 It is, of course, a matter of debate whether the existence and transmission of continuous records about school children is desirable. Quite apart from whether social agencies can provide a continuous picture of family background, it is in some cases school policy to disregard any record of the pupil handed on by the previous school, on the principle that the child should make a fresh start in a new institution.

6 The pupil population of a primary school may include a nursery class of pre-school age children, and some secondary schools have 'sixth form' groups of pupils aged 16+. In any one institution, however, the majority of pupils are of compulsory school age. Notable exceptions are the sixth-form colleges which, although subject to Schools Regulations, teach only post-compulsory pupils. Such institutions are part of the 'bizarre variety' in educational provision referred to by Craft.

7 Welton, J. NAPCE seminar discussion, Warwick University 1984.

8 Kingston, W. and Rowbottom, R. Working Paper – 'The new NHS districts and their units', HSORU, BIOSS, Brunel University 1983.

9 For example, Open Door and other youth counselling groups attract adolescents who are unwilling to work with more formal agencies. These groups recruit their funding from a number of sources.

10   By contrast, in United States' high schools a 'school counsellor' is first and foremost an education counsellor, advising the student about courses of study.

11   The 'Policy and Provision for Special Needs' project, led by John Welton at the London Institute of Education, will look into this question among others.

12   See Johnson, D. 'Research into home-school relations, 1970–80' in Cohen *et al* 1982.

13   The liaison role might, for example, be exercised by the school counsellor, or the deputy head (pastoral care). Some schools had two such liaison persons, for boys and girls respectively.

14   Some of the implications, both for agencies and schools, of these and other 'alternative educational settings' were explored in Bird *et al* 1981, pp. 101–112.

Parents, schools and pastoral care: Some research priorities

Alastair Macbeth

Do teachers concerned with pastoral care regard parents as fellow-practitioners? Often it would seem not. Should they? I think so.

Research should break new ground. Of course there is a case for consolidating and refining in old territory, but researchers should also be peering beyond established frontiers. It is therefore in a questing spirit that this paper considers how research in the field of pastoral care might give greater attention to school-home relations. Although British authors on pastoral care devote space to parents in their writings,[1] families are generally seen as forces influencing the effectiveness of schools (for better or worse) rather than as educational and pastoral care structures located outside the school. Yet when we examine the published definitions of pastoral care, guidance and counselling, most of them could apply to the parental function if the word 'child' replaces 'pupil'. Consider, for instance, 'looking after the total welfare of the pupil' (Marland 1974, pp. 8–9), 'taking of that personal interest in pupils as individuals which makes it possible to assist them in making choices or decisions' (Scottish Education Department 1968), 'the kind of work which is done to promote the personal development of pupils' (Dooley 1980, p. 24), and the notion of a 'child agency' to assist the child to greater autonomy (Freeman 1983). Even when one breaks the function down into educational, vocational and personal elements or assesses 'fundamental principles' of guidance such as considering the whole child, understanding him as an individual, assisting him in times of need, emphasising prevention rather than correcting maladjustment, use of persuasion rather than coercion, assisting his talents to flourish and provision of information (Auld and Stein 1965, pp. 9–10), the description can still apply to caring parents and Dooley (1980, p. 16) draws our attention to the 'fatherly' nature of pastoral care. The United Nations Declaration of the Rights of Children (1959) proclaims that the child shall have special protection 'by reason of his physical and mental immaturity' and it adds that 'The best interests of the child shall be the guiding principle of those responsible for his education and guidance; that responsibility lies in the first place with his parents.'

It is worth bearing in mind that most parents *are* providing pastoral care anyway in parallel with the school. The differences are that schools have access to certain kinds of specialist information (e.g. about careers) to which parents generally do not, and guidance staff may have had frequent experience of certain kinds of problems common to pupils and may handle them with more confidence and less emotion than might the child's parents. However, evidence suggests that the psychological influence of parents on their child's attitudes and motivation may be greater than that of the school; in Moore's (1973, p. 22) words 'When home-based educational objectives clash with school-based objectives, the student normally resolves the conflict by rejecting school.' Also it is probable that parents know much more about the child and his personality (though perhaps less analytically) than do his teachers. Thus, there are two pastoral care structures concerned for the child, family and school, each with differing but overlapping stores of information, advice and influence on the child's thinking, but with similar objectives. The theme of this paper is that research might be directed towards finding ways to bring these two pastoral care forces into mutually-supportive operation.

The parental dimension of pastoral care has been somewhat neglected by schools other than to regret the adverse effects of insufficient or uncaring parents. Another way to say the same thing is that school-based pastoral care is too inward-looking. In part this seems to stem from haziness and maziness about guidance within schools and from the multiplicity of operational dilemmas thrown up as systems developed. These problems include the pastoral/academic divide deplored by some (e.g. Marland 1974, pp. 1 and 11) but seen as a basis for development by others (e.g. Best, Ribbins, Jarvis and Oddy 1983). Related to this is the specialist/generalist debate which, in turn, gives rise to questions about professionalism and training. There is the issue of the extent to which pastoral care services should deal with disciplinary matters. Then there is the structural problem of whether a vertical (house) or a horizontal (year) structure is best, or whether combination schemes such as schools-within-schools or teams are preferable. There are questions about whether guidance should more concern personal or vocational issues; should focus on present or future problems; should be curative or preventative. Best *et al* (1983, p. 252) have referred to the 'lack of precision in many people's conceptions of the objectives of pastoral care' and Milner (1980, p. 124) asserts: 'Probably the most that we can say about guidance in education at this stage is that it is a conglomeration of ideas and practices that different schools organise in different ways.' With such internal uncertainty it is perhaps not surprising that links have not been forged universally with familial pastoral care processes.

The issues mentioned above and the problems of intermeshing with other welfare services (Johnson *et al* 1980) have been analysed by others and I merely record the problems as impediments. However I would like to touch on one feature which seems to me to have bearing on relations with parents but has not been considered sufficiently. This is the question of individual versus group functional emphases.

In their interesting final analysis, Best *et al* (1983) conceptually separate discipline from pastoral care and present the academic, pastoral and disciplinary functions as three overlapping circles in a model which helpfully depicts each as distinct but related to the other two. What does not receive sufficient attention, in my view, is that each circle has a different level of functional emphasis; pastoral work is primarily focussed on the *individual* child, education is mainly organised in learning *groups*, while discipline is rooted in a *whole school* approach. There are overlaps of course. Some pastoral care functions are in years or houses and therefore grouped. The educational element is usually in a basic unit of the class (set, stream) which is timetabled as a group, coordinated as a group and often taught as a group, but there are also periodic facilities for individuals to pursue their own interests or to go at their own pace. Despite these overlaps, pastoral care is in emphasis individual; teaching is generally carried out in groups. Teachers theorise in terms of service to the individual (see almost any list of the aims of education[2]) but, for resource reasons, they provide teaching for clusters of children en bloc. It is akin to the airlines' advertisements which emphasise personal service as the overtly-projected image for what is fundamentally a group process. By contrast, what parenting and in-school pastoral care have in common is a focus on one child at a time.

The difficulties which secondary schools have experienced in liaising over educational matters with parents in part stem from the limited extent to which a pupil is known to each specialist teacher; the issue is easier to handle in primary schools where the teacher sees each child for most of the day and more readily adopts the pastoral role. It may therefore be that liaison between parents and secondary subject teachers should differ in nature from that between parents and those with pastoral duties. Written school reports and face-to-face meetings with subject teachers (the former, as an agenda, always immediately preceding the latter one may hope) are certainly useful, but the German system of periodic class meetings of parents, perhaps as sub-units of the PTA, to discuss coming curricula, textbooks and ways in which parents can assist in the home (see Macbeth *et al* 1984, pp. 26–27 and 55–57), may be especially appropriate for *group*-based liaison. Alternatively, year-group meetings may assist.

For pastoral contact the focus must be more on the individual. The Danes have a useful arrangement of pastoral care which is neither vertical nor horizontal, but mobile. The tutor joins her group when it first enters the school and she takes it for one subject in the week so that she gets to know the children both as individuals and academically. She then moves up the school with them year by year. This means that she has close contacts with the parents who have time to get to know her personally. Parental contact is more frequent and informal in Denmark than in Britain; evening telephone calls and the home-school contact book (carried daily to and from school by the pupil) less formally help to individualise a class-based system which depends on children staying in the same group for several years.

In brief, the family is also a pastoral unit and in considering how it and the pastoral facilities of the school can relate and the directions which research might take, I shall divide my argument into three main parts:

1 The parental dimension.
2 Six circles, not three?
3 Research proposals.

The parental dimension

Rights and duties

Questions of rights and duties in education are philosophically complex and the topic of current debate. There is insufficient space to pursue that debate in detail here, but some fairly simple assertions may suffice to introduce the relationships of home and school in regard to pastoral care.

The dispute about whether 'natural' or 'human' rights can exist uncodified may be avoided by agreeing that rights can be socially determined or man-made. They may appear in laws, regulations or inter-personal agreements. British law tends to be administrative rather than philosophical and it is untypical when we encounter a 'general principle' being enunciated in our educational legislation to the effect that, with two reservations, children are to be educated in accordance with the wishes of their parents.[3] Alternatively rights may arise out of responsibilities. If someone has a legal *duty* to do something, that confers a commensurate *right* to do it. The important issue here is the answer to the key question: 'Who, in law, has the duty to educate the individual child?' The answer (until the child is 16 years old) is parents.[4] It is a concept common to all countries in the European Community for instance (Macbeth *et al* 1984, pp. 19–32), and it recognises the family as the basic unit of society and the child's prime educator. It may be noted that parents' responsibilities (and therefore rights) do not end at the school gates since parents do not divest themselves of their duty on passing a child to school; authority may be delegated but not responsibility. It is therefore appropriate that schools are required by law to educate in accordance with parental wishes. Further, the law says nothing about parental preferences being limited to choice of school only. The education authority (I use the Scottish term since I know of no education authority which is any longer 'local') must, by law, *make facilities available* to ensure that parents can carry out their educational duty. That parents are responsible for their child's education makes them, in my view, by definition, the school's clients (pupils the consumers) until the child is 16.

One may disagree with the law. Personally I do. I consider that the age of about 14–16 should be a period of gradual transition during which the young person assumes more (but not all) responsibility for his/her education. But as the law now stands that is not the case. Therefore, since rights are man-made, the prime accountability of pastoral care staff (and all teachers) is to parents until the young person is 16 years old.

This raises the question of the teacher's professional autonomy. Teachers often nurse the argument that since they are professionals they are answerable to their consciences and to their peers. However, theories of professionalism are not as simple as that. There is some agreement (e.g. see Cogan 1953, Millerson 1973, Langford 1978) that expertise, service to a client, ethical standards and responsibility are criteria for a professional. These are duties, but the rights associated with them must be those necessary to fulfil the duties and it may be questioned whether a high level of autonomy is essential, especially if service to the client is a prime criterion of professionalism and education is to be provided in accordance with parents' wishes. Further, Hoyle (1974) has drawn the distinction between the ideal (professionalism) and practice (professionality) and there can be much variation in practice between individuals, between occupations and between criteria in the extent of professionality. Indeed, it may not be possible to draw a useful distinction between professions and non-professions at all. If teachers are to base their claim to autonomy upon a general presumption of professional status they may be on weak ground.

It is easiest to defend a teacher's claim to professional status (but not the claim to autonomy) in terms of service to the client. But who are the clients? I suggested above that parents are. Most authors on pastoral care assume that pupils are the clients, an assumption which is legally valid for 16+ young people. Vaughan (1975, p. 11) has regretted the use of the word 'client' for the 'person who comes for counselling', but on grounds of association of the word 'client' with commercialism. In my view it is more helpful to think of parents as clients because of their legal obligations, but to recognise that there are times when a teacher must help a child to overcome the handicap of an uncaring or incompetent family, in which case the teacher's right to action must be safeguarded.

By the same token, parents must have some real redress in the case of an uncaring or incompetent teacher, but that is not an issue for this paper.

Allied to the question of professional relations with clients is the issue of accountability. There is no consensus about the meaning of the word and accountability is multi-dimensional (see, for instance, Sockett *et al* 1980, Becher and Maclure 1978, Macbeth *et al* 1980, pp. 46–54, and Elliott *et al* 1981). Taken at its simplest level of 'rendering an account' or explaining, there would seem to be a mutual obligation upon both teachers and parents, as co-educators both concerned with a child's pastoral care, to keep each other informed. If the view is accepted that parents are the school's clients while the child is of school age, then the teacher's accountability to parents may require the involvement of parents in key decisions about the child (e.g. what courses he shall pursue and at what level). The concept of teachers being *in loco parentis* (not, incidentally, included in statute law to my knowledge) does not remove the obligation of teachers to consult with parents who still remain responsible for their child's education even when he is in the school.

Parental influence on pupils' in-school attainment

There is insufficient space here to summarise the world-wide research evidence (and anyway it is generally known among teachers) that in-school attainment of children correlates with home background, especially parental attitudes. Some, such as Marjoribanks (1979 and 1983) have given emphasis to the complexity of interacting variables in and between home and school. Others, such as Miller (1971) have argued that although there may be a correlation between social class and school success, the terms 'social class' and 'home background' may be too broad and too vague and that causal factors *within* a child's home environment, especially parental attitudes, are not *necessarily* tied to social class (even though they may correlate with it) and may therefore be open to modification; Lady Plowden (1971) has seen this as ground for optimism: 'Parental attitudes appear as a separate influence because they are not monopolised by any one class.'

We may add to this the gradual demise of the 'parental apathy' myth and the growing evidence that 'not only are the huge majority of parents *not* apathetic but very concerned' (Marland 1983, p. 4). They may be apathetic about parents' evenings where they are treated like sheep, about PTAs whose activities are seen as irrelevant to their child's experience or concentrate upon fund raising, but they are generally not apathetic about their child's progress. If that is so, and if their attitudes influence children's in-school motivation and attainment, then presumably it is the professional duty of teachers to harness the home forces.

That is not easy. As Marland has written (1983, p. 3):

> Teachers are no more 'typical' than parents, but it is probably fair to say that they almost all appreciate parental interest, and would in principle be happy to increase it. Some, indeed, already go to considerable lengths. However, the constraints are great, and many are caught in limitations of tradition and practicalities.

I shall return below to the practicalities and the ways in which research in regard to pastoral care might assist.

Families as pastoral care structures

I have already argued that families are pastoral care structures which have the same broad aims as those formalised in schools, but that the nature of their psychological impact and the range of their knowledge are different.

An additional point deserves attention. Some authors have noted that families may have a damaging effect upon their child's development. It may be a question of a father wishing to retain his authority over the child rather than encouraging self-development (Dooley 1980, p. 23) or parents not recognising their child's potential and being under-ambitious for him (McGeeney 1974, p. 141, Roberts 1980, pp. 41–55). Johnson and Ransom (1983) found that parents often saw the secondary school as a phased introduction to the outside world and therefore, as parents, they became less directly involved; part of this appeared to be related to an assumption that their children would get counselling from the secondary school, which hints at a dependence upon a level of personal service from the school which may not be as full or as perfect as they imagine (or would like to imagine) it to be.

The danger in cases of parents being over-trusting is that the family, as a major guidance force and with knowledge and insights which could help in consultations, may either 'leave it to the experts' or may fail to communicate essential information to the school for fear of being 'interfering', or may advise the young person in a way which conflicts with the advice of the school to the detriment of the pupil. The case for regular three-way consultations would appear to have *prima facie* validity.

Six circles, not three?

To illustrate the potential dove-tailing of school-based and family-based pastoral care I shall return to the three circles model of Best *et al* (1983, p. 272). It shows the three interrelated circles representing *education* (academic), *welfare* (pastoral) and *order* (disciplinary). Families may also

120

be seen as pastoral care units carrying out the same functions but in different ways. For most schools and families there is a very small pastoral overlap which may be depicted by adapting the Best *et al* diagram as shown in Figure 1. It illustrates what is the common *practice*. However, one may argue that the degree of partnership and joint planning/action for the child should be much greater than is normally the case, especially in regard to the educational functions. The model might therefore be adjusted as shown in Figure 2.

Figure 1

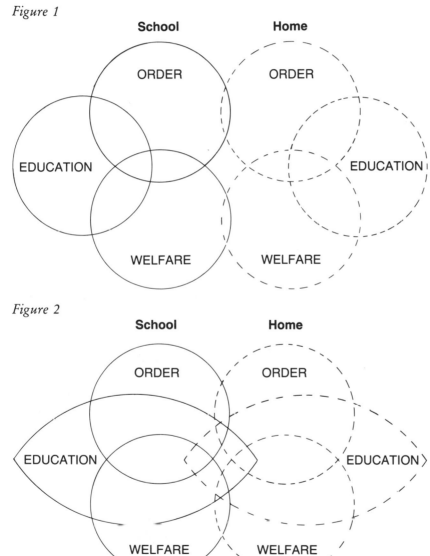

Figure 2

We may then consider some of the recommendations of Best *et al* and see the way in which the revised model has implications for them. Following Marland's argument (1980, ch.11) for a 'pastoral curriculum' to help heal the pastoral/academic split, they urge (p. 281) that 'a pastoral or welfare curriculum should figure prominently in a school's curriculum policy and implementation.' Marland's examples (1980, pp. 151–53) take him well down into the age group for which parents are responsible for their child's education, and rightly so, and most of the topics are issues upon which parents have impact.

Curricular teaching is organised by groups, so that a group arrangement for involving families might be appropriate, such as the class meetings at which the curriculum for the coming month (or term) may be discussed to enable parents to assist in the home element of education or perhaps to influence the nature of in-school provision. If health education is to be a theme, then the school's approach might be explained, work sheets shown and copies of instructional leaflets or textbooks handed out. The learning process initiated by the school can then be reinforced through home-learning deliberately designed to coincide with the curriculum.

Next, Best and his co-authors recommend that 'all members of staff need to reach a common understanding of the nature of pastoral care and how it relates to the other facets of a school's provision' and that such understanding should be converted into practice. If understanding of pastoral care is important to all educators of a child, then parents as co-educators should surely be among these. In other words, there is a publicity function which can be led by guidance staff. But if *action* is also important, the question of supportive home practice (encouragement, discussion of issues, advice) is also needed. The attitude of reliance by parents on schools reported by Johnson and Ransom (1980) should, presumably, be countered if it is over-reliance or opting-out by parents. Current schooling appears to encourage parents to opt out of their pastoral role.

The idea of 'schools-within-schools' (mini-teams) is applauded by Best *et al* (p. 285). Such an approach has some attractions, not least of which is that it enables staff to get to know 'their' parents more closely. (I have seen this in operation in a Norwegian school where teacher-parent relations are strengthened in an educational setting by the device of termly community-based study projects on topics such as old age, money or pollution. The nature and implementation of these projects is determined jointly by parents and teachers who get to know each other better in the process. Each project lasts for several days and replaces normal classes.) The idea of schools-within-schools gives rise to the question of parental choice of team. Parental choice of school is based upon the principle of education in accordance with parents' wishes. As in the case of mini-schools involved in the Alum Rock voucher scheme (the Jencks scheme; see Maynard 1975), parental choice between teams deserves attention.

One may similarly approach the other recommendations of Best, Ribbins, Jarvis and Oddy by inserting the parental dimension. Teacher training should include it; discussion with all staff can then involve all parents (a *real* task for the PTA?); listening to parents' views as well as those of teachers; and so on. With the educational and personal importance of parents and their potential contributions in mind, we may now turn to the issue of research priorities.

Research proposals

Most discussion of pastoral care has concentrated on the secondary school level (because organisational problems have made it more difficult in the large comprehensive school, with its subject specialisms) rather than in the primary school where every teacher is more readily seen as being concerned with caring and knowing both pupils and parents personally. However, many of the following suggestions can apply to primary and middle as much as to secondary schools. Since what parents think, say and do influences children's attainment in school and since educational opportunity depends on equality of parental input at early as much as later stages (indeed, perhaps more since it has some preconditioning impact upon the extent to which a pupil can benefit from secondary schooling) then it would seem wrong to think of pastoral care as being a secondary school problem. My suggestions therefore apply to all levels.

I have argued that the parental dimension of education is not just important, it is also relatively neglected as an *active* ingredient of schooling. 'Allowing' for home background, permitting parents into the school to do trivial and menial tasks, the PTA and fund-raising, reporting to parents – none of these is the same as harnessing home-learning. My broad contention is that *research should make assaults on ways to convert the well-known correlation between home background and school attainment into practical steps for making the pastoral care forces of the home and those of the school mutually-supportive.* Wolfendale (1983, p. 10) has recently called for 'an articulated consensus over the areas of enquiry rather than a perpetuation of unrelated small-scale projects.' I think that she is right.

Present practice

The first, obvious stage is to ascertain to what extent joint home-school pastoral care is operating at present. This may be carried out at two levels. The first would be a 'broad sweep' study (perhaps by questionnaire) to pastoral care staff across the country on a random basis. Such a sweep might give indicators of staff attitudes and may throw up examples of exciting innovative practice. The second level is a matter of examining in depth several case study schools selected either because they are relatively typical or (and I consider this to be more helpful) because they are interestingly untypical and have attempted new practices which could guide us. A study sponsored by the Scottish Education Department is currently being carried out by John MacBeath, Dave Mearns and Maureen Smith at Jordanhill College in Glasgow and is looking at ways in which guidance systems in four secondary schools make contacts with homes. Such studies at different parts of the country could be valuable.

Useful glimpses of practice do already exist. Marland's (1974) book contained case studies; Mortimore and Blackstone (1982) quote many studies in relation to disadvantage; and Wolfendale (1983) does the same for parental participation, Johnson et al (1980), for the welfare network. These and others provide an excellent starting-point, but they tend to concentrate on scattered formal studies and inevitably miss many of the rich pickings of local initiatives.

The place of the home-school liaison teacher

Craft (1980, p. 43) has argued 'Home-visiting is so time-consuming that it is doubtful whether any of the other roles of a school welfare team could be combined with it.' Yet there is no need to regard home visiting as the only or even the main function of a home-school liaison teacher. For instance, Simpson (1983) has broken down his task into three main categories: *problem-solving, image-making* and *specialist resource* by which he becomes an agent for mutual understanding between homes and schools and an enabler rather than just a trouble-shooter.

The French have a word 'animateur' as someone who brings something to life, and 'animateurs' have become important in some aspects of parent-teacher relations (Macbeth *et al* 1984). We have no comparable word in English. Neither 'stimulator' nor 'motivator' nor 'enabler' nor 'catalyst' nor 'middle-person' reflects the range of functions. However that may be, the potential role of pastoral care staff as 'animateurs' could be considerable.

The extent to which this role can best be realised by a specialist home-school liaison service (as part of a welfare team), or by all teachers in a school-within-a-school approach or by other means warrants research. However, it does seem that the necessary 'animation' for meshing home and school pastoral functions is frequently missing. It deserves study.

The triangle of consultation

I have already expressed concern that pastoral care happens in two different and largely unconnected units, the home and the school.

Sometimes their separation can have value, especially when the home is the cause of the problem and the pupil is seeking a sympathetic ear; but even then it would seem to me that a three-way discussion (parent-pupil-teacher) might be an objective. It should also not be overlooked that families are constantly dealing with what pupils perceive to be school problems. The self-satisfied way with which much writing assumes that it is school guidance staff, like knights in shining armour, who are compensating for home deficiencies may lead us to neglect the way that families may have to compensate for school deficiencies. In either case, a mode of three-way communication would appear to have attractions.

There are serious practical problems of time and resources, and in some instances letters, telephone calls and requests via pupils may have to substitute for a meeting. However, research might be directed to two issues:

1   the extent to which teachers and parents can be stimulated to inform and consult with each other in regard to pastoral matters; and
2   active consultation over key decisions.

In amplification to (2) above I would like to refer to Danish educational law which, incidentally, is written for citizens rather than lawyers and is admirable in its clarity. It requires that the three parties must meet and consult in regard to certain key decisions, especially as the pupil approaches the age of 14 when the courses and sets (fast or slow groups) for each subject must be determined. What is of special interest is its specification of whose view should prevail in the event of disagreement: it is the *parents'* since they are responsible for the pupil's education at that age. As the pupil approaches 16 a similar meeting must happen to decide what subjects he will sit in the public examinations and, in recognition of the self-development of the young person and the transfer of responsibilities, it is the *pupil's* view which must prevail in the case of disagreement. A study of comparable consultations in Britain could be revealing.

Curriculum: group contacts and the pastoral curriculum

A study of the ways that parents might be involved in groups with the curriculum, especially Marland's pastoral curriculum, both in formulating its content for the class in which their children learn and in extending that learning into the home, would be valuable.

Records of personal achievement held in the school: parental access

Separate papers in this publication by Andy Hargreaves and Patricia Broadfoot helpfully concentrate on the developing nature of records of personal achievement. If parents are responsible for their child's education and if pastoral care is a joint home-school process, then the questions of what information should be sent to parents (Are school reports and school brochures *really* adequate bases for partnership?) deserve more investigation as does the question of *access* by parents to further information held on their child by the school. The work of Bastiani (1978) and Atherton (1982) has provided a starting-point in regard to brochures and Hargreave's paper *ibid* gives useful references to studies of personal records and profiles. It may be that access should be a matter for legislation. In the United States federal laws were enacted in 1974 (see Peterson, Rossmiller and Volz 1978) which require that parents and students over 18 years should have access to official school records and that nothing may be communicated to any outside person or body which is not recorded on the child's official record, thereby reducing the likelihood of unofficial records replacing the official ones. The questions of communication of information and parental access deserve initial research which may grapple with conceptual problems of confidentiality and may survey practice.

The family as a pastoral care unit

Much of the foregoing has made the assumption that families do act as 'pastoral care units.' On the face of it that is a reasonable assumption. Yet in what ways do they do so? How do they vary in their provision? What are the emphases, the biases, the distortions? Does the existence of pastoral care facilities in schools lead some families to opt out of their familial responsibilities on the grounds that they are 'leaving it to the experts?' Do attitudes vary from one part of the country to another? The work by Johnson and Ransom (1983) has thrown useful light on some of these areas and research needs to follow on with more detailed investigations of parental actions and assumptions. The extent to which parents need aid in their pastoral function and the ways in which the school might provide help deserve consideration, as does the relationship of parenting styles to delinquency rates, school attainment and social interaction in schools.

What part can the PTA play?

It has not been conventional to consider PTAs in pastoral care terms, except perhaps by home-school liaison teachers who have a specific task to encourage their growth (Simpson 1983). Their image has been one of fund-raising, social events, occasional dry meetings and assistance with the more menial aspects of peripheral school activities. That image is not always fair, especially when the variety of parental organisations encountered on the Continent is considered (Macbeth *et al* 1984, section E). Could PTAs and PAs become more involved in educational and the broader aspects of pastoral interchange between schools and homes? The

Scottish Parent Teacher Council has defined a PTA as 'a group of people who recognise that the education of a child is a partnership between parents and teachers, and who wish to take joint action to improve the quality of that partnership.' It may be noted that education is seen as its main focus, a message which has not always been greeted with enthusiasm by teachers.

Could research be carried out looking at PTAs which have broken away from the traditional mould of organisation? Could action research projects be initiated to experiment with the effects of new approaches to the PTA, for instance making home-school action in regard to education its main concern, avoiding fund-raising except for communicating to all parents, and being organised (like Swedish PTAs) on a 'cell' basis in order to reach out to as many parents as possible?

A school-home contract or signed understanding?

If parents bear the responsibility for their child's education and the school provides a service to assist them to fulfil their obligation, there is an implied contract between home and school. Since parental attitudes affect the degree of benefit a pupil obtains from schooling then the parental contribution to such a contract becomes more important than was hitherto assumed. Would an *overt* contract or an annually signed agreement between home and school reinforce to parents that education *is* their business and that they should be providing more than just the delivery of the body at the school gate each day? I have argued elsewhere (Macbeth *et al* 1982 and 1984) for such a signed understanding, constructed at political levels and enforced through the social account-ability function of a governing body or school council (one for each school) at the participatory level. A signed understanding, renewed annually, would be preferable to a contract in order to avoid drawing in the law courts.

Parents, for their part, would undertake (in return for school services) to support the school, attend specified consultations at mutually con-venient times, attend class curricular meetings, provide appropriate homework conditions for their child and give informed encouragement. The school, of course, would have to provide the counterpart liaison facilities (such as class meetings of parents to discuss the curriculum) as well as a professional educational experience for the child.

Such a scheme could be introduced experimentally by an authority in selected schools, and a monitoring, evaluating action research programme should be part of any such experiment.

Attitudes: a publicity campaign as action research

When the Carreras Rothmans factory at Basildon closed in January 1984 a spokesman said that a prime cause was that cigarette demand in Britain had dropped by 18% in three years, partly because of expense and partly for health reasons. The anti-smoking campaign, based upon the correlation between smoking and various illnesses, is determined, widespread and well-organised. Its message emerged from the medical profession. Its target is attitudes.

In the world of education we have a correlation also: between home background and school attainment by the child. It is now a quarter of a century since Elizabeth Fraser's (1959) study pointed to parental attitudes as a key factor. After all that time, have we not yet reached a stage where our profession can advance with confidence a popular campaign based on our correlation? If we did, then pastoral care staff would be at its heart. It may be argued that publicity campaigns either do not have the intended impact or that it is difficult to assess the impact. It may be felt that, since it is a form of advertising and advertising is not a traditional feature of the professions in Britain, such a step would cheapen the image of schools. These are serious arguments; but clear, tastefully-projected messages need not damage schools' image and widespread acceptance of the parental contribution to education may help to legitimise and give general credence to an activity which is sometimes falsely regarded by both parents and teachers as improper 'interference' in school matters. Exhortation (e.g. in the Plowden, Warnock and Taylor reports) within the world of teachers has not resulted in great changes in practice and a public campaign might be as important in affecting the attitudes of teachers as those of parents.

A campaign could be attempted initially as an action research project. The first stage would be a careful sifting of research findings to date to decide what messages can be advanced with confidence to the parents (and schools) of Britain. Only when these have been agreed would professional publicists convert these messages into popular statements and design modes of projection. Our profession might not like some of the emerging themes at first since they might conflict with treasured illusions. Would one slogan, for instance, be 'Families educate. Schools assist'? Would another be 'Parents! Your school needs you.' I must not prejudge the outcome of the first stage, but I suspect that those teachers who currently shy away from contact with parents might feel ill at ease with such publicity. For implicit in such messages would be expectations of change. Indeed one reason for such a procedure would be change. As Rutherford and Edgar have argued, a prerequisite for parent-teacher partnership is that 'teachers must believe that parents have a role in the education process' (1979). Just as doctors had to be persuaded before the anti-smoking campaign had force, so must teachers.

The third stage would be a national multi-media drive and the fourth an evaluation. All, of course, would depend on the profession being able to agree on the messages. However, assuming that it could, then the pastoral elements of schools (however organised) would be central to the difficult tasks of making adaptations in schools and implementing modes of pastoral liaison with parents. It would be a tough assignment, but it might provide school-based pastoral care with a unity of objectives which to some extent it seems at present to lack.

Notes

1   A very rough indication of the proportional attention paid to families is to express the number of referenced pages of a book referring to 'home', 'family' and 'parents' as a percentage of the total number of pages in the book. By this crude measure Marland (1974) scores 25%, Best *et al* 1980 and Best *et al* 1983 both score 14%. By contrast, the American books on guidance which I have checked devote much smaller amounts of space to these topics.
2   See, for instance, White's (1982) *The Aims of Education Restated*. A typical list of 'tentative' aims which has met with approval from other philosophers is O'Connor's (1957, p. 8).
3   For England and Wales the principle is laid down in section 76 of the 1944 Education Act; for Scotland it appears in section 28 of the Education (Scotland) Act, 1980.
4   For England and Wales section 36 of the 1944 Education Act; for Scotland, section 30 of the Education (Scotland) Act, 1980; for Northern Ireland, section 35 of the Education and Libraries (Northern Ireland) Order, 1972.

Personal development

Richard Pring

Introduction: education and personal development

Education is about the development of persons.

This is a conceptual point that needs explaining. We can train people to do certain things – to mend cars, to knit pullovers, to decorate houses – without affecting them *as persons* in any significant way. They could, despite a most thorough-going training, continue to have the same values as they had before – the same attitudes towards other people and the same basic understanding of themselves and of the world in which they live. In an important sense (to be explored) they may remain unaffected by their training at a deeper personal level. In educating people, by contrast, we have in mind a transformation of how they see and understand the world and themselves within that world. Such a transformation (gradual though it may be) will include not only 'knowledge about' and 'understanding of' but also 'valuing'. The education of the very young child (from vicarious experience, maybe, but also from the introduction to a range of cultural and family influences) lies in the slow acquisition of a language, in a conceptual structuring of experience, in the formation of deep-rooted judgements, and in different levels of attachment to objects, people and activities. Formal education pushes this development in particular directions. It provides new skills, more sophisticated understandings of experience. It provides opportunities for new and different valuings and attachments. Often of course it fails in this, but such failure in no way affects its aims. Often, too, formal education not only fails but gets in the way of further development – blocks the route to new understanding by turning young people away from the excitement of learning and from the exploration of fresh opportunities for finding value in things. As Dewey argued, formal education can be *mis*educative.

What this means in detail is of course open to argument. Once formal education intervenes in personal growth, important decisions have to be made about the direction of that growth – about experiences and knowledge that are significant in personal development and that will, to be a little tendentious, shape persons in a particular way. The sort of person I am is the result of many different influences, but some of those influences are the literature I have been introduced to, the objects and activities I have come to love through school and university, the grasp (adequate or not) I have acquired through study of *my* place in space and time, the religious and moral ideals that give meaning and inspiration to my life.

These points need stressing for three main reasons. First, there is currently an emphasis in our schools and training programmes upon personal development. But we should not lose sight of the fact that personal development is part and parcel of the whole educational enterprise – and is as controversial in nature as is the very concept of education. Such controversy relates centrally to the values and to the kinds of knowledge, that we think young people should be introduced to and be made competent in. Certain areas of the curriculum are more central than others – literature and the humanities, the arts, religious education – because they are at the centre of persons' exploration of relationships, valuings, and feelings, but there is nothing that, taught in a particular way, should be excluded from the process of personal transformation. We must not, therefore, in the pursuit of personal development locate this in a separate part of the curriculum whether it be in tutorial groups, in separate subjects, or in a structure called pastoral care. A policy for personal development is an educational policy for the school and for the curriculum as a whole. It is the case unfortunately that, in many new pre-vocational educational and training programmes, personal development has been seen as a matter of skill acquisition isolated from a deeper educational tradition which, as a result, is in danger of being curtailed in the pursuit of a more utilitarian concept of preparation of young people 'for life'. At the heart of this is an impoverished concept of 'being a person'.

Secondly, in establishing the connection between personal growth and education, we cannot avoid, in our concern for persons, the controversial questions about what constitutes 'the worthwhile life' to which we want to introduce young people. That is the very stuff of curriculum decisions. It is at the core of our selective tradition in literature; it shapes the historical perspective we transmit to pupils; it is embodied in the values transmitted through the very ethos of the school; it is reflected in the concepts and skills that are taught through science. And a diminution of the arts or of the humanities in the emerging 14 to 18 curriculum (there is a need for more room on the timetable for computer science) reflects a changed set of values, an altered vision of what is significant in personal development.

Thirdly, 'education' and 'training' are not to be seen as mutually exclusive. Any training programme *can* be educational. To train to be a decorator or to be a doctor can, if conducted in a particular way, have a profound effect upon a person's conception of his or her own powers or upon that person's sense of responsibility. To be trained *may* be an educational experience; whether or not it is depends on how the trainee is affected. I see nothing wrong, despite the objections of many liberal-minded educationists, with vocational training for young people, if that training is conducted in an educational manner. There is no *necessary* contradiction between education and training, although there is always a danger, under the influence of a narrow conception of training and of an attenuated vision of its purpose, that training programmes will fail to prepare young people for living in any deeply personal and educational sense. The growth of training and educational programmes that have isolated a special component called 'personal effectiveness' or 'personal and social education' demonstrates a certain impoverishment of thinking – a failure to see the educational possibilities in any training and the continued relevance of the arts and the humanities to personal development.

Education therefore is about the development of persons. And pastoral care – the conscious effort to help young people in one way or another to develop as persons – must examine closely its relation to the overall educational enterprise. The establishment of a distinct organisation must be an enhancement of what, in theory at least, is already aspired to, not something distinct with different aims in mind. Furthermore, it cannot either in its organisation or in its objectives escape from the complex moral problems that lie at the centre of all educational debate. The kind of pastoral care you provide depends on how you answer the question: what is a worthwhile life to lead?

Concepts of pastoral care

There are two senses in which I detect the 'pastoral care responsibilities' of a school to be understood. First, there is the sense in which it is broadly identified with all that goes under the description 'personal and social education'. This would include, but not be identified with, 'vocational guidance'. Secondly, there is the sense in which 'pastoral care responsibilities' refer to the way in which schools cope with 'personal crises' – either in a responsive way or in anticipating personal crises through systematic classroom instruction.

If we take the first sense, then, as I explained in my introduction, this is to be identified with the educational enterprise as a whole. It does not follow however that there is no need for any specifically pastoral care organisation. Far from it. There is a need for a school to ensure that the different aspects of the curriculum and of school life are contributing to personal development as they should be and that gaps in this development are filled. That of course requires some school-based analysis of what is meant by personal development, and of the underlying values – a job for the pastoral care system of the school.

If we take the second sense, then different demands are made upon the school. In any large group of people there will inevitably be certain individuals who have difficulty in adjusting to the social environment in which they are obliged to spend their time. They will manifest behaviours which the classroom teacher will not have the time or skills or knowledge to cope with. Expert help will be needed – the experienced counsellor, the psychological advisory service, various branches of the social service. Part of the expertise of the teacher (the year or the house tutor) will lie in the knowledge of when and where to go for help. There are of course dangers in this because it is always possible that one ascribes to psychological or to social inadequacy problems that are really created by the school system or by an inappropriate curriculum. Although this is increasingly recognised in academic accounts of education, one would like to see more case studies of how schools have responded to manifestation of personal crises through a re-examination of curriculum.

As I explained above however, the responsibility for 'personal crises' may not be purely responsive. There are certain aspects of 'personal growth' that require systematic teaching. McLaughlin (1983, p. 95) refers to those principles that '. . . can be invoked to determine the particular problems, decisions, and adjustments facing the individual . . .' in the absence of which there are *likely* to be crises. McLaughlin suggests a curriculum programme will need to satisfy four conditions:

1 it will equip the young person to deal with a range of problems, decisions or adjustments that are likely to confront any person in our society;
2 the ability to deal with such 'problems, decisions, and adjustments' is not likely to be brought about by other means;
3 it will ensure the school has the relevant expertise;
4 it should not get in the way of the primary task of the school, namely, a liberal education.

Such a conception of pastoral care seems correct, although it demands close examination of what are critical phases in, say, adolescence that can be anticipated and made part of the curriculum. This has, of course, been attempted in various ways. For example, McPhail's survey of what adolescent boys and girls thought moral education should be about is one instance (McPhail *et al* 1972), and doubtless Marland's suggestions for a pastoral curriculum arises out of similar considerations (Marland 1980).

In conclusion, therefore, pastoral care does have two connected but different orientations: the first being to the personal development as a whole, the second being to coping with or anticipating individual crises. If we take the first sense, then pastoral care has to cope with some rather difficult problems that affect its practice – and of course affect research into it. These I want briefly to point out. If we think of pastoral care in the second sense, then different kinds of research problems arise – namely, how to identify phases of development that are critical and how to anticipate them in the curriculum.

Major problems

I have picked out three major difficulties that affect research into pastoral care.

Values

As I explained, pastoral care, in that it aims to promote personal development, cannot avoid ethical questions about a worthwhile form of life. Intervention in the personal growth of individuals presupposes a moral view about the kind of life worth living. Values are built into our selection of literature, into the kinds of relationships we promote in the classroom, into the proper conduct of scientific enquiry. Some of these values will be political. Indeed just as the extension of education was, before 1870, seen quite explicitly to be socially dangerous, so too there are those in position of power today who express similar views (Simon 1984). The encouragement of the spirit of criticism and of enquiry at the very time when there will be fewer occupations even for well-qualified people has its social dangers. What kind of persons is it sensible to develop in the unstable economic environment we are entering into?

Conceptual

As I have already indicated, personal development can, in one sense, be identified with the whole educational enterprise. But that creates conceptual problems, because such an enterprise is extensive indeed. Thus there is a need to 'break down' the concept of personal development into various components or features. And that in turn requires some philosophical analysis of 'growth' or 'development' as persons. An interest in research must not deflect us from the confusing conceptual issues that so often lie beneath what, on the surface, appear to be straightforward empirical questions. There are many competing concepts of what it means to be a person, and it is important to make clear how these different concepts relate to distinctive pastoral care programmes (think, for example, of the philosophical ideas that underpin programmes of behaviour modification – see Pring 1981).

Organisational

There are problems to be faced in how to translate into an effective structure the promotion of personal growth where this permeates so much that the school is doing. How can one take on responsibility for something that is so general and all pervasive, without limiting and impoverishing the very aims of personal development?

In tackling these different problems it is clear that one must begin with some view of what it means to be and to develop as a person.

Personal development

My account can be but brief and dogmatic. To be a person is to have (a) a mind of one's own, (b) a will of one's own and (c) a capacity to exercise that mind and that will in a responsible manner.

With reference to (a), as a person I have acquired a way of understanding the world and myself and others within that world. I am a centre of consciousness with an ability to reflect, to think, to argue, to reason and to criticise. My development as a person lies in the gradual extension and enhancement of those mental capacities. To that extent the whole curriculum of the school can contribute to personal development; that depends on whether the different school subjects and experiences really do stimulate the imagination, provide a more adequate hold on experience, or provide the intellectual rules for critical questioning or enquiry. Part of this intellectual development will lie in my understanding of other people as persons, with their own particular ways of seeing and appreciating things.

With reference to (b), my growth as a person lies, too, in my ability to behave intentionally, purposefully, and effectively within the world as I understand it. I do not simply have to follow the crowd or react passively to whatever fashions or forces happen to be around. I have the capacity to deliberate, to formulate my own principles of action and to create my own distinctive mode of living.

With reference to (c), such active involvement in the world leaves me open to praise and blame in that my action either does or does not come up to certain standards. I am increasingly held responsible not only for specific actions, but for more general failures to sort things out in life as a whole. Not only is my life mine and no-one else's; it is also my responsibility. Part of this responsibility lies in coming to see others and oneself as persons, and thus worthy of respect.

If we had time to dissect further these features of being a person, we could see how each can be seen developmentally and how the promotion of these capacities is and always has been central to the educational task of the school. But certain features need to be picked out for particular attention. First, there is an underlying sense of autonomy as an aim of personal development where this means the capacity for independent and critical thinking. This may not fit easily with an impoverished sense of personal effectiveness in a context where deliberation, and critical reflection, are to be discouraged. There is, as a consequence, evidence of fear in some circles of too much education for young people.

Secondly, there is an underlying sense of autonomy where this means the capacity for independent action (the ability, for example, to sort out one's own learning needs, or to have the flexibility and the confidence to assess oneself and to go one's own way). But this requires the development of self-respect, of confidence, and of those emotions and sense of personal worth without which the young person will not be able to persevere.

Thirdly, there is an underlying moral sense of autonomy, where this refers to the recognition of oneself and of others as worthy of equal and respectful treatment as a person – the bestowal of a sense of dignity and of worth.

There is much to be said in detail about particular personal qualities and about the systematic development of these through specific school activities and subjects. But for the moment it is sufficient to point up the broad features and what these entail for the school, college or training scheme as a whole. For there is a danger that, influenced by a general concern for personal development, we avoid the central issues by creating a special subject called 'personal development' or by initiating a training course in 'life skills'.

Implications for the school and for research

Impact of the curriculum as a whole

The central issues can be reached initially by asking: what impact upon personal development, as I have described it, has the experience of the curriculum as a whole? For example, does the curriculum as a whole:

1 demonstrate a respect for the student's or the trainee's capacity to reason, to reflect, and to be critical?
2 provide a sense of achievement and of personal worth?
3 promote a respect for others irrespective of ability, colour, or class?
4 develop a sense of responsibility for their own learning and courses of action?

Hargreaves (1982) speaks of the experience of schooling of many youngsters as 'a destruction of their dignity which is so massive and pervasive that few subsequently recover from it.' This may not be true of the experience provided by many schools, but the indictment is sufficiently strong that our concern for personal development must begin with a rebuttal (where possible) of that. And that in turn requires some attention to what it means to be a person and to respect oneself and others as persons.

Impact of the institution's ethos

Closely connected with the curriculum, but worthy of separate mention, is the impact of the hidden curriculum – the implicit values and atmosphere of the school as a whole and of the system of which it is part. Kohlberg (1981 and 1983) demonstrates the importance of a just community if one is to promote a sense of justice. Wasserman and Garrod (1983) illustrate what this can mean in practice. It is clear from Piaget onward that one of the most significant elements in the development of autonomy is how authority is exercised, but we need sensitive instruments for analysing this in the complex practical world of the school. (See, for example, Murphy 1984.)

Mapping the curriculum territory

No amount of general questioning, however, about the impact of the curriculum or institution as a whole can get rid of the need for detailed curriculum questions about the contribution of different subjects or topics to an overall view of personal and social education. I have devised a matrix (see page 138) of the different general and specific aspects of personal and social education, so that teachers of different subjects could ask systematically how their own subject or teaching method did, or could, make a contribution. Doubtless many will be critical of this particular mapping of the territory, and will want to adjust it in some way. What is important, however, is the value of an instrument like this for a school to begin to examine the different ways in which aspects of personal development are, or are not, being encouraged. Indeed, it is often not until one has to make explicit, for such purposes, a detailed analysis that teachers begin to think more philosophically about something they take for granted as important. The result of such school-based deliberation may not be agreement on a new subject or new pastoral care organisation, but a revision of the content and learning styles of existing provision.

Organisation

Even if the 'internal enquiry' described above resulted in no more than a re-examination of existing provision, there would be a need for some organisational development to make sure that this was achieved. Where a school has a 'language across the curriculum' policy, there is still need for someone to co-ordinate the policy. Similarly it is the case with the pastoral care policy where this is equated with personal and social

Figure 1

	Cognitive capacity *Note a*	Facts to be known	Attitudes, feelings, dispositions	Practical application *Note b*
A General considerations (i) **Being a person** (including the capacity for entering into personal relations) *Note c*				
(ii) **Moral perspective**				
(iii) **Ideals** (including religious and other styles of life) *Note d*				
B Specific application (i) **Moral rules,** behaviours and so on				
(ii) **Social issues** (a) race (b) sexism (c) nuclear war (d) environment (for example, pollution) *Note e*				
(iii) **Politics** (a) citizenship or membership of the state (b) community participation (c) the rule of the law				
(iv) **Place within society** (a) occupation (b) status and class (c) economic and social needs				
(v) **Health** (a) physical (b) mental				

development and where it begins with an examination of the impact of the curriculum as a whole.

However, pastoral care does mean something else besides, as I have pointed out. What organisation within the school best provides the 'response to crisis'? When in the curriculum can one systematically anticipate 'typical crises' in a pastoral curriculum?

Assessment

Any kind of development that is important enough to promote is important enough to be assessed in some broad sense of that term. If one knows what personal development means, then one must have some rough idea of what counts as having achieved it in some respect. One must be able to state what counts as appropriate evidence of success. It is therefore important to attend to ways in which both the school and the individual are succeeding – the school in helping the individual to develop as a person, the individual in his or her own personal development. If it is argued that personal development is much too subjective or private an affair for any form of assessment, then one should retort that it is much too subjective or private an affair for the school to get involved in. But that is not to say that personal development

---

Notes

(a) **Cognitive capacity** – this includes reasoning ability, understanding, acquisition of relevant concepts.

(b) **Practical application** – how a person actually behaves, plus habits and skills required to behave appropriately. These are distinguishable sub-categories that could appear as such if one did not mind a very complicated matrix.

(c) **Being a person** – this includes general social growth, social awareness, and so on, since development as a person is inseparable from coming to see oneself in relation to others, coming to see things from another's point of view, and developing some sense of reciprocity and community.

(d) **Ideals** – too often personal growth is seen from a purely psychological point of view and moral growth is seen in the context of principles and duty. But the place of ideals in development, going beyond what is obligatory, needs to be explored. In a secular education, religion might be seen as one way of providing ideals that transcend the needs of everyday transactions.

(e) **Social issues** – these will no doubt change from society to society, but in our society the ones listed seem to be issues in which respect for persons, social awareness, and moral ideals have current significance. Different schools might wish to add other issues to the list.

should be assessed through tests or examinations. It does mean that one has to make judgements, and that to make judgements one needs to think by what criteria and on what evidence is one to make them. The Rutter Report, for example, did suggest broad criteria for assessing the effectiveness of a school in providing an appropriate ethos for personal achievement (Rutter 1979).

At the personal level, there is a lot of exploratory work on profiling of pupils in which there is recognition of personal experience and endeavours. This may be in its early stages, but considerable progress is being made. And so it needs to be made, because there is now considerable evidence to show that many employers place much more importance upon personal achievement (a developed sense of responsibility, an ability to work cooperatively, a flexibility of approach, a readiness to face new problems) than they do upon academic success.

School to work

A lot has been written about this subject but two points need to be made. First, it is highly unlikely that, in the near future, it will be expected of any young person to be employed in the normal sense of the word before 18 or 19. Until then he or she will be either in full-time education or on a training programme. This affects profoundly the attitude of young people to school and what it has to offer – the perceived relevance of the school and the kinds of relationships that will be found acceptable. The school in its turn will have added responsibility for preparing young people not only academically but also psychologically for a much less secure future which, for many, will involve periods of unemployment.

Secondly, for most young people the way into employment will be through a government-financed training scheme, and therefore the connection between full-time education and such schemes must be worked out and understood within each local area. This creates additional burdens for the guidance and advice aspects of the school – an extra duty to know the quality of different training opportunities.

Learning styles

We recently conducted a one hour interview with each of 230 students on a TVEI course. The account of their experiences suggests, first, a quite remarkable increase in self-confidence arising out of a sense of achievement and out of the more frequent interaction with adults, whether teachers or visitors; secondly, a greater sense of responsibility towards their work due to increased participation in the deliberations over aims and activities; and, thirdly, a sense of cooperative endeavour due to the group approach to activity-based learning. It is impossible to judge the long-term effect of this programme, or indeed to disentangle the various contributions to the changed perceptions and sense of responsibility of

140

these students. But there is a *prima facie* case for arguing that a shift in relationships and learning styles has been a strong and positive influence in the growing sense of personal worth and personal power. And why not, since the relationships and learning styles embody those very values?

Conclusion

This paper is indeed sketchy. It aims to do no more than to show the vast area that is the responsibility for any pastoral care system. At the same time it tries to point both to the central unifying concern of 'development as a person' and to different features of a system that takes this seriously. The encouraging point is that already so much excellent curriculum development is taking place that is relevant to this development – in developmental group and active tutorial work, in systematic guidance and counselling, in moral education, in profiling, in experience-based learning, and so on. What are, in my view, required are the detailed examples of how schools tackle these issues as a whole – developing a coherent policy in which key questions are systematically asked, the territory is mapped out, the structures established, the curriculum changed or extended and teaching and learning styles adapted to embody the very values being promoted.

Research needs in pastoral care – the vocational aspect

A. G. Watts and Bill Law

Helping students with their educational and vocational choices is an important part of the 'pastoral' responsibility of schools. Its essence is a focus on the individuality of each student, recognising and enhancing the 'thumbprint' which each individual places on his or her way of doing things – in school and out of it. Whereas much of the curriculum of schools is concerned with imparting a body of knowledge which is the same for everyone, career development is essentially a personally owned and personally created experience. Insofar as pastoral care is distinctively concerned with the wholeness and the uniqueness of the individual, careers guidance must be a crucial aspect of its concerns.

At the same time, careers guidance cannot be seen as the exclusive property of a school's pastoral-care system. In the first place, there are specialists available in the form of careers teachers and of careers officers. Secondly, careers guidance is also linked in a variety of ways into the wider curricular and organisational structure of the school – not least through the career 'channelling' that takes place through this structure. And thirdly, many students are less influenced by schools and official agencies than by the informal contacts available to them in the community through their family and friends.

The last decade or two have seen an increasing interest in recognising and broadening these various forms of help. A particularly important development has been the incorporation of careers education into the curriculum, as a systematic attempt to develop attitudes, skills and knowledge related to (a) self-awareness (What kind of person am I? What kind of person do I want to become?), (b) opportunity awareness (What kind of opportunities does the adult and working world offer to me?), (c) decision learning (How am I to make the choices that face me?) and (d) transition learning (How am I to implement these decisions, and what transitions will they imply?) (Law and Watts 1977, see also Hayes and Hopson 1972, DES 1973). In some schools this is done on an 'addition' basis, with careers education being placed on the timetable like other subjects, with its own specialist staff, syllabus, financial allocation, and so on. In other schools it is done on an 'infusion' basis, in which the aims and objectives of careers education are incorporated into the work of other subject departments (e.g. awareness of local industry in geography, structure of wage packets in mathematics, preparation for interviews in drama), with varying attention being given to co-ordinating the various elements into a coherent and reasonably comprehensive programme.

Careers education can be seen as an important part of what Marland (1980) called the 'pastoral curriculum': a recognition that 'the art of the pastoral system is to help all the individuals without always giving individual help' (*ibid*, p. 153). Its key is that the learning process should make full allowance for the individuality of each student's career development. Some schools have indeed come increasingly to link careers education with other elements in the curriculum which are similarly focussed around students' individual lives – social education, moral education, health education, education in personal relationships (e.g. Wilcox and Lavercombe 1984). In recognition of Marland's dictum, some schools have begun to integrate these areas of the curriculum with the pastoral-care system, seeing tutorial periods as a key 'delivery point'. In such schools, careers education has become part of 'active tutorial work' (Baldwin and Wells 1979–81).

At the same time, careers education has also become linked with other trends in schools. One of these has been the concern with strengthening school-industry links (Jamieson and Lightfoot 1982). The roots of this lie not in notions of influencing individual career development but in political and economic education: the central concern is that all school pupils – regardless of where and when they are to work themselves – should be taught to understand the place of 'industry' in our society. Nonetheless, the experienced-based methods used by the more innovative school-industry projects – notably the School Curriculum Industry Project (SCIP), with its emphasis on work experience, work simulation, and the use of 'adults other than teachers' in the classroom (Jamieson and Lightfoot 1982) – have been symbiotic with parallel developments in careers education and guidance (Law 1982, Watts 1983a). Such methods have also been encouraged by other developments, such as the Technical and Vocational Education Initiative (MSC 1984) and the Certificate of Pre-Vocational Education (Joint Board 1984). These trends have all been clearly linked to the effects on schools of the fracturing and deferring of entry to employment which growing youth unemployment and policy responses to it – notably the Youth Training Scheme – have caused (Watts 1983b).

Careers guidance is thus much less clearly 'bounded' in organisational terms than used to be the case. The effect has been an increasing concern

Figure 1   Examples of levels of integration

		Key question
High differentiation ↑	(a) *Specialist teacher* as 'head of careers' teaching an insulated course within a modular social-education programme for the fourth and fifth years. Few direct links with the pastoral and academic systems, even at option choice. Autonomous and insulated contacts with outside agencies (speakers, visits).	How might the careers teacher achieve a 'role-change' *vis-à-vis* colleagues?
	(b) *Careers co-ordinator* co-ordinating a small careers 'team' and resourcing its classroom activities. Little formal contact between team and pastoral and academic systems. Limited use of external contacts.	Can co-ordinator develop influencing skills to build links with school departments?
	(c) *Social education team* on cross-disciplinary basis with careers element included in programme for third, fourth and fifth years (tutor groups in fifth). Wide range of staff and contact with all students but no formal links with academic department. Considering the development of neighbourhood contacts and resources.	Will this team remain a separate element within the school?
	(d) *Community curriculum working party* – cross-disciplinary group, including the careers teacher, headed by science teacher. Considering means of using out-of-school experience (e.g. work experience) across the school curriculum. Organising events which bring non-teaching adults into school and send students out into the neighbourhood.	Can this group combat exam pressures?
	(e) *Integrated course* to be taught by a cross-disciplinary team to students in the fourth and fifth years. Intended to assist students to reflect and review experience in anticipation of school-leaving.	How will this course be organised and managed?
High integration ↓	(f) *Cross-disciplinary tutor group* and no careers 'specialist' in school. Careers work is individual – the shared responsibility of form tutors, backed by contributions from different areas of the school curriculum. Co-ordinator in an administrative role. Close links with Careers Service which 'resources' tutors.	Does the system still need a specialist input to resource careers work?

Source: Evans and Law (1984)

with 'integration' of the various potential sources of career-development help both inside and outside schools. A NICEC action-research project, sponsored by the DES and EEC, identified various levels of integration strategies, arranging them along a continuum from 'high differentiation' to 'high integration', and identifying key questions related to each level (Figure 1). The project also revealed clearly the difficulties of seeking greater integration, and the organisational obstacles which have to be surmounted. In particular, it confronted the question of 'Who controls the process of integration?' It accordingly came to draw a distinction between *integration* – which is the process the student engages in – and *co-ordination* – which is the responsibility of staff, and assists the student to integrate varied experiences related to their choices and transitions (Evans and Law 1984).

Some research needs

Research has a number of contributions to make in improving careers guidance in schools (Killeen and Watts 1983). The first is the *conceptual* function of helping guidance practitioners to understand the processes in which they are attempting to intervene. All guidance practices are based on practitioners' assumptions about these processes. Research can draw out such assumptions and scrutinise them; it can also seek to offer alternative conceptualisations and to test one against another. A variety of different theories of career development have been developed, all of which suggest different kinds of interventions (Watts *et al* 1981). For example, such research has indicated the importance of the attitudes and dispositions which are developed in the pre-adolescent years, including sexual and ethnic self-images. This suggests that interventions in the process need to start before the third or fourth years of secondary school, at which point careers-education programmes conventionally tend to begin.

A second contribution is the *technical* one of providing data-based tools and procedures to be used in careers guidance. This might, for instance, include classifications of abilities, interests, personality, and so on. It might also include psychometric tests for measuring these attributes. Again, it might include the systematic collection and analysis of occupational data which can then be used for guidance purposes.

A third contribution is the *evaluative* one of analysing the process of guidance, describing ways in which it can be provided, and measuring its effects. There have, for example, been a number of studies which have attempted to evaluate the outcomes of careers guidance (Watts and Kidd 1978, Clarke 1980). More specific questions can be posed too. What, for instance, are the relative merits of group work as opposed to individual interviewing? How effective are the new computer-aided guidance systems that are now being developed (Watts and Ballantine 1983)? Such questions can be approached either in 'summative' terms, or in more dynamic 'formative' terms which provide a springboard for further development.

It is in this third category that issues related to the specific relationship between careers guidance and pastoral care can be addressed. Some of these questions are concerned with organisational *roles*. How reconcilable is the disciplinary and administrative role of the pastoral-care tutor with a careers-guidance role? What levels of 'system orientation' (Law, 1978) do pastoral-care tutors have, and what levels are most functional for effective careers guidance? Other questions are concerned with organisational *structures*. What links and boundaries do different schools establish between their pastoral-care systems and their careers-guidance systems? What tensions do they experience between the two? What are experienced as being the advantages and disadvantages of different patterns? Further questions are concerned with organisational *change*. What are the conditions that need to be satisfied before such changes can occur (*cf* Evans and Law 1984, Law and Roberts 1983)? What strategies of change seem to be most effective?

Another more specific set of research questions might be related to the organisational implications of introducing particular techniques or procedures, for example, profiling. The formative use of profiling (Law 1984) potentially offers a powerful link between the guidance roles of careers officers and careers teachers and the guidance role of tutors, in which all are encouraged to collaborate in helping students to review their progress, to use feedback, to articulate their sense of self, and to negotiate their progress through appropriate learning experiences towards their career and other goals. Not only does this bring careers guidance and pastoral care together, but – if integrated into the process of curriculum development – it could bring them close to the centre of this process. Research issues here include: What are experienced as the advantages and disadvantages of different methods of profiling? and How do different organisational structures impede or facilitate the use of these methods as tools for curriculum development?

A second example is the use of the 'pastoral curriculum'. What sorts of help are tutors in a particularly good position to offer? What difficulties are experienced in involving them actively in incorporating careers education into their tutorial programme? On what matters do they require specialist support? What forms can this support take?

A third example is the use of community resources. Unlike most subject teaching, pastoral care by definition requires teachers to cross the boundaries of the school and to seek links with parents and appropriate community agencies. This offers a further potential link with careers guidance, which is concerned in an important sense with helping *students* to cross the boundaries of the school, and accordingly should properly make full use of links with community resources (Law 1981). Research issues here relate to the forms which such links can take, the problems encountered in establishing them, and the benefits which can ensue. A recent development of particular interest in this respect is the Grubb Institute's 'Transition to Working Life' (TWL) project, which uses a lot of the 'apparatus' of pastoral care (small-group work, emphasis on relationships) but with 'adults other than teachers' in the 'tutorial' role (Reed and Bazalgette 1983).

In these and other respects, research can contribute to enhancing the vocational aspect of pastoral care. It may not be able to answer many of the questions we have posed – most interesting and important questions are incapable of yielding definitive answers – but it should be able to illuminate them, thereby helping teachers to develop their own responses.

Motivation versus selection: A dilemma for records of personal achievement

Andy Hargreaves

> (The Record of Achievement) would detail activities within school and outside it. . . . Qualities such as self-discipline, persistence, enthusiasm, drive and the ability to get on with other people, all characteristics that it would be useful for an employer to know about, could be included. It could increase motivation of those children who, at the moment, may not feel that their achievements are fully recognised.

On 28 November, 1983, the Secretary of State for Education and Science, Sir Keith Joseph, pledged to earmark £10 million of government money to support the development of Records of Achievement for all school leavers. The purpose of these records, he stated, is the assessment of skills, personal qualities and achievements beyond the usual subject attainments. The two reasons for this initiative to which Sir Keith drew particular attention and which appear to be of pressing concern to both schools and employers were the need:

1   to acknowledge 'the totality of what pupils have done in order to improve their motivation and help schools identify their needs more closely.'
2   to provide 'a testimonial respected and valued by employers and colleges.'

In the draft policy statement, 'Record of Achievement for school leavers', these aims were stressed yet again and with even greater emphasis. The Secretaries of State, the draft policy statement said, wanted the Records of Achievement:

> . . . to improve pupils' motivation. There is evidence that some pupils who are at present poorly motivated would aspire to higher standards of attainment if they knew that their achievements and efforts would be formally recognised. (DES 1983a, p. 3)

At the same time, it was the aim of the Record

> ... to offer pupils a certificate which is recognised and valued by employers and institutions of further education when the pupils seek work or admission to a course. The intention is that most potential users ... should gain from records of achievement a more rounded picture of candidates under consideration for jobs of courses; and that many should make direct use of this information in deciding how the applicant could best be employed, or for which jobs, training schemes or courses he should be advised to apply. (DES 1983a, p. 3)

Two of the dominant, publicly-proclaimed purposes of Records of Achievement are that they should meet pupil *motivation* needs on the one hand, and employment *selection* needs on the other.[1] I want to argue that these two publicly-respected and professionally shared 'needs' may well be contradictory; that one set of needs will tend to be met at the expense of the other; that pupil motivation will actually be improved only at the expense of efficient employer selection or vice versa. The consequence, it seems to me, is that teachers and schools are and will be forced to prioritise one set of 'needs' over the other in their approach to recording pupils' achievements: to be primarily *motivation-directed* (to recognise pupils' worth and personal achievements, however unconventional) or *selection-directed* (to document the kinds of achievements, qualities and activities which they feel employers are likely to value) in their policy and practice. Teachers, schools, LEA and Exam Board consortia and the like will of course vary amongst themselves in just how they overcome this dilemma. But whatever particular strategy is adopted, these attempted resolutions of the motivation/selection dilemma will have a broad impact on at least two aspects of this new innovation: on the form that the final Record of Achievement document takes, and on the process through which the statements ultimately included there are negotiated between teachers and pupils. These two areas, I want to propose, should be important research priorities for people who are seriously interested in evaluating the extent to which the process of recording pupils' achievements meets the stated aims of its supporters.

The form of the record

There are many different systems for recording personal achievements. Hitchcock (1983) identifies four generic types – profile grids, criterion checklists and comment banks – all slightly different versions, overt or disguised, of ranking pupils' personal achievements according to rather narrowly-defined pre-specified criteria – and more extended forms of pupil self-recording. In all cases, as Balogh (1982) and Goacher (1983)

have noted, the enhancement of pupil motivation was a prime consideration in their development; the heads in particular giving emphasis to this
factor. However, the effectiveness of systems of recording in meeting
motivation needs has varied very much with the type of system adopted.
At the extremes are extended systems of pupil self-recording on the one
hand, and the various types of grid-like profile on the other (including
comment banks and checklists as more disguised versions). I shall now
evaluate these in turn.

Pupil self-recording

Most systems of pupil self-recording derive from a model developed by
Don Stansbury in the Swindon area in the late 1960s: the Record of
Personal Achievement (RPA). Variants and derivatives of this model
include Stansbury's own later version, the Record of Personal Experience
(RPE) and the Schools Council's funded development of this scheme, the
Pupils' Personal Record (PPR). Though there are differences between
these schemes, they all revolve around entries made by pupils on a variety
of headed cards – Hobbies, Family, etc. – which are then stored in a file.
The file is controlled by the pupil and access to it can only be gained with
the pupil's permission. This 'wodge' of material can later be made
available to employers and other potential 'users' if pupils so wish.

Personal recording systems seem to have met with some success in
improving pupil motivation, particularly among the less able for whom,
incidentally, most of the schemes were initially and primarily designed
(Swales 1980). The privacy and control afforded to less able, sometimes
deviant and potentially disaffected pupils, and the possibilities this
has created for them to record experiences and activities which would
probably otherwise be at best neglected and at worst frowned upon
elsewhere in the schooling system, has almost certainly been helpful in
this respect.

Against the success of the schemes in *motivating* many of the less able,
must be matched their virtual worthlessness to employers as aids to
selection. The sheer bulk of the final 'wodge' of materials and the
difficulty of knowing just what sense to make of its voluminous contents
has seriously undermined the credibility of personal recording systems
with employers (HMI 1983). Moreover, as Swales (1980) points out
in his evaluation of RPA, when schemes of personal recording were
extended to include the more able, this group of pupils held serious
doubts about the schemes' value, and their parents, indeed, were often
anxious that the schemes presented a serious and damaging distraction
from 'real learning'. In the case of more able pupils, it seems, for whom
future occupational success is a very real possibility, success through
formal selection via the conventional external examination route at 16
plus, is motivation enough. To sum up: where success in conventional

exam-based selection is unlikely, schemes of personal recording make a strong, compensatory contribution to the development of pupil motivation, but they improve the process of non-exam based selection not one jot. Schemes of pupil self-recording, that is, apparently score high on motivation but close to zero on selection.

Grid profiles

In the case of grid-type profile summaries of pupil qualities, skills and achievements, the tendency is precisely in the opposite direction: towards efficient non-exam based selection, and away from the development of pupil motivation, even though motivation (albeit the extrinsic motivation of meeting short-range targets and objectives) has ranked highly among the aims and intentions of those developing and adopting profile systems. The Scottish Council for Research in Education (1977) led the way in developing profile systems with its own *Pupils in Profile* scheme, but elsewhere, profile grids have perhaps been most widely used with the 16–19 age range; the major initiatives being made by the Further Education Curriculum Review and Development Unit (FEU), the City and Guilds 365 scheme and the Manpower Services Commission.

As with forms of pupil self-recording, the exact nature of the grids and checklists vary, but most include a list of qualities (leadership, initiative, punctuality, etc.) or skills (talking and listening, use of powered machinery, etc.) and an assessment of whether and how far pupils/ students possess those qualities or have mastered those skills. Such systems of evaluation are usually teacher-dominated or even entirely teacher-controlled, but there are a number of important exceptions (e.g. SCRE and FEU) where pupils or students participate in and negotiate the construction of their profile with their teachers or tutors.

Of all the systems of recording personal achievements, employers seem to respond best to these (Jones 1983). They are brief and easily scanned; they are standardised across all pupils participating in a single institution and in some cases across many institutions; and the skills and qualities listed have at least a superficial resemblance to those in which employers appear to have an interest. From the employers' viewpoint, grid-type profiles are simple and relevant: they can be significant aids to the process of *selection*.

However, as the work of Goacher (1983) and others (e.g. Education Resource Unit for YOP, 1982) suggests, an assessment and recording system neatly tailored to the needs of employers may be less than beneficial in boosting pupil motivation. Aside from all the criticisms that can be made of the terseness of the categories on the profiles and checklists and of the misunderstandings that can therefore commonly occur about their meaning, and apart from any worries one might have that the 'gaps' between different grades of skill mastery often appear inconsistent and uneven, one of the most distressing features of the operation of grid-like profiles is that in many cases they seem not to increase pupil motivation at all but if anything to depress it still further. It is not difficult to predict the effect upon a pupil of ticks being consistently placed in boxes which attest only to the most elementary levels of skill mastery, especially where he or she is witness to and at least nominally involved in the production of this authoritative statement of his or her apparent incompetence. As Goacher (1983, pp. 31–32) points out in his work with schools developing some form or other of recording personal achievements, the very descriptions of elementary skill mastery in some of the grid-type schemes he reviewed 'can handle *simple* tools with safety', 'understands *simple* scientific language', etc. (my italics) – only served to undermine pupils' sense of worth and to instil deep resentment among them. Equally, after examining the grades used in profile schemes used by Manpower Services Commission and the Further Education Unit, a group of Scottish evaluators concluded that:

> The grades are . . . vague, uneven, and far too widely spaced to register progress. . . . We feel that they work against the central MSC principles of progression, motivation and catering for young people's needs. The grades look as if they belong to a labelling strategy rather than a learning strategy. (Education Resource Unit for YOP 1982, p. 14)

Perhaps it is because of these threats to motivation implied by grid-like schemes that the DES in its recent draft policy statement directed that:

> One feature of some existing schemes which the Secretaries of State would not wish to see imitated is the practice of grading personal qualities in the form of ticks or letters whose significance is not clear, however conscientious the attempt to define the grade descriptions. Such gradings contain unsupported and often negative judgements and are open to misinterpretation. (DES 1983a, p. 7)

To sum up: although developers and adopters of grid-type schemes of profile assessment have been at least as interested in improving the motivation of pupils unlikely to succeed in conventional CSE and 'O' level assessment at 16, as they have been in providing information of use to employers, in practice it seems that once more, motivation needs and selection needs are in conflict with one another. Goacher (1983, p. 15) may be right when he remarks that this system of recording pupils' personal achievements (and the lack of them!) should not 'be expected to perform a motivating function except in a very general way by encouraging, for example, attendance.' Getting pupils to underwrite their inability (or unwillingness) to succeed in employer-desired skills and competences will do little to improve their motivation or their sense of worth. Grid-type profiles and checklists, that is, seem likely to score high on selection but largely at the expense of pupil motivation.

Alternative options

As a way of circumventing these difficulties, of trying to achieve a more equitable balance between motivation needs and selection needs, and in a way that will optimise the fulfilment of each, a number of schools and, it seems, consortia of Examination Boards and LEAs – in the emerging Oxford Certificate of Educational Achievement for example (OCEA 1984), appear to be gravitating towards a third kind of summative document – the succinct prose summary of pupil achievements in and perhaps also out of school. It appears that the preferences of the DES (1983, p. 7) are currently inclined in this direction too. They say:

> There are strong arguments in favour of designing records in such a way that personal qualities and skills are mainly inferred from accounts of actual achievements in activities in which the pupil has participated – or from the absence of such information.

Although the arguments surrounding this proposal are speculative and await confirmation or refutation by much needed research, there does seem to be at least some possibility that a record of achievement taking this form could meet motivation needs by affording a more rounded and positive picture of a pupil than seems feasible in grid-type schemes, and by involving pupils themselves in a long and continuous formative process of self assessment and reappraisal which many see as essential to the construction of the final document. Moreover, it is also possible that employers *might* be persuaded to see the selection implications of a document of no greater length than, say, one side of A4 paper – if only for the purposes of interviewing applicants.

In the succinct prose summary of pupil achievements, then, we may have a form of summative statement which does not pose too many threats to the enhancement of pupil motivation and which does not appear to be unduly prejudicial to the interests of employer selection. Proponents of what, until very recently, has been an uncoordinated and rather inchoate movement towards recognising pupil achievements beyond those which are acknowledged by the conventional system of external examining at 16 plus, perhaps have good cause to feel optimistic that in the succinct prose summary, they have at last devised a type of summative document which has a reasonable chance of overcoming the motivation/selection dilemma.

The negotiation of the record

However, notwithstanding the importance of the form that the final document takes, it would be unwise to assume that the construction of an appropriate summative document will, of itself, resolve the motivation/selection dilemma. All that the construction of a concise yet open summative document may do, in fact, is to displace that dilemma into the detailed process of interaction between teachers and pupils through which the final document is ultimately constructed. It is in this process, in the perspectives held by teachers and pupils respectively, in the meanings that pass between them, and in the capacity of one party to impose its meanings upon the other, that pupil motivation needs or perceived employer selection needs are likely to make themselves felt most powerfully and decisively.

There are, Janet Balogh (1982, pp. 41–42) argues, 'good reasons for involving pupils in their own assessment: improved motivation, the fact that they may have the best knowledge of their own strengths and weaknesses and that there are few areas where they could be considered not to have the right to make a judgement.' Some writers, like Burgess and Adams (1980) go further than this still, and propose that the negotiation of assessment between a teacher and a pupil can provide the basis for and be a constitutive part of a new learning, curriculum and assessment contract, negotiated between them on open, democratic terms. Indeed, in a commentary on the Secretary of State's initiative, Burgess and Adams take issue with the draft policy statement's suggestion that the record of achievement should be the responsibility of the school and propose instead that it should be the responsibility of the pupil. The benefits to the student of the record of achievement, Burgess and Adams (1984) suggest

> are better served if students themselves are offered initiative in their own learning and responsibility in compiling their records. In particular, motivation is greatly enhanced where students exercise such initiative and responsibility. (p. 4)

Nor, they continue, will the benefits of democratic involvement accrue solely to the student, for

> the motivation of students and the perception of teachers would alike be enhanced by being expected to discuss together the programmes of work under consideration for school groups and individual students. (p. 5)

Whatever the worth or feasibility of this democratic ideal, it has to be said that the actual *practice* of negotiated assessment all too often tends to fall well short of it. Negotiating a pupil's assessment with him or her can too easily be discharged in a swift, perfunctory manner and, as Goacher (1983, p. 35) has observed, may even involve the teacher putting pressure on a pupil to alter that assessment. 'Authority,' remarked Willard Waller in his classic text *The Sociology of Teaching*

(1932), 'is on the side of the teacher. The teacher nearly always wins. In fact he must win or he cannot remain a teacher.' (p. 196). It is because of this insight, perhaps, that Waller felt drawn earlier in his book to advancing the following view of the self-governing school.

> Self government is rarely real. Usually it is but a mask for the rule of the teacher oligarchy. . . . The experimental school which wishes to do away with authority continually finds that in order to maintain requisite standards of achievement in imparting certain basic skills, it has to introduce some variant of the authority principle, or it finds that it must select and employ teachers who can in fact be despotic without seeming to be so. (p. 9)

Negotiation, however open and fair teachers and heads may declare it and perhaps believe it to be in principle, is nonetheless usually and perhaps inevitably very much one-sided in character. This may or may not be a good thing: but whatever one's beliefs and preferences, its existence has to be conceded.

Roy Hattersley gives us a salutary insight into this fact in his recollections of life as a second year pupil at Sheffield City Grammar School. He recalls receiving his end of year report and remembers being delighted with the immense improvement in his test results and class position. Yet he was also incensed that:

> . . . the comments alongside the figures bore no relationship to my achievements. They were just the same as the year before when I had been near to the bottom of almost anything. The judgements lacked originality as well as relevance – 'could do better if tried' . . . 'must work harder' . . . 'greater effort needed'. (Hattersley 1983, p. 147)

The admirably impetuous Hattersley stormed off to the staffroom in protest and after a brief unsatisfactory encounter with his form-teacher, marched towards the study of the man who 'instead of striking out the libels on my year's industrious progress . . . had lamely added his name in confirmation of the calumny' – the headmaster. Fortunately for Hattersley, he was intercepted outside the head's study by A. W. Goodfellow 'senior master head of the history department, sometime Commandant of the Sheffield Air Training Corps, President of the Local History Association and man of general cultivation and refinement!'

> I looked at him – gleaming shoes, pinstripe suit into which no crease would ever dare to intrude, stiff white collar and clipped moustache – and I explained. I think that the phrase 'not fair' was repeated half a dozen times in a single spoken paragraph. 'These', he said, 'are extremely good results',

pausing to allow his emollient message to sink in. 'But you can hardly expect the comments simply to make the same point. If the results and the comment columns said the same thing, the comment column would be wholly unnecessary. Take the two things together – top in English and History but could do better still'. He emphasised the 'still' as if the word actually appeared on the offending report card. 'I would', he concluded, 'be proud to take that report card home.'

'To this day', Hattersley concludes, 'I do not know if I walked out of the school office a more rational human being or the victim of a confidence trick.'

Now readers of Hattersley's autobiographical account might reasonably argue that the stuffy days of pupil deference to gentlemanly authority that characterised life in boys' grammar schools in the 1940s have long since passed. They might equally object to the candid if somewhat vitriolic remarks which Waller passed upon many of his apparently authoritarian colleagues in teaching, on the grounds that these were made more than half a century ago and no longer apply to the more open and democractic educational institutions in which pupils participate today.

Would such criticisms and their implicit optimism about current educational practice be justified, though? Research studies of attempts to democratise and widen choice in other parts of the state education system are not encouraging. At the level of primary schooling, for instance, the trend towards individual choice and self-direction in pupil learning in the 1960s and '70s was largely restricted to the level of educational rhetoric and seemed to impinge little on the daily realities of classroom practice (Sharp and Green 1975, Berlak *et al* 1975, A. Hargreaves 1977). Teachers did not abrogate their control over the curriculum. Nor did they hand over learning decisions and choices to pupils in any fundamental way. They simply disguised their control and interventions by exercising them in a more subtle less overt manner: 'leading from behind' as it was commonly called. The characteristic pedagogy of the so-called progressive primary school was, as Basil Bernstein (1976) pointed out, one where the principles of teacher control were relatively 'invisible' to the outside observer. But this did not mean that control had diminished. If anything, rather, its influence became increasingly pervasive as more and more of the pupils' conduct and activity was covertly subjected to teacher assessment. Like fugitive criminals pursued by resourceful and relentless detectives, pupils often found that for them 'progressive' teaching simply amounted to there being, in the words of the old detective serial, 'No Hiding Place' (there is a message in this for the Record of Achievement movement too!). At the secondary level, similar processes could be discerned in the broadening of option-choice systems at 14 to pupils participating in the expanding comprehensive sector. Yet, while in principle this offered many pupils a far greater latitude of choice, in practice it simply placed more of an onus of guidance and selection on to the individual teacher's shoulders – a duty which often involved 'persuading' pupils who had made 'wrong' choices to choose again (Woods 1976, Ball 1981).

In both cases, it seems – progressive primary teaching and subject option choice – the more that the business of choice and negotiation is conducted through the details of teacher-pupil interaction, the more the outcomes of those choices and negotiations become subject to teachers' judgements and stereotypes of what is appropriate for particular pupils given their perceived ability, their behaviour, their sex and so on (Nash 1973, Sharp and Green 1975, Woods 1976, Ball 1981, King 1978, Grafton *et al* 1978–1983). The more informal the process of guidance and choice, that is, the more likely it is that pupils will be channelled along routes which conform to teacher stereotypes of their potential.

Is there any reason to believe that things will be any different in the case of informal, negotiated processes of pupil assessment? Is it likely that secondary school teachers who will continue to be bound to their subject specialisms (perhaps even more so if DES (1983b) recommendations on tightening up 'subject match' through initial training and teacher appointments are followed through) and who will continue to spend much of their time teaching for the 16 plus examinations (for few advocates of Records of Personal Achievement, least of all the DES, have seriously proposed the abolition or even substantial reduction in scope of such examinations), will be any more sensitive, open and democratic in responding to their pupils' personal and educational needs than their 'progressive' primary colleagues? Under these kinds of continuing pressures – the pressures of dealing with records of achievement alongside existing and perhaps mounting commitments to examinations and subject specialist teaching – it is difficult to see how secondary teachers can, even if they would wish to be, *that* responsive. Certainly, Broadfoot's (1982, p. 51) anxiety that informal processes of pupil assessment 'will be subject to the well-known disadvantages of . . . the halo effect, social class bias and personal antipathy' seems worthy of further exploration.[1]

What meanings will teachers bring to their encounters with pupils when assessments are negotiated with them? Will they, intentionally or unintentionally perhaps, mediate employer values by encouraging pupils to record only those activities and achievements which have the ring of such qualities as loyalty, dependability and leadership – scouting and guiding, playing in the school orchestra, running the fishing club, for instance? And how will they react to those pupil activities which might not chime so sweetly in the ears of employers – to Rastafarianism, feminism, peace campaigning and the like? Will they discourage pupils from recording activities and achievements of these kinds – and what would be the consequences of this denial of experience for pupils' sense of worth and motivation? These are – or at least they ought to be – real dilemmas for practising teachers.

Similarly, in the case of pupils, in what ways will their approach to the recording process vary? In all other aspects of their school lives, we know that pupils differ a great deal in their response to school, from enthusiastic or less enthusiastic brands of conformism through to cynical instrumentalism, total indifference or even outright opposition (Hargreaves 1982, also Woods 1979, Fuller 1980, Turner 1983). There is no reason to believe that the approach of pupils to profile assessment will be any less varied than elsewhere. It is therefore worth asking which pupils, in line with the aims of the RPA and PPR schemes, for instance, will use the assessment process to define and declare their identity, no matter how unusual or unappealing that might be to potential employers. And how will such students fare when they 'negotiate' their assessments with their teachers? Which pupils, by contrast, will need no guidance, no pushing or prodding by their teachers to be made cognisant of what employers might want, but will already have a sophisticated sense of those activities and achievements which signal employability, perhaps self-censoring their own entries in order to maximise their own chances in the job-selection stakes? Clearly, the dilemmas for pupils engaged in this tricky process are equally serious.

In the case of teachers and pupils alike, the choice of either option has a 'Catch 22'-like quality about it. Declare pupil activities and involvements, however unconventional and you will probably enhance pupils' motivation, but only at the cost of their job prospects. Stick to recording only clearly 'reputable' activities and achievements and you will communicate a more positive sense of a pupil's employability, but only at the expense of failing to declare and therefore implicitly denying vast chunks of the more unconventional pupil's experience and identity. The consequences of such a denial for a pupil's identity and motivation are potentially very serious; for whereas poor performance in conventional subject examinations possibly labels a pupil as an academic and intellectual failure, the public excision of large parts of his or her identity entails failing that pupil utterly as a person. Thus, the more all-encompassing the assessment, the more total and damaging will be the consequences for the identities of those more unconventional but by no means worthless pupils who are subject to it, even more so if they actively participate in the construction of that assessment, if they actually underwrite this public statement of apparent personal failure. Clearly, when pupils and teachers are playing for stakes as high as these, for declarations or denials of personal worth, no less, the task of identifying the meanings which different types of pupils and teachers attach to the recording and assessment process, and of evaluating the ways in which those meanings come to be negotiated between them is surely an urgent research priority.

Conclusion

In their incisive account of the reorganisation and reconstruction of secondary education in Scotland since the war, John Gray and his colleagues (1983) point to three problems which have accompanied educational expansion: problems of difficulty, selection and motivation. One combined effect of these problems, they argue, is that in the interests of fair, meritocratic *selection*, the examination system has been extended to encompass a wider and wider section of the ability range. But, they go on, this has only served to subject many pupils of moderate or low ability to forms of assessment of very great *difficulty* and to exam-directed courses of little intrinsic interest. This, in turn, has affected pupil *motivation*, particularly among the less able as they experience courses in which their prospects of failure or of only the most limited kinds of success are very great.

In the conventional examination system, it seems that with less able pupils, selection needs and motivation needs are very much at odds with one another. Whether restructuring of the examination system through the new GCSE will alleviate these difficulties at all remains to be seen. But how sad and ironic it would be if more open forms of assessment, one of whose central purposes is to provide alternative ways of generating pupil motivation *despite* the exams, actually turned out only to depress motivation still further among many pupils, particularly the unconventional and 'unclubbable'. If we are to stand any chance of avoiding these difficulties, a number of research and policy priorities seem worthy of further exploration.

Research priorities

1 Studies of the effects of the *form* of recording personal achievements on pupil motivation and on the value of the document to employers and other 'users'.
2 Observational and interview studies of the actual process by which teachers and pupils negotiate meanings through the assessment process, and of the effects of that negotiation on pupil motivation.

These are not, of course, the sole research priorities in the case of records of achievement, as the companion chapter by Broadfoot in this volume should make clear, but they are the ones that will have most bearing on the motivation/selection dilemma. Findings on these matters might, then, provide us with some guidance on the following policy issues.

Policy issues

1 It would be useful if we were able to provide some dependable, research-based advice about those forms of documentation which are most likely to benefit pupil motivation and/or employer selection.
2 It would be useful to have a sensitive research-based understanding of the meanings that pass between and are negotiated between teachers and pupils during the business of assessment, so that guidelines for the in-service training of teachers who will be involved in the assessment process, could be established. Such in-service training and the research basis on which it could be mounted could be designed to help teachers

   (i)   be aware of the dangers of stereotyping and of the forms that stereotyping might take during their guidance of pupils;
   (ii)   be aware of the influence they have upon pupils in the negotiation process and develop the skills to manage that influence knowledgeably and sensitively;
   (iii) be clear about and discuss with their colleagues in a rigorous way the values that are involved in the assessment process: in particular, to come to recognise and appreciate the value of certain pupil activities and achievements not normally recognised as worthwhile by schools and employers.

3 It would be useful to consider whether motivation needs are being and can be met in a recording system which does not replace but runs alongside conventional examining at 16 plus. What relative importance do teachers and pupils attach to records of achievement and conventional examining respectively, and what proportions of time and commitment do pupils, teachers and schools in general attach to these different parts of their work? As an urgent policy matter, therefore, we should ask the unaskable: is the success of records of achievement actually contingent on the elimination or at least the substantial reduction of conventional examining at 16 plus? Educational research might help to give us some answers to this.
4 Lastly, it is important to ask whether motivation needs can be compatible with selection needs in any recording system which has employer involvement. It is customary, indeed it seems to be almost obligatory to involve employer representatives in the construction of records of achievement, and to regard them as one of the major users of such records. Yet, while one can understand the fearful keenness with which educators court employer involvement in an educational

and social system which is becoming increasingly directed towards industrial values, one cannot also help wondering whether the extent of employers' involvement might be far outweighing their practical importance. I have already pointed to some of the negative backwash effects that employer values can have on the assessment process. The fact that employers are simply there, as potential users, is probably enough to guarantee this. Their involvement in the actual design of records just makes such effects more certain still. But with so few students now going direct into employment at 16, and so many going on to further education or training, might it not be argued that the use of records of achievement as a selection device for employment could reasonably be deferred until post-compulsory education, thereby releasing records of Personal Achievement in the compulsory stage to concentrate exclusively on the satisfaction of motivation and personal development needs alone?

The initiatives, both local and national, to develop Records of Personal Achievement for secondary school pupils promise to realise a number of long-hoped for and worthwhile human ideals in education concerning the development and personal growth of young people, and the encouragement of their own active involvement in that development. Few people would argue that, in principle, this is a bad thing. Yet amid the educational consensus which is emerging behind this movement, a movement whose passionate educational optimism has sometimes reached proportions not far short of religious fervour, it would be a pity if we could not produce and in due course turn for guidance to a sound and rather more dispassionate research-based evaluation of this initiative. This would help us identify different forms that records of achievement might take and assess their consequences in each case; it would help us pinpoint difficulties and obstacles regarding their implementation and suggest practical guidance for overcoming them; and, not least because of the intensity of almost religious conviction behind this innovation, it would help keep a few sobering heretical thoughts (abolition of exams? exclusion of employers?) on the policy agenda.

Note

1   At the end of 1984, the DES and Welsh Office updated their draft policy statement into a final document *Records of Achievement: a statement of policy*: The statement of this document on the relevance of records of achievement to purposes of pupil motivation and employers' selection are fundamentally the same as those included in the earlier draft. Among the 'four main purposes' which records of achievement and the associated recording systems should

serve' according to the Secretaries of States are:

(ii) Motivation and personal development. They contribute to pupils' personal development and progress by improving their motivation, providing encouragement and increasing their awareness of strengths, weaknesses and opportunities.

(iv) A document of record. Young people leaving school or college should take with them a short, summary document of record which is recognised and valued by employers and institutions of further and higher education. This should provide a more rounded picture of candidates for jobs or courses than can be provided by a list of examination results, thus helping potential users to decide how candidates could best be employed, or for which jobs, training schemes or courses they are likely to be suitable. (DES 1984, p. 3)

Profiles and pastoral care:
Some neglected questions

Patricia Broadfoot

In 1977 the Scottish Council for Research in Education published the results of a four-year research study entitled *Pupils in Profile*. This study, which was conducted in conjunction with the Headteachers' Association of Scotland, set out the arguments for 'profiling' and reported the results of extensive field trials of a prototype profile in Scottish secondary schools. More than five years later, this Scottish publication appears to have been all but forgotten in the rash of development work which has accompanied the growing interest in the institution of such 'profiles' in England and Wales. Indeed, Sir Keith Joseph's policy statement on 'Records of Achievement' published in June 1984 makes no mention of this early work. But to cavil at the fickleness of an educational public which so soon forgets the origin of an educational idea is in itself absurd. What matter the biography of a policy provided it is a good one? Apart from a few Scottish extremists, teachers, pupils, parents and the public appear to be showing a rare unity in their support for the idea of profiles. The only faint tarnish on the lustre of the new policy is the possibility that it may help to perpetrate the divisiveness of existing certification procedures whilst doing nothing to hasten the demise of the dual system of 16+ examinations. But even those few who have only half-hearted praise for Sir Keith's initiative, seem content to accept that even if it does no good, at least it will do no harm.

The contrast between this attitude and those encountered ten years ago when the earliest 'field trials' of such records were conducted in Scotland is striking. *Pupils in Profile* recounts faithfully the suspicion and scepticism which were characteristic of attempts to institute profiles at that time. Teachers felt they did not know pupils well enough to make such detailed records. They were sceptical about the existence of cross-curricular skills like 'visual comprehension' and 'oral expression'. They feared the enormous additional workload of mundane clerical tasks such records appeared to require. Above all they were hostile to the overt recording of assessments of what were then called, somewhat euphemistically, 'work-related qualities'. Even designated 'guidance teachers' who were officially responsible for pastoral care, professed their inability to judge 'leadership', 'social competence' and 'reliability', and feared the proliferation of pervasive, possibly computerised 'dossiers' which would herald a quite unacceptable invasion of personal privacy. So controversial was the proposed recording of assessment (albeit positive) on personal qualites that the early Scottish Council for Research in Education prototype, designed by a working party of the Headteachers' Association of Scotland, abandoned all but two of such qualities for inclusion on the profile, leaving only the relatively uncontroversial creativity ('inspiration') and effort ('perspiration'). Despite this, the term 'profile' rapidly became almost synonymous with 'personality' assessment provoking a storm of criticism within the profession which has been well-documented in the press.[1]

What then happened to bring about such a radical change in educational opinion? The conquest of teachers' innate conservatism? The pressure for accountability? The 'great debate' on standards and with it the more effective articulation of employers' concerns? The changing nature of the job market and the demise of the examination meal-ticket? Undoubtedly all these factors played a part in changing professional opinion and with the passage of time one would like to think that considerations of justice also prevailed, with the recognition on the part of the teachers and policy makers of the absurdity of comprehensive schools which must disenfranchise a significant proportion of their pupils.

However, whilst the available literature suggests all these factors had a significant part to play in elevating the early commitment to the institution of a common, comprehensive and cumulative record for all pupils into a major policy issue, it does not explain the radical change that has taken place in teachers' attitudes to making assessments of personal qualities. In place of the worry that existed ten years ago about the possible advent of a Big Brother-style of control if teachers were allowed or indeed required to formalise on a record what could only be very impressionistic data about pupils' personal characteristics, is a growing feeling that schools must be concerned with educating *the whole person* and thus must be prepared to make such a concern explicit in their assessment policy. Now not only is some information on 'personal qualities' normal on summative 'records of achievement' but more and more profiling schemes are blurring the traditional distinction between 'cognitive' and 'affective' development in a new generation of predominantly formative profiles concerned with pupils' development during their school career.

One increasingly popular basis for such records is the institution of pupil recording or of some form of statement, negotiated between teacher and pupil, which avoids any pretence to be more than it palpably is – a careful descriptive comment. Yet, although a shift in emphasis from summative to formative profiles, from grades to descriptive statements and from teacher to negotiated assessments may not seem in itself particularly significant, the very novelty of these approaches has so far largely obscured their potentially fundamental implications. To be done properly, such profile initiatives require a significant elevation in the status and, hence, the time given to the 'pastoral curriculum'. In many cases these profile initiatives imply the institution of a negotiated individualised 'curriculum contract' if teachers are to have the right sort of relationship with pupils. Thus, contrary to many first impressions, the implications of profiles are potentially fundamental, requiring a much greater change of curriculum focus than a simple grafting exercise. Just as formal, external, written examinations played a key part in the nineteenth-century institution of school organisation and curriculum content as we know it today, so their progressive replacement by 'profiles' may well be regarded as the sign that such curriculum models are about to become as outdated as the technology that gave them birth.

In this respect, profiles are far more than just an attempt to redress the imbalance caused by a divisive public examination system – important as this is. Rather they are a manifestation of the changing character of schooling itself. In place of the narrow concern with academic progress reflected in traditional forms of assessment, is a much broader, explicitly pastoral, commitment to the support and development of each pupil as a whole person. This is the explanation as to why teachers are less and less hostile to comprehensive profiles of which statements about personal qualities form an integral part. To the extent that this is so it emphasises the need for the profiles movement to be seen alongside other initiatives such as Active Tutorial Work or the founding of NAPCE itself as part of the more general upsurge of interest in pastoral care. And, like other aspects of pastoral care, the profile movement has been equally neglected by the research community.

As is so often the case with educational policy-making, the 'bandwagon' phenomenon means that development and dissemination activities are not supported by an equivalent volume of impartial evaluation and research. Whilst considerable effort is currently being expended by a variety of institutions and authorities up and down the country concerned to develop their own prototype 'profile', relatively little effort has so far been put into testing out the assumptions on which such profiling is based. We do not know, for example, if pupils will be motivated by the provision of such records. The piles of uncollected CSE certificates in headteachers' offices suggest there are already substantial grounds for doubt in this respect – at least as far as summative statements are concerned. Again, we do not know what effect such records will have on employers' selection procedures. Above all, the available experience can still offer very little guidance on just how the appropriate assessments are to be made. The briefest of incursions into the realm of criterion and norm-referencing, graded and standardised tests, is sufficient to reveal a Pandora's box of technical dilemmas on a scale far greater than those associated with public examinations – and these are proving intractable enough.

The euphoria produced by the grand vision of a newly-humanistic curriculum is no substitute for critical evaluation. Far from welcoming such a change in assessment and curriculum practices, more than one voice has already deplored the advent of 'child-centred' assessment as the basis for a new more insidious basis of social control.[2] Given teachers' acknowledged tendency to stereotype pupils and to extrapolate assumptions about ability from observed behaviour, it is quite possible to argue that continuous, comprehensive and cumulative records will provide an effective and insidious means of reinforcing existing educational disadvantage. Certainly this has happened in countries, such as France, where a form of profiling has been in use for some years.[3]

Respect for evidence is characteristic of the Scots – as is a certain phlegmatic restraint. In Scotland the initial development of the profile idea depended on a careful and sustained programme of research and evaluation, research which attempted to answer some of the fundamental questions which profile recording poses, such as whether teachers can discriminate in their assessment between the different attributes of a pupil or whether the assessments of teachers in different subjects reflect common or specific abilities. Now that the idea of recording is firmly entrenched on political and professional agendas, it is all too easy for such questions to be overlooked. Despite the £10 million of Government money set aside for development studies on Records of Achievement, there is little sign that any of this money will be spent questioning the educational desirability of profiles *per se*. Yet whilst the issues of teacher time, school organisation and employer reaction which currently dominate the evaluation agenda are critical,[4] they are no substitute for a fundamental and measured study of the implications of profiles and the claims made for them.

Particularly pressing is the need for research that locates profiling within a broader programme of enquiry which is concerned with the whole range of pastoral care procedures. As long as the summative *selection* function of profiles is allowed to dominate the research agenda, the more important task of examining the revolutionary potential of such records to change the whole emphasis of schooling away from its traditionally instrumental emphasis in favour of a greater stress on personal development, will continue to be neglected. What is required now therefore are research studies which go beyond the practical problems of implementation which dominate the little research that has already been initiated, to address more fundamental issues such as:

1 What are the implications of the various profile recording assessment techniques currently in use for the effective provision of pastoral care?
2 What happens when teachers and pupils work together to build up a negotiated record?
3 How do such opportunities appear to pupils? Do they encourage motivation, self knowledge and confidence as intended or are they perceived by pupils as 'just another brick in the wall'?
4 How do profiles relate to a school's more general programme of pastoral care in providing for the success of both?
5 What balance between the formative and the summative aspects of profiling provides the best compromise between the educational, pastoral and selection functions of profiles?
6 What relevant experience is available from other countries?

It is a compliment to Sir Keith Joseph that he has not suffered the fate of an earlier opposite number in France, René Haby, when the latter tried to introduce computerised pupil 'dossiers' in 1965 and was greeted with opposition so vitriolic he was forced to abandon at least the computerisation of the dossiers as a formal policy. Undoubtedly the 'dossier' issue was at least one factor in Haby's political demise. Since then French teachers have found other, less confrontary, means of boycotting the dossiers, such as not filling them in. But they remain unpopular. It is a curious irony in English educational policy-making that the very absence of central government machinery to enforce individual policies removes the suspicion and defensiveness that might otherwise hinder the development of bandwagon issues. As it is, these are characteristic and the educational history of recent decades may be read as a sequence of such enthusiasms – child-centred education and curriculum development in the 'sixties, standards, accountability and recession in the 'seventies, vocational training, profiles and pastoral care in the first few years of the 'eighties. Where commitment to an idea pushes policy and practice too far ahead of research evidence – as has happened with the advent of profiles – there is a danger that a potentially good idea will founder for lack of the critical evaluation which would have allowed the anticipation of potential problems. The lack of clarity about where education is going which is increasingly characteristic of a society tortured by its own insecurity is thrown into stark relief by the profiles' issue. Goodwill and enthusiasm are ultimately no substitute for evidence. When the initiative has such portentous implications, this is no mere nicety.

Notes

1 See, for example, Brown, S. 'Pupils in Profile: Enter the Slot Machine Mark II', *TES*, March, 1977; Spooner, D. 'The Profile as a Weapon of Destruction', *Education*, 6 March 1981.

2 See, for example, Jackson, M. 'New Profiling Draws Heavy Criticism', *TES*, 17 August 1982; Ranson, S. 'Towards a tertiary tripartism: new codes of control in the 17+' in Broadfoot, P. (ed.) 1984 *Selection, Certification and Control*, Falmer Press, Sussex.

3 See, for example, Broadfoot, P. 'From public exams to profile assessment: The French experience' in Broadfoot, 1984. Also Broadfoot, P. 'Alternative to public examination in Nuttall, D. (ed.) (forthcoming) *Assessing Educational Achievement*, Falmer Press.

4 See, for example, NAS/UWT 'Pupil Profiles', 1982; NUT 'Profiles', 1983.

Taking the consumer into account

Peter Lang

Introduction

> There is only a limited number of studies of the pupils' point
> of view of schooling in Britain available: therefore a first
> conclusion is that it is a neglected issue in educational
> research. (Meighan 1981)

What Roland Meigham says here refers to research into schooling
generally; if we consider only those aspects of schooling that relate to
pastoral care and personal and social education, his comment appears
almost as an understatement.

Why should pupil perceptions have been so neglected? A number of
explanations have been advanced. Rogers sees it in terms of the attitudes
of researchers and talks of 'A pervasive bias throughout educational
research, namely that it is the teacher who is the significant member of
the class and the one who is most worth studying' (Rogers 1982). Others
have seen the explanation in broad structural and idealogical terms.
Calvet (1975) suggested:

> The reasons for the neglect of the pupils' view may be related
> to the low power and status of both children's and pupils'
> role. The existing definition of the situation appears to
> consider teaching as more important than learning and the
> teacher's activity as more central than pupils.

and Meigham (1981) pointed out that:

> As structural functional views tend to dominate educational
> thinking, so investigations of pupils' views are often seen as
> radical even when they are not.

My own research suggests that as far as schools, as opposed to
researchers, are concerned the neglect is due to the existence of a 'conventional wisdom' (Lang 1982). This parallels Best, Ribbins and Jarvis'
notion (Best *et al* 1983) of the 'conventional wisdom' of pastoral care;
which they describe as a body of worthy, reassuring, unsubstantiated and
unchallenged views about the nature and purpose of pastoral care.

I found that in the schools I investigated a similar 'conventional wisdom' existed that teachers knew and understood what pupils felt and thought.

One important argument of this paper is that a clear understanding of how pupils view things is of great importance if we are to develop more effective and, as far as pupils are concerned, meaningful pastoral care and personal and social education. However, as the quotations above make clear the information presently available is limited, thus a second argument is that research into pupil perspectives should be a priority. The quotations also suggest that the reasons for the neglect of pupil perspectives are something more than mere oversights, and it maybe that a deep-rooted resistance to such investigations exists amongst some of those who control the processes of schooling. Though it is not the intention of this paper to examine this particular possibility, the fact that this could be so is one reason why the case for research into pupil perspectives will be made as clearly and strongly as possible.

I intend to suggest a number of reasons why research into pupil perspectives is needed, and briefly review the work undertaken so far. In the section below I describe the results of a piece of research I undertook into pupil perspectives, and use it to illustrate the value of such research and some of the problems associated with it. Finally, I will discuss the implications of this particular research and more generally the need for further work.

The case for investigating pupil perspectives

The introduction to this book stresses the contribution research can make to the future development of pastoral care. If we accept this need the logic of the research process itself implies that pupil perspectives should be an area for investigation. What real sense does *descriptive* research which leaves out pupils make? In the same way, *prescriptive* research which is intended as a guide to action makes little sense if it does not include some investigation of the effects on pupils, and their understanding. Similarly, action research which involves only teachers can be seen as contrary to its own logic.

There are also several arguments directly relating to what goes on in schools for finding out about the perceptions and feelings of pupils. I have already considered some of these in detail previously (Lang 1983). The most important of these arguments involve the avoidance of waste and the aims and objectives of pastoral work.

Without some attempt to investigate the feelings, understandings and reactions of pupils much of what is done in relation to pastoral care and personal and social education may be misdirected and wasteful. My own research, which is considered in more detail below, has shown that there are significant discrepancies between the assumptions schools make about the problems pupils have and their use and understanding of pastoral systems, the 'conventional wisdom', and what the pupils actually do and feel.

In the case of aims and objectives many of these, if fully articulated, clearly imply some consideration of the pupils' views, feelings and understandings. Work directed towards the personal development of individuals or more effective group relationships must have as one objective the articulation of their views and feelings by the pupils themselves. If it does not it should not count as the activity it claims to be. If we take one of the most frequently-cited and general developmental aims of pastoral care, namely, that of assisting pupils' growth towards personal autonomy, the individual pupil's views and feelings must by definition be central to the concept, and judgements made purely on external teacher-devised criteria are invalid.

For pastoral care and personal and social education to be effective both from the teacher's and the pupil's point of view, pupil perspectives must be understood.

Pupil involvement

The debate about if and how pupils should be involved more directly in their own schooling is not a new one, however, it is now rapidly becoming something that most schools have to consider. This is partly due to the fact that it is frequently a significant element of a number of new initiatives, particularly the personal profiling movement. It is also something which schools may embark on as they find traditional approaches ineffective in the face of the disaffection, apathy and disillusionment common amongst a number of pupils. It is significant that the so-called Hargreaves' report on 'Improving Secondary Schools' stresses the need for pupil involvement and participation (ILEA 1984). If pupils are to be involved more an important first step should be an attempt to understand pupil perspectives, something only achievable through research.

A final point is that if we move towards the situation where teachers are regularly assessed a case could well be made for pupils playing a part. However, such an approach would have to take place within a framework of understanding of the nature and operation of pupil perspectives, which does not exist at present.

Pupil rights

At a rather different level to the arguments presented so far a case can be made that pupils have a right to have their views, perspectives and understandings very much better understood than they are at present. An example of this kind of argument can be found in Shostak and Logan (1984) in their conclusion to 'pupil experience'.

> The task of the educationist is to ensure meaningful participation in social decision-making through resourcing educative experiences. This involves elucidating the meaning social phenomena have for the participants and exploring through thought and action the possibilities inherent in the given situation. Such a conception places a duty on teachers to listen, to respond and de-mystify the received views of the world through critical reflection. Those on the receiving end of adult educative acts have the right to comment critically or appreciatively otherwise it is undemocratic and ineducative. Unless teachers and pupils join forces to reconsider how education may be operated better within society the freedom of the individual is at risk.

Though this argument is perhaps not directly relevant to the case for research into pupil perspectives, it can be seen as adding weight to it.

Existing work on pupil perspectives

Research into pupil perspectives has displayed a range of purposes and methods. As regards 'purposes', research which has involved some consideration of pupil perspectives can be divided into two main categories, (a) where pupil views were sought in relation to some wider question, and were therefore only considered in so far as they related to this question and (b) where the pupil perspectives were essentially the subject of the research work.

Examples of the first category are Ford's investigation of social class in the comprehensive school (Ford 1969), Banks and Finlayson's study of the causes of success and failure in secondary schools (Banks and Finlayson 1973), and Rutter analysing what seemed to differentiate good from bad schools (Rutter *et al* 1979). All included pupil responses in their investigations but only in so far as they contributed to the wider concerns of the study. At the other extreme Willis' (1977) study of the schooling of working class 'lads' in a boys' secondary modern in the Industrial Midlands is entirely focussed on the attitudes and perceptions of the pupils, and the book's argument is constructed from this perspective.

Kitwood's study 'Disclosures to a Stranger' (1980) provides some interesting material and insights as regards the feelings and perspectives of young people. It is based on interviews with a wide sample of adolescents which allowed them a free reign in terms of the topics they discussed. Kitwood's conclusions focus on the themes and patterns that emerge from what the youths said and felt. A number of the conclusions in fact have considerable implications for schools, particularly in connection with young people's views on self-image and the significance of peer group support. One further contribution should be mentioned, this is *Pupil Experience* (1984) edited by John Schostak and Tom Logan. All the papers in this collection do in fact deal with pupil experience and perspectives and many of them are based directly on what pupils have actually said – indeed many of the papers quote pupils at considerable length. The book's approach is well characterised in the following quotation by Schostak:

> I argue that in revealing the world of pupils we either reveal a world unproblematically framed within adult fantasies or see the world of pupils as problematic. Then we may see them caught and perhaps struggling within a net of manipulative intents sometimes achieving a sense of self-responsibility, sometimes failing. I would suggest that researchers must do the latter and try to describe the social structures which facilitate or repress this process.

Though some of the arguments presented would be seen by many as either too radical or too abstract or, perhaps, both, the book does make a significant contribution to the area. This is especially through its emphasis on the need to let pupils talk and to listen to them, and by its stress on the essentially difficult and problematic nature of research into pupils' perspectives.

In relation to 'method', research undertaken to date has involved techniques which cover the full range of traditional research methods. Most typically the views of pupils have been sought through questionnaires in work such as that carried out by Rutter *et al* (1979). In some cases pupil perspectives have been partly inferred from observation, for example, in the case of both Hargreaves and Furlong whose work is discussed below (Hargreaves 1967 and Furlong 1976). Finally, pupil perspectives have been sought through the use of direct interviewing, both structured and unstructured, and also through what is more appropriately described as discussion.

Willis' and Corrigan's studies are based on the use of interviews, conversation and discussion (Willis 1977) and (Corrigan 1979). My own research considered later in this paper involved both the use of questionnaires, and interviews and conversations with pupils.

Problems

There are several problems about the work described below. What has been done does not really amount to a cumulative picture with pieces of research complementing each other, rather it is a set of fragmentary and partial insights. Equally, the work does not provide much in the way of clear guidance as to how further work might be undertaken, particularly by the practising teachers to whom this paper is mainly directed. Finally, it raises a number of unanswered theoretical problems, these are considered below.

Theoretical problems

There are two significant theoretical problems which arise in relation to the work undertaken so far – the problem of reality and problem of grouping. The problem of reality concerns the way pupils' perspectives should be developed on the basis of their responses. My own research and a comparison of that of others suggest that *how* pupils respond to attempts to understand their views may depend on a number of variables including who they are talking to, where they are talking, and what they perceive the purpose of the conversation to be. Thus when discussing the same topic it is likely that pupils will respond differently to a social worker, a researcher, a subject teacher or their tutor. On one occasion when undertaking research in a school I found a significant difference in the way pupils responded when I changed the interview venue from a head of house's room to the home economics flat.

These variations in pupil responses can in fact be interpreted in three different ways. The assumption can be made that what pupils say is more valid under certain sets of circumstances, an assumption in fact made by some researchers, i.e. pupils only really reveal their perspectives to those not involved in school. It can also be assumed that nothing pupils say can be really taken as a valid reflection of reality, that they are in fact unreliable and changeable by nature, a view occasionally taken by a small number of teachers. Finally, the variation in pupil responses can be interpreted in terms of a reflection of a multi-faceted reality, the fact that pupils, like most social beings, do not possess a clear and consistent world picture. If this is the case, different inquirers and different situations will gain access to different parts and aspects of pupil perspectives. I would suggest that this final alternative is in fact the most productive one, and it is one that provides the possibility of making sense of the data. In terms of developing a picture of what pupil perspectives are and how they should be understood, it has to be admitted that this view of pupils' reality makes the development of a theory much more complicated. Nevertheless the development of some sort of explanatory theory to help both researchers and teachers understand the nature and implications of the variations in pupil perspectives is a clear priority.

The way that pupils relate to each other in terms of grouping is another problem raised, but not answered by research so far. How we understand pupil groupings in school has considerable implications for our interpretation of their perspectives. Here again there are two possible views, one sees pupils as belonging to a relatively constant grouping of peers which can be defined in terms of subculture. This view can be related to that which sees pupil perspectives as based on a single view of reality and is reflected in the work of Hargreaves (1967) and Willis (1977). A second, more fluid view of pupil groupings is proposed by Furlong (1976), partly in opposition to Hargreaves' subcultural view. Furlong's study consists of a detailed set of observations centring on one particular pupil – Carol. The main point to arise from study was that any attempt to define the informal peer groups of which Carol was a member would give only a poor indication of the pattern of her interactions. Furlong shows that as the events of the day unfolded so Carol moved from one set to another, interacting closely with some people at one moment but then being quite separate from them, although perhaps still in the same room. The 'interaction sets' that Furlong discusses are primarily defined by shared perceptions. Those pupils who share an understanding of any particular event will be able to communicate this to each other, often by non-verbal means, and thus establish an interaction set.

It is of course likely that both views of pupil groupings have some validity, but Furlong's notion of interaction sets is a helpful one, in that it relates clearly to the idea of a multi-factual reality which is reflected in pupil responses. Pupils involved in a number of different interaction sets might well view things differently at different times.

Research project into pupil perspectives

So far I have argued the case for research into pupil perspectives in relation to pastoral care, and reviewed the work that has been undertaken to date. Now I wish to present an example from my own research to illustrate the value of such work.

The purpose of the research

Both Lang (1977 and 1980) and Best, Jarvis and Ribbins (1977 and 1980) examined the contradictory and problematic nature of pastoral care as it exists in most secondary schools. In my own case this initial interest lead to a specific examination of pupils' views in relation to pastoral care. I hypothesised that just as there was a conventional wisdom about the way pastoral care operated (Best et al 1977), there seemed to be one in relation to teachers' beliefs that pupils adequately understood the nature and function of pastoral care. As I have already implied at the start of this paper this hypothesis turned out to be valid. The research aimed to:

1 provide preliminary information about pupils' feelings about, attitudes towards, and understanding of a number of aspects of pastoral care and roles related to it;

2 give some indication of what the problems were that pupils felt confronted them;

3 explore the extent to which the contradictions noted in the structure and process of pastoral care were reflected in pupils' views;

4 ascertain the key problems pupils saw themselves as experiencing and the range of these problems;

5 map the range of elements pupils saw as going to make up teachers' pastoral roles.

Outline of research and results

A pilot stage involved a number of interviews, discussions and some observation in several different schools. From this work a questionnaire was constructed. In the main research samples were drawn from twenty-four secondary schools throughout the West Midlands' area – in all 393 pupils completed questionnaires. The pupils ranged from the first year through to the upper sixth. The sample included almost equal numbers of boys and girls, and the pupils were drawn from the full range of ability as designated by the schools themselves. An important point was that much of the actual research work involved was undertaken by practising teachers.

The first section of the questionnaire contained four groups of specified problems which piloting had suggested were of concern to school students: these were grouped under the headings 'worries about yourself', 'worries about home', 'worries about other people', 'worries about school'. To each specified problem the respondent had the option of choosing between the following responses:

'hasn't worried me at all'
'worried me a bit'
'worried me a lot'

and, of course, the option of not responding at all. Analysis of the responses showed that the problems included on the questionnaire were significant ones for pupils, in that all pupils answered that at least two had 'worried them a lot', and a number of pupils identified up to ten problems in this category. Equally all problems produced some responses in the 'worried me a lot' category. There was not a great deal of difference between the responses of boys and girls. Girls expressed slightly more worries, while those pupils designated by schools as 'lower ability' expressed more worries.

The following tables (1–4) indicate those problems in each category where over 10% of respondents indicated that it 'worried them a lot'. In cases where the combined percentage for the categories 'has worried me a lot' and 'has worried me a bit' was over 50% this percentage is stated in brackets as this seems to suggest a significant level of importance.

Table 1   Problems grouped under: Worries about yourself

Problem	'has worried me a lot' (%)	Combined 'has worried me a lot' and 'has worried me a bit' (%)
Problems about money	11	—
Being given a bad name I don't deserve	18	—
Having too much work to do	13	—
Being attacked	24	(58)
My future career	38	(80)
Being unemployed	44	(81)
Losing my temper	12	(51)
Not being able to keep up with schoolwork	17	(59)
Lack of confidence in yourself	10	(55)
Keeping myself organised		(58)
Problems about how you feel about yourself		(52)

Table 2   Problems grouped under: Worries at home

Problem	'has worried me a lot' (%)	Combined 'has worried me a lot' and 'has worried' me a bit' (%)
Not really getting on with my parents	20	(51)
Too much pressure on me from my family	13	—

These responses can be used to provide a number of insights and paths for future investigation, particularly by schools themselves. They indicate some of the things which seem to worry pupils most. They also suggest how a profile of the range of worries that young people may have during their secondary school career could be developed, and could form the basis for the development of further research into pupil problems. The pattern of responses could also be used to raise questions about some of the current preoccupations of pastoral care and to indicate some areas which might be profitably covered.

Table 3 Problems grouped under: Worries about you and other people

Problem	'has worried me a lot' (%)	Combined 'has worried me a lot' and 'has worried me a bit' (%)
Other people getting you into trouble	15	(63)
Not getting on well with your friends	15	(53)
Problems with particular friends	14	(57)
Problems with boy/girl friends	13	—
Getting into fights	14	—
People gossiping about me at school	16	(53)

Table 4 Problems grouped under: Worries about school

Problem	'has worried me a lot' (%)	Combined 'has worried me a lot' and 'has worried me a bit' (%)
Problem with being bullied	10	—
Examinations	38	(85)
Not understanding school work	10	(64)
Not being able to do the subject you want	13	—
Problems with staff you feel don't teach you properly	15	(54)

The next section of the questionnaire posed a set of ten problems. A number of the questions were school-based, for example, 'being set more homework than you could cope with'. Pupils were asked to indicate who they would go to about each of the problems. A detailed analysis of the responses to this section has been undertaken, the most significant results being that individuals other than teachers – particularly parents, relatives and peers – were much more frequently mentioned than teachers, and teachers with specifically pastoral roles were mentioned infrequently. This result is particularly worthy of further investigation as, if those for whom pastoral systems are designed are generally unlikely to use them when they have a choice, major questions about the effectiveness of such systems have to be raised. The evidence also provides support for Alastair Macbeth's point made in a paper in this book that 'families should be seen as parallel pastoral systems'. However, answers to questions about the role of the tutor and house/year head were more favourable (discussed on p. 181). The possibility of the differences of reality in different situations arose. It seems that pupils may use these systems more than they feel they would want to in an ideal situation.

The questionnaire also dealt with pupils' views of their teachers. When asked about what they felt concerned teachers most, 80% mentioned getting good exam results, 51% mentioned making sure everyone keeps the rules, 38% keeping pupils quiet and obedient, while 47% mentioned looking after pupils. When asked what makes a really good teacher the single thing mentioned most often (18%) was 'someone who stops and helps you when you need it'. Pupils were also asked what they liked most about teachers. It was possible to sort these responses into a number of categories, these are listed in Table 5 in order of frequency of mention.

The results of the questions about pupils' ideas in relation to teachers are important for several reasons; they suggest that pupils would often like teachers to be more concerned with things other than what pupils think they are primarily interested in. The sort of person a teacher is, and the kind of relationship it is possible to establish with them, are seen as more significant than teaching ability and disciplinary skills, though these are not seen as unimportant. This result is one that gives considerable support to those who stress the importance of pastoral perspectives within schools. It also raises further questions about variations in perspective depending on circumstances – pupils' central concern with discipline and effective teaching has been well-documented in other studies. When pupils were asked what they saw as most important to

Table 5   What pupils liked about teachers

Category	*%*	
Accessibility	33	(includes informal approach, will chat, listens to you, will have a joke, you can talk to them)
Supportive	20	(includes understands pupils, is helpful, understands when the work is too much for you, helps with problems)
Teaching skills	15	(includes teaches well, teaches interestingly, explains, does not set too much homework)
Attitude	14	(includes fair trustworthy, kind, honest, treats you as an adult, strict but not too strict, not nasty, tells you about themselves)
Personality	11	(includes good-natured, not bossy, not boring, nice appearance)

them about their future life, qualification and job-related aspects were mentioned more often than interpersonal-related topics.

Pupils were also asked what two things had worried them most over the last year, and what they thought worried other people of their own age most. The responses were sorted under a number of broad headings according to the general area they related to and Table 6 shows the percentage of responses falling into each category.

Table 6   Pupils' own worries and those attributed to others

Problems	*Boys' problems*		*Girls' problems*	
	Own	Others	Own	Others
School-related	41	24	42	22
Friendship-related	11	14	11	24
Appearance-related	1	8	2	10
Future work-related	5	11	6	10
Personality-related	—	1	1	1
Family- and home-related	8	5	11	6

These results broadly confirmed those from the first part of the questionnaire. They also showed that most pupils felt they had worries, and that they were able to articulate them. The comparisons of the two sets of responses raised a number of significant issues which could well form the basis of further research. For example, it seemed possible in the case of certain more personal problems that pupils projected their own worries on to others.

Pupils were also asked how happy their previous year at school had been. The responses here seemed particularly significant: 53% reported that their last year had been very happy or happy, 34% not too bad or not very enjoyable, and 5% miserable. From the point of view of pastoral care both ends of the scale are important – it is encouraging that over half the pupils are happy but equally worrying that a small but significant percentage admit to being actually miserable. It should be noted, of course, that had it been possible to include those pupils who were not at school in the survey these results could have been different.

Pupils were asked what they thought the most important things about the house/year heads' and tutors' job were and why they thought they had tutorial time. The responses to these questions were sorted into a number of fairly specific categories such as 'fairness' and 'to punish wrongdoers' for heads of house 'knowing the pupils' and 'organising trips and activities' for tutors, and 'talking to your friends' and 'discussing rules' for tutorial time. These categories could well form the basis for the construction of a semantic map of the full range of pupil perspectives of each subject. In the case of house/year heads 36 categories were established; 33 for tutors and 33 for tutorial time.

Table 7   Categories mentioned by more than 10% of respondents

Category	%
House/year head	
Helps with problems	30
Understanding	19
Concerned with discipline and control	13
Concerned with maintaining order and good behaviour	11
Being helpful	10
Tutor	
Helps with problems	23
Understanding	16
Helps/helpful	14
Good relationships, friendly	12
Concerned with control and discipline	12
Tutorial time	
Do homework, catch up on work	21
Getting on together, getting to know people in group better	20
Building relationships with tutor	19
Receiving information	15

The results of these three questions are generally encouraging for pastoral care, though the responses regarding tutorial time are less so. The replies also represent a swing from earlier work during the piloting stages where less favourable responses prevailed (Lang 1981).

One final question should be mentioned, this asked pupils what things they liked most and least about school. At this stage a preliminary examination of those responses suggests that, the single most important positive thing about school for many pupils is that it is the place where they meet their friends. Amongst the negative things appear factors which may seem quite trivial to teachers, but clearly do not appear so to pupils. High amongst the negative feelings are access to the school generally and to toilets particularly, and also the smelly unpleasant nature of many toilets and their lack of paper. An important point about the data from this question was that it often provided significant feedback for the particular schools the pupils attended, if they were prepared to act upon it.

An overall examination of the data revealed a number of other points of interest. The responses quite clearly indicated different levels of awareness in relation to pastoral care amongst pupils; pupils did not necessarily see care and control as mutually exclusive or control and discipline as necessarily bad; strictness, firmness, ability to control were quite often mentioned in favourable terms, together with care, understanding and helpfulness. One function of pastoral care mentioned quite frequently was maintaining the school's good name. Whilst some pupils seemed to see pastoral care as specifically linked with problems of school only, others saw it as concerned with both school, personal and home problems. Administration as a function of pastoral care was clearly central to a number of pupils' perceptions, while fairness and lack of bias were seen as crucial qualities for teachers involved in pastoral care, as was not being too nosey and the ability to talk to pupils as people and equals rather than just pupils.

What the research suggests

The research set out to be a shallow scan of a broad territory; shallow because its rigour was limited, because very small samples were taken in each school and because resources could not stretch to anything other than a fairly basic analysis of the data; broad both because of the large overall sample and its distribution (24 schools), and because of the range of material covered in the final questionnaire. The aim was therefore to acquire as much information as possible of a kind which would provide a basis for further work, both by roughly mapping the area and by highlighting those aspects most needing development.

I have already highlighted a number of hypotheses which had been developed along the lines of grounded theory from the pilot stages of the research (Lang 1983). How have these emerged from the full analysis of the data? *Some pupils are unaware of the contradictions and problems of pastoral care while others recognise them; and pupils vary in their levels of awareness in relation to pastoral care and school generally.* The responses to the open-ended questions generally supported the original hypothesis, certainly to the extent of justifying a more detailed study of what is likely to be an important variable in pupil perceptions. Very much the same could be said of the hypothesis that *there were substantial variations in the degree to which pupils understood the nature and purposes of pastoral care in the school.* The answers given suggested that this was the case.

As regards pupils' feelings towards the pastoral system and role in their school, the original hypothesis was that *these tended towards the unfavourable.* As has already been stated, this view has had to be modified in the light of a substantial number of favourable responses. This supports the theory that pastoral care has recently become more effective, at least in terms of how it is perceived. The hypothesis that *many pupils tend not to use the pastoral system* has found very considerable support from the completed analysis of the data, as did the hypothesis *that pupils regard accessibility, and a humorous and open interpersonal approach* as the most important things about teachers they like and regard as good.

The final contentions that (a) *pupils encounter a number of problems and worries at school* and (b) *the most significant of which are not necessarily those which are mainly dealt with by pastoral care* has received strong support in the case of (a) and general, though not conclusive, support in the case of (b).

The work also confirmed that what has been described as the 'conventional wisdom' of teachers regarding the problems experienced by pupils, and pupils' perceptions and understandings of pastoral care, is to some extent at variance with reality. This underlines the argument of this paper and the importance of investigations of this type by schools themselves. From an analysis of the data it is possible to focus on what seem to be the key problems for pupils and, also, the range of problems that pupils may encounter. It is thus possible to map out the key features of pastoral roles as seen by pupils. In both the cases above the insights provided do not only provide a greater understanding of the present but have implications for the development of pastoral care in the future.

The significance of the research project

The research project described above illustrates several of the points made in this paper. It demonstrates the need for research in terms of its function of highlighting some of the mistaken beliefs schools have about pupil perceptions, i.e. the 'conventional wisdom' held by teachers. It shows the value of such enquiries in terms of the data obtained and the insights gained. In that much of the work was carried out by practising teachers it demonstrates that it is quite feasible for schools to undertake further work of this kind themselves.

Finally, the data underlines some of the problems that have been referred to earlier. Pupils' perceptions are not always consistent and there is a need for analytic and explanatory theory to aid a fuller understanding. The final section of this paper will now consider the major needs and priorities for the future.

New directions

Talking of building up a corpus of data about pupil views that will be of value to teachers, Cohen and Manion (1981) said:

> Although both normative and interpretive studies play an important part in this area, the latter are of particular value to

us for the frequently disturbing way in which they force us to question, and sometimes reject, our commonly accepted assumptions about what we imagine pupils think of their schools, schooling and fellow inmates.

The points that they make reflect very closely the main arguments of this paper, that is, in order to understand pupil perspectives more than commonsense and personal views are needed; an approach involving the methodology of research must be employed if we are to find out what pupils really think, as opposed to what we think they think. Similarly, they suggest that schools often misunderstand what their pupils think. They also support the view that if pupil views are researched the implications of the findings are likely to have a significant effect on schools. The argument of this paper goes even further, suggesting a number of reasons why it is important for schools to undertake such work. Though some research into pupil views has been undertaken by full-time researchers, there is little record of such work being undertaken by practising teachers as individuals or schools as a whole. (This is not to say that no such work is being done, this is discussed below.)

The major new direction suggested in this paper is that teachers individually, schools and groups of schools should set out to research the perspectives, understandings and meanings that pupils have of, and give to, all aspects of pastoral care and personal and social education. This should be undertaken in a much more systematic and coordinated manner than has so far been the case. Clearly it is hoped that full-time researchers will also undertake a great deal more research than has so far been undertaken, but it is to teachers and schools that this paper's message is addressed. My own research has already demonstrated that they can most profitably engage in such undertakings. However, if these developments are to be successful there are a number of points that need to be considered.

Methodology

Cohen and Manion have suggested that interpretative studies will be particularly valuable in gaining understanding of pupil views. Certainly qualitative methods which involve the interpretative approach do offer schools some of the best chances of fully understanding their pupils' perspectives. Involvement, observation and conversation are ways through which the complexity of pupil perspectives may be revealed, nevertheless, it would be a mistake to over-emphasise a particular approach. Burgess (1983) in a useful paper on research specifically states:

> However, as I have commented elsewhere, to equate ethno-graphic methods merely with observation is too narrow and can result in some misinterpretation of the data that

184

are collected. Accordingly, I choose to define ethnographic methods to include observation, participant observation, interviews and documentary evidence.

Teachers and schools are in fact confronted with a number of methodological and related options.

There are what might be described as curriculum options – basically, whether the research is undertaken as a separate activity or incorporated into the curriculum in some way. For example, the research could be written into a personal and social education course and, therefore, undertaken on a regular basis. There are also options in terms of the frames of reference adopted. This particularly relates to whether the research is seen as being aimed at greater understanding and clarity for those who undertake it and the schools on whose behalf it is undertaken, or if it is intended to have an evaluative purpose in relation to some aspect of the school's work. It is also possible that the intention may be to endeavour to increase the involvement of pupils. Alternatively, the research may be conceived as having some form of comparative intent.

The most appropriate range for the research is also something that has to be considered carefully and this in part relates to the frame of reference. The target range may be a single group, several groups within one school, or a group spanning several schools. The actual methods which might be used will also need considerable thought. In terms of qualitative methods the most appropriate are listed by Burgess above, with the possible addition of informal conversation and group discussion. However, there will be occasions where a more quantitative questionnaire-based approach will be most appropriate.

A final question relates to whether the research is best conducted by an 'insider' or 'outsider' to the school or schools. There are problems connected with teachers researching the perspectives of pupils with whom they are too directly involved, though these are by no means insurmountable. However, there may well be a case for schools cooperating on research projects into pupil perspectives, the idea being that groups of teachers should act as researchers in each other's schools.

Practical problems

There are several practical problems which, though not involving the practice of research, relate to its outcomes. The first concerns the ways in which information and understanding obtained through research should be used. Knowing more about pupils, in itself, will make little difference. Also, there is evidence that in some cases schools mishandle information about pupils and on occasions use it in a way that is, at the least, unhelpful to the pupil concerned. Thus schools will have to consider carefully not only how to obtain information but also how it should be used. Closely related to this is the problem of teacher acceptance of pupil perspectives. There is a tendency amongst some teachers to be very resistant to pupils' views and dismissive of them. These teachers are those whose existence is implied in the following statements from two pupils in my research, each answering the question: 'What makes a good teacher?'

> someone who treats you as a person and not just another boy
> someone who doesn't treat us as a crowd of zombies

There will be little point in research providing greater understanding of pupil perspectives if these are then rejected by teachers. The problem of teacher resistance is one that not only needs to be recognised but one which will require positive action on the part of schools.

Finally there is the problem of pupil involvement. Simply to find out what pupils think without responding in some way could well have a negative effect on pupils, especially in the older age range. However, it is in fact quite difficult to involve pupils in a way that seems real to them. Indeed this very point is intimately related to their perspectives. This is certainly a problem that schools undertaking this kind of research will have to address.

Needs

I have considerable evidence of teacher-initiated research into pupil perspectives which has or is being undertaken. However, as yet, most this work has attracted no attention except at a local level. There is a major need for a data bank, at a national rather than local level, which will provide information on all work undertaken or in progress. Such a facility would in itself provide a considerable incentive to further teacher research. However even more than this is needed. Schools and individual teachers need encouragement to embark on research – and once committed they need support and guidance. The collection of more data alone will be counterproductive – this paper has referred on a number of occasions to the problems of interpreting data on pupil perspectives – it is essential that along with increasing amounts of data there is a parallel development of theory to facilitate its interpretation. The provision of such a data bank, of relevant support and guidance and the development of related theory should be a priority amongst NAPCE's aims. In fact it is hoped that the pastoral unit set up jointly by NAPCE and Warwick University will play a significant part in its realisation.

Acknowledgements

I am indebted to Robert Burgess who provided comments on an earlier version of this paper.

The research into pupil perspectives discussed in this paper was supported by a grant from the University of Warwick Research and Innovations Fund Sub-Committee to whom I am most grateful.

Documenting pastoral care: Strategies for teachers and researchers

Robert G. Burgess

Traditionally, much educational research that has taken place in schools and classrooms has utilised questionnaires and interview schedules as many researchers have been concerned to conduct wide-ranging surveys. Yet, as Wax and Wax (1971) have indicated, such a research strategy suggests a 'hit and run' tactic on the part of the researchers who have relatively little involvement with the institutions or the people who become the 'subjects' of study. To overcome some of the problems associated with this style of investigation some researchers have engaged in a style of research known as ethnography or field research or case study. Such research is characterised by a close relationship between the researcher and the researched. It involves the study of people *in situ*. It involves the study of individuals, their actions and their activities in a natural setting. As a consequence of this approach researchers are required to spend time in a school or a classroom making observations, conducting interviews, engaging in conversations and collecting documentary evidence. These research strategies might, therefore, be said to complement those strategies that are commonly associated with the survey tradition. But we might ask about the character of the data that are collected and the involvement of the researcher with those who are researched.

In some studies that utilise an ethnographic approach the researcher has adopted a researcher-teacher role as this facilitates ease of access and allows data collection to take place. Among the researchers who have adopted this stance have been Hargreaves (1967), Lacey (1970), Ball (1981) and Burgess (1983a). All these researchers took a teacher role which involved them teaching a small number of lessons while doing research. In turn, Burgess (1983a) used his teacher role not only to penetrate the world of the classroom but also to take part in the house system and parts of the administrative structure of the school that he studied. In all these investigations, the researcher-teacher role was taken by sociologists who were not only interested in exploring the world of schools and classrooms but also in examining critical debates in the literature of education and the social sciences. Accordingly, some teachers might quite properly ask about the extent to which the findings reported by these researchers are relevant for them.

It is with a view to addressing such issues that commentators such as Stenhouse (1975) have suggested that teachers should not only be the 'subjects' of research enquiries but they should engage in research activities; that is, they should adopt the role of teacher-researchers. Such a role it is argued will result in reflection and evaluation on the part of the teachers concerning their own activities. Accordingly, the issues and questions on which they focus will be concerned with professional activities rather than with the concepts, categories and debates to be found in the literature.[1] However, such investigations share a common set of research strategies with those of the researcher-teacher, for Nixon (1981) has suggested that the most appropriate style of investigation involves qualitative methods such as participant observation, unstructured or informal interviews, and documentary evidence.[2]

Nevertheless, although a common set of research strategies are in use the researcher-teacher and teacher-researcher are rarely brought into contact with each other. In turn, there are too few projects where researchers and teachers work cooperatively together. All too often researchers view teachers as 'subjects' to whom and on whom they do research rather than as individuals *with whom* they may work with a view to producing material that will feed into the professional interests of both groups. Accordingly, many opportunities are lost for cooperative research to take place that would be of direct benefit not only to researchers from higher education but also to teachers in schools.[3] It is the purpose of this paper to examine ways in which some ethnographic or fieldwork methods can be used by researchers and teachers working together to investigate dimensions of pastoral care.

Among those investigators who conduct ethnographic or case study research the emphasis is upon those actions and activities that can be directly observed. Such an emphasis results in research where documentary evidence is overlooked.[4] Yet many contemporary institutions are crammed full of documents, and schools are no exception.[5] In turn, individuals are accustomed to using documents of different kinds in their day to day work and, therefore, it is suggested that these could be used in the conduct of research on pastoral care. In particular, we shall briefly explore the potential of written evidence such as diaries, visual evidence such as photographs, and audio-visual material such as short documentary films. It is these three forms of documentary materials that could be used as a basis for cooperation between researchers *and* teachers working together on studies of pastoral care.

The diary

Diaries are examples of first-hand accounts which may take the form of intimate journals, memoirs or logs of activities (*cf* Allport 1942). However, in the conduct of research, diaries can be used to record and reflect by both researcher and researched. Ethnographic research reports are often based on the materials that are in the researcher's diary, while material that has been recorded by a teacher-informant may give access to areas of a school, to meetings and to classrooms where the researcher has not been present (*cf* Burgess 1983a, pp. 208–235). It would, therefore, appear that diaries might have some potential in research conducted by researchers and teachers, but how can these be devised and used?

The researcher's diary might include three basic forms of notes: substantive accounts, methodological accounts and analytic accounts (*cf* Burgess 1981 and 1982).

Substantive accounts

These should include as much detail as possible about situations that have been observed, events in which the researcher has participated, and activities which others have recounted to the researcher in conversation. In particular, such notes might address the questions: Who? What? When? Where? By addressing these questions the researcher, who might be attending an assembly in a house hall, will be encouraged to write about the people who are present, the activities which occurred, the time period over which they occurred and their location. Such notes can be supplemented by diagrams which allow the researcher to establish ideas about social groups and the various categories of group membership in terms of age, sex, status and race. Such records provide a continuous description of observations and conversations that can be used to help formulate the final report.

Methodological accounts

These accounts may provide a series of first-hand reflections on the research process and the research experience. Once again, such an account has to be constructed with certain questions in mind. First, how were the observations made? Secondly, what role or set of roles was adopted by the researcher? Thirdly, what individuals were selected for study? Fourthly, what kinds of problems occurred throughout the research? If the researcher addresses these questions a continuous account will be provided of the research process that will complement the substantive account, provide a means by which the researcher may identify gaps in the research design, and reflect on possible ways in which data analysis may occur.

Analytic accounts

These may avoid a situation whereby a researcher amasses a vast store of data that are to be sifted and analysed at the end of a project. Analytic accounts might take various forms and could include a note of the key questions that were used to orientate the study, suggestions about concepts that might be used to analyse data, and reflections on data that have been analysed with teachers and other informants who have participated in a study. The researcher might, therefore, use such accounts to record the categories and concepts used at different points within a study to develop hunches and insights about the research data. Data such as these might be subsequently used to form the basis of a research report.

But we might ask: how can this material be used with teachers when investigating dimensions of pastoral care? It is here that the teacher-informant's diary becomes an essential resource that can be used in conjunction with the researcher's substantive account.

The teacher-informant's diary

It is evident that the researcher cannot be present at all situations, events and activities that are relevant to the topic under study. For example, in a comprehensive school that might be subdivided into eight houses, it is impossible for a lone researcher to observe in all these locations during the same time period. Accordingly, a researcher might ask those teachers who are involved with the pastoral system to keep diaries about the activities in which they are engaged in order to extend the process of data collection. For example, in the comprehensive school that I am currently studying I wanted to be able to compare the activities of house heads over a four-week period, yet I knew it would be impossible for me to observe even a small number of the day to day activities in which they engage. Accordingly, I asked house heads to become actively engaged in my research by keeping diaries. However, it was important to outline what I wanted them to do and why. To begin with I wrote a short letter to each house head (Figure 1). On the basis of this letter all but one house head (who thought the record would not be representative) agreed to keep these diaries.

To assist these teachers to record their observations I included the following note in the exercise books which I provided for the diaries:

Diaries

As part of my research I am interested in the work you are doing in the house system. It would help if you could record any events, situations or activities you feel are relevant. You may wish to focus on a particular activity each day or to record details of meetings or conversations in which you are involved. It will be useful to say *who* is involved, *what* is involved, *when* the activity occurs and *where* it occurs. The period to be covered is 11 June to 6 July 1984. It would help if you could provide any background you feel is relevant. If you have any questions please do not hesitate to get in touch with me.

Thank you for your help.

Bob Burgess

Figure 1   Specimen letter

Department of Sociology,
University of Warwick,
Coventry CV4 7AL

3 June 1984

Dear (name of house head)

As you know, one of the areas in which I am particularly interested in connection with my research in the school is pastoral care. Obviously it is impossible for me to spend time in all the houses, but I would like to get some impression of the jobs that a head of house has to do. Accordingly, I did wonder if you would be prepared to keep a brief diary for me between Monday, 11 June and Friday, 6 July. This covers four weeks and I think it would help to give me an impression of the pace at which a head of house works. I would supply an exercise book in which you could record your comments.

I do hope that you will be willing to keep a record as this would be useful to me, no matter how brief it might be. If I do not hear from you by break time on Friday, 8 June, I shall assume that you are happy to do this for me and I will leave an exercise book in your pigeon-hole.

With best wishes,

Yours sincerely,

Bob Burgess

Such notes were written in the hope that the units of study on which the teachers would focus would be sufficiently clear for them to be compared.[6]

The diaries that were returned provided some insight into the ways in which house heads use their time and define their roles. Many of the diary entries refer to the kinds of duties in which a house head is involved. For example, one house head recorded a day's activities:

8.45	Arrive: unlock house-block, go through post.
8.55	Supervise furniture layout in hall for assembly with the Head.
8.57	Information about the day given out to tutors.
9.05	Registers called in assembly.
9.10	Head arrives and conducts assembly.
9.25	Supervised clearing away of furniture.
9.30	Invigilation in exam hall.
10.10–10.40	Bringing pupils' files up to date.
10.50	During break discussed with another teacher some problems with two second-year girls.
11.00	Interviewed girls concerned re: behaviour to one another/other pupils.
11.40	Concluded interview with each promising not to name call/be violent. Shook hands on the agreement. Filed their statements and promises.
11.40–12.10	Arranged a lesson for tomorrow.
1.00	Staff meeting.
1.15 – 3.35	A variety of house administrative tasks. Filing, writing reports of incidents to update files. Rang parent to arrange interview time. Some time spent arranging a trip.

At first glance, it might appear that this is a rather bland catalogue of the events in which a house head is engaged. Yet this record, when compared with other records in the same teacher's diary, reveals a set of categories: conducting interviews, taking statements, handling incidents and writing reports on these activities that recur not only in this teacher's diary but also in other diaries that were returned to me. However, it was not merely those teachers who completed diaries who provided data on activities associated with pastoral care, as I found when I approached those house heads who had not returned their diaries to me. When I asked these individuals for their diaries, explanations were provided to illustrate why they had not maintained a record. For example, a male head of house explained that he had not kept a diary by saying:

> It's like this, Bob – in my house this year the fourth years are really no problem and therefore I have had nothing to write about.

Such a comment might appear to be straightforward in a house which only contained fourth-year pupils, but in a house to which pupils from years one to five were present we might ask *why* he chose to focus on one particular year group. A similar question might also be asked of a woman teacher in another house who remarked:

> I usually spend all my time with fifth-year girls who are always in trouble but as they have gone now (they were on examination leave) I have nothing to put down.

Taken together such evidence suggests that house staff in the school in question appear to spend a disproportionate amount of time with pupils who are involved in a range of misdemeanours. Furthermore, questions can be raised about the ways in which these two members of the house staff interpreted pastoral care for pupils in years one to three.

It is on the basis of such material collected through a researcher's diary and through the diaries of teacher-informants that the potential exists for discussion and dialogue to take place about the ways in which pastoral care is defined, how pastoral staff are used and how time is utilised. However, this is not the only way in which pastoral staff may work collaboratively with a researcher in the course of monitoring their activities as there is further potential in the use of photographic evidence.

Photographs

In common with diaries, photographs have an everyday use. They are a record of events in the past, they are a momento of life and may be classified as public or private documents. The private photograph may be a portrait of a family member, or of a situation or event in which we have participated, while a public photograph is of a situation or event with which we have no direct connection. Yet, as Walker and Wiedel (1985) have indicated, photographs about activities such as classroom life may be private documents that become public when displayed beyond the setting in which they were originally taken.

Like diaries, photographs are often under-used in ethnographic work. Yet ethnographers such as John Collier (1967) have shown the potential of photographic evidence to 'open up' social situations in elementary school classrooms in the United States. Similarly, other social scientists have illustrated the potential of collaborative work between themselves and photographers which has resulted in further sets of data and a greater degree of understanding in a variety of social situations (*cf* Agee and Evans 1969, Berger and Mohr 1967 and 1975, Marsden and Duff 1975). In the course of studying schools and classrooms Rob Walker, working with the professional photographer Janine Wiedel and a mathematics teacher in a comprehensive school, has shown the potential of photographic evidence for collaborative work and for understanding the social world of schools and classrooms.

In writing up their collaborative project Walker and Wiedel (1985) illustrate how a set of photographs taken as part of a fieldwork exercise can be used. Janine Wiedel spent some time observing a mathematics class where she took numerous photographs which could be used by Walker to enter into conversations with teachers and pupils about the activities that occurred in the classroom. In their article, they provide the photographs together with comments which were made by teachers and pupils about the situations portrayed and the discussions that were held with other members of the Mathematics Department about the subject and about methods of teaching.

It would appear that photographs have considerable potential to stimulate collaboration between various groups and individuals. But how could they be used to stimulate a collaborative enquiry in the area of pastoral care? There is the potential for a social and educational researcher not only to work with members of the pastoral team and professional photographers from outside the school but also with photographers drawn from staff members and pupils within the school. Indeed, this approach has the potential not only to be used by those from outside the school but also by small groups of teachers who could utilise this approach to analyse *how* time is spent by a member of the pastoral team in a comprehensive school. For example, just as the diary of a house head gave a written account of the daily routine, so in turn this might be accompanied by a photographic record. The resulting material would then be available not only for collaborative work to take place between teachers and outsiders but also among fellow teachers within a school. In turn, collaborative photographic exercises could also be conducted by pupils and teachers.[7] In a similar way, film-making has this kind of potential.

Film making

As many accounts of documentary materials have indicated the term 'document' is no longer reserved for the collection of written materials that are available in the conventional city record office or county archive. Instead documentary materials include audio and video recordings (*cf* Burgess 1982, pp. 131–160; Burgess 1984a, pp. 123–142). Indeed, the world of schools and classrooms have become a centre of interest with such classic ethnographic studies as Frederick Wiseman's film *High School* made in the USA, and the work of documentary film makers in Britain, such as Roger Graef and Richard Denton. Roger Graef's documentary film *School*, in the *Space Between Words* series, and Richard Denton's *Public School* – a film of the life of Radley College, and *Kingswood* – an account of life in a Northamptonshire comprehensive school, have not only caught the attention of educationalists but also the 'popular press'. Meanwhile, fictional accounts of comprehensive schooling have also loomed large in the popular imagination of both adults and children who have been regular followers of the *Grange Hill* television series.

While it could be argued that a series such as *Kingswood* involved a television producer living on a school site with a film crew, the potential exists for more modest attempts at sound and video recording to occur in our schools. For example, it should be possible for those involved with audio-visual services in a large comprehensive school to plan, perhaps with pupils, a project which would involve collaborative work between different teachers and pupils who might make a documentary record of 'A day in the life of a house head'.[8] Such activity would not only involve collaboration between teachers, but also between teachers and pupils who might come closer to understanding what constituted 'pastoral care' and what activities were involved. Yet, as Graef (1980) has indicated, work involving documentary film-making does involve a number of research problems and ethical problems. In this sense researchers and teachers who work together on collaborative research projects need to be aware of the issues that are involved in the use of written, oral and visual documentary materials.

Some problems in collaborative documentary research

For the purposes of this paper we have focussed on different forms of documentary evidence that might be used where researchers and teachers work together. Although the researcher and the teacher may be working with different kinds of documentary materials the practical, political and ethical problems with which they are confronted are broadly similar.

First there is the issue of selection. Here, we return to the Who? What? When? Where? questions that were raised earlier in relation to written documentary evidence.[9] Similar issues are raised in the selection of photographic evidence, and the material that is either included or excluded in the production of a documentary film. In short, any researcher has to decide on the focus of a particular investigation concerned with pastoral care; a situation that will result in the researcher and the teacher considering the extent to which the setting they are examining is 'typical' or 'natural'.

Secondly, there is the question of privacy and confidentiality. In some senses this is particularly acute where photography and film-making are concerned. Accordingly, provision has to be made so that individuals can decide what material can be included or excluded from a project.[10]

Thirdly, the investigations focus on natural settings rather than contrived events. Accordingly, this involves a situation whereby the researcher needs to negotiate access to a social setting and to seek permission to utilise data that are drawn not merely from formal encounters but also from informal settings, casual conversations and a variety of different locations.

Fourthly, there is the question of reporting, whereby the researcher and the teacher need to be clear about what can be reported to whom and under what circumstances. This point of procedure touches on a crucial political aspect of a research project, the issue of consent and avoiding any harm to individuals.[11] For example, Graef (1980) indicates that in the production of a documentary film any secrets or irrelevant personal remarks are normally deleted, other than in circumstances where their inclusion has been negotiated with those individuals concerned on the basis of relevance.

Fifthly, there is the question of control over data and who holds rights over data that have been collected but are not used and who owns the data that have been collected.

Such issues are common to much ethnographic research where professional groups such as the American Anthropological Association (1971) and the British Sociological Association (1973) have attempted to establish 'codes' of ethics and statements of ethical principles concerning the conduct of such research. In turn, documentary film makers such as Graef (1980) have established sets of 'rules' that attempt to come to terms with the practical, political and ethical problems that surround the conduct of any social enquiry. While many commentators (Roth 1970, Barnes 1979, Burgess 1984a) have indicated that a set of rules are of little value, they do point to the importance of establishing frameworks where moral compromise is essential. It is, therefore, important for teachers and researchers to consider the extent to which a framework is important for those engaged in collaborative research.

Conclusion

At this point we might consider the relative merits of a collaborative research enterprise between researchers and teachers in the field of pastoral care. Among the uses of such collaborative enquiries are:

1 As a means of providing a record of what constitutes pastoral care in different institutions.
2 As a means of providing different sets of data that may be compared.
3 As a means of stimulating reflexivity and critical awareness among teachers and researchers with a view to narrowing, if not closing, the gap between theory and practice.
4 As a means of encouraging teachers and researchers to critically evaluate systems of pastoral care and to create knowledge that would be of relevance to further practice and policy.

It would therefore appear that there is much potential in developing research where researchers *and* teachers work cooperatively with each other as both professional groups may benefit. Here, we have merely focussed on documentary evidence being used to study pastoral care but other research strategies need to be considered when developing collaborative investigations not only on pastoral care but on other dimensions of the familiar world of schools and classrooms.

Notes

1 For a further elaboration of this idea by Lawrence Stenhouse, see Stenhouse 1979 and 1981, and for discussion of the way in which this strategy might be used in an analysis of pastoral care, see Burgess 1983b, Winter 1983, Burgess 1984b.
2 For a discussion of some of the problems involved in using this research strategy to conduct teacher-research, see Burgess 1980.
3 In addition, a collaborative project involving accounts from teachers as well as researchers would involve the principle of triangulation of investigators; an aid to research reliability and validity (see Denzin 1970, Burgess 1984a, for further discussion).
4 For a discussion of the problems involved when historical and documentary evidence is omitted from view, see Burgess 1982, Goodson 1983, Woods 1983, Goodson 1985.
5 For a detailed discussion of the potential of documentary evidence in social research see, for example, Bertaux 1981, Plummer 1983.
6 For a critique of this style of diary-keeping by teacher-informants see the discussion provided by Hilary Burgess on the basis of her work with primary school teachers (*cf* Burgess, H. 1983 and 1985). In turn she also suggests a more structured approach to diary-keeping by teacher-informants.
7 For a discussion of collaborative projects between teachers and pupils, see Pollard 1985.
8 For an audio-account of a day in the life of a house head see

Schostak 1984. Copies of this paper can be obtained from the author at the School of Education, University of East Anglia, Norwich, England.

9 For a discussion of some of these issues, together with other problems associated with keeping diaries on a research project, see Griffiths 1985.

10 For example, members of the Centre for Applied Research in Education, University of East Anglia, have entered into discussions with all those with whom they conduct research work. As a result, teachers are given the opportunity to view the data that are collected by researchers and can delete or veto elements of the material. In turn, they are also invited to sign the following form.

CENTRE FOR APPLIED RESEARCH IN EDUCATION

University of East Anglia, Norwich NR4 7TJ

I am prepared to give authority for the transcript of this interview of myself by (name of fieldworker) to be reproduced in an anonymous form for use in conferences, teaching and research and for lodgement in an archive in print or microfiche which shall be open to researchers.

Signed ....

Date ....

Source: Stenhouse 1984, p. 227

While such a strategy might seem to point towards reports which are heavily censored, Stenhouse (1984) indicates that this rarely occurs and that only minor amendments are made.

11 For discussions of informed consent see Barnes 1979, Bulmer 1982, and for the difficulties in handling this principle in the field see Burgess 1985.

Acknowledgements

I am indebted to Hilary Burgess, Gordon Griffiths and Peter Lang who provided comments on an earlier version of this paper. The research that is briefly referred to in this paper is part of a larger project that was made possible by a grant from the University of Warwick Research and Innovations Fund Sub-Committee to whom I am most grateful.

The future research needs of pastoral care in education

Peter Lang and Michael Marland

The following material contains the editors' summary of the main issues that were raised during the final discussion sessions of the Warwick seminar (1984). These were focussed on the future research needs of pastoral care. Though what follows takes the form of a useful agenda for future developments, it is the editors' construction of a wide range of ideas and suggestions. It should not therefore be taken as necessarily reflecting the precise views of any particular seminar participant.

Introduction

Research has so far contributed little to thinking about pastoral care and its practice in an educational context. This is for the simple reason that, until the 1980s, little research had actually been carried out. Consequently, pastoral care suffers from a lack of knowledge about itself and its role in the educational process; about its relationship to other caring agencies; and about the connections that could exist between schools and these other agencies.

The purposes of this agenda are:

1 to make evident to a broadly-conceived research community the opportunities for research and the areas for research within pastoral care in education;
2 to alert national and local governmental and funding bodies that much research needs to be carried out into pastoral care.

Researching issues of principle

All those concerned with pastoral care in an educational context should analyse, clarify and justify the concept of pastoral care in education as manifested in specific aims, attitudes, practices and organisational systems. A wide range of problems, often not recognised or acknowledged, can be created by different perceptions of pastoral care and the various related justifications made on behalf of pastoral care in individual schools and across a wider spectrum.

Research should draw out and clarify:

1   the asssumptions made about the nature and value of pastoral care and whether they are justifiable;
2   the conception of education which underpins what is done in the name of pastoral care and the notion of personal and social education, and its relationship to pastoral care and to education generally;
3   the respective rights and duties of the various parties – teachers, pupils and parents – involved in the pastoral care process;
4   problems of value which arise from the practice of pastoral care in state schools within a pluralist democracy, identifying whether any determinate conception of human good – or of human life as a whole – is being presupposed and what values should underpin pastoral care in this context;
5   how far pastoral care work recognises, reinforces, cross-cuts, or denies the diverse beliefs and practices of different cultural groups in society;
6   the philosophy and processes of pastoral care both as it is perceived by teachers, parents, schools and other institutions and agencies, and as it is practised;
7   the methodologies appropriate for the design, conduct and evaluation of research on pastoral care systems.

Researching fundamental empirical issues

Research should establish what actually happens in schools under the description of pastoral care and should analyse the assumptions, shared or otherwise, on which teachers base their pastoral care aims and activities. It should also establish which groups in society share particular assumptions about pastoral care in education and should explore why they hold the assumptions they do.

School-based development of pastoral care

Schools should be helped to consider their objectives effectively, to set out the criteria and methods for making decisions about pastoral care and to develop and use appropriate strategies for implementation. The role of case studies in helping schools with this task should not be neglected.

Perceptions of pastoral care

Teachers, parents and pupils should be helped to perceive the various goals of pastoral care that exist in different sorts of school. These are often related to different conceptions of what it is to be a pupil, and different expectations of those occupying that role.

Pupils and pastoral care

The pastoral dimension of learning requires research into how personal and social development can be promoted throughout pupils' school and classroom experience, particularly through the curriculum and through aspects of introduction to the classroom and the school.

Work is needed on pupils' own perception of pastoral care and on whether they see their needs being met. Research should include:

1 analysing school practice so as to understand the processes through which children learn to take up the pupil role and own it for themselves;
2 helping pupils to define, negotiate, understand and make use of their role in school and what might be involved in taking on a particular pupil role;
3 helping teachers to identify, understand and evaluate the various roles they make available to the pupil as learner;
4 studying pupils' routes through the pastoral care and pastoral curriculum arrangements in schools, how pupils experience them, and what factors – such as gender – shape these experiences;
5 analysing what pupils themselves see as their needs which require attention in pastoral care;
6 discovering the pastoral care needs of 16–19 year-olds who are not in educational institutions, and of people of all ages who have special needs because of particular disabilities.

Home/school links

Fundamental questions remain as to how to bring home and school together most effectively. Research should concentrate on the relationship between the pastoral care provision in the family and the pastoral care system in the school, and how the two can be mutually supportive. More specifically, research should investigate:

1 what parents see as the responsibilities, obligations, capacities, caring styles and wishes of teachers, and what teachers see as those of parents;

2 the tensions arising from different perceptions of the relative responsibilities of teachers and parents in a pluralistic society;
3 the circumstances in which families have to cope with the deficiencies of the school, and vice versa.

The relationship between pastoral care and other aspects of school

The way a school is organised and the style and role adopted by a headteacher are often crucial to the harmonious integration of pastoral aims and structures with the other aspects of what a school is trying to do. Much depends on who controls pastoral care within a school.

Research should seek to identify:

1 how far pastoral care in educational institutions is restricted by inappropriate administrative structures;
2 when the aims of pastoral care are being hampered by the decision-making processes established to put them into effect.

It should also seek to:

1 aid the development of school-based solutions to problems hindering harmonious integration and the effective delivery of services;
2 help to develop general support services for pastoral care staff.

The school and other caring agencies

The possibilities of cooperation between schools and caring agencies outside the school should be investigated. In addition, research is needed on points of conflict arising, for example, from the different aims, ideologies, bureaucracies and views of professional status.

Research should investigate how agencies outside the school may help teachers effectively fulfil their pastoral care responsibilities towards all pupils, and not simply those pupils about whom the caring agencies are specifically concerned.

Confidentiality

Research should be carried out into issues of confidentiality between teachers, parents and pupils, between schools and other agencies, and between professions concerned with children. Particular emphasis should be put on school records and profiles.

Handling conflict: culture, ethnicity and gender

Research should help schools face and resolve conflicts of value, attitude and perception over pastoral care and its role in a multi-cultural society.

The literature of pastoral care has, to date, hardly addressed itself to equal opportunity or to multi-cultural education. If equal opportunity is to be a real educational issue, it must be located in the central guidance processes of the school: pastoral care. Therefore, research into pastoral care in education should also focus on issues of culture, ethnicity and gender. Wherever possible, research in this area should take account of the key variables used in traditional educational research. Such an approach would facilitate secondary data analysis.

There should be a comparative case-study between the maintained and private sectors of education, and within different societies, in order to highlight the relationship between pastoral care practice and its social purposes and consequences.

Pastoral care and special educational needs

In the light of the 1981 Education Act, research is needed on the contribution of pastoral care to the development of pupils' and teachers' behaviour and attitudes with respect to disability.

Research should investigate:

1 the contribution of pastoral care in meeting the special educational needs of pupils with learning difficulties and pupils who present behavioural problems;

2 the contribution of pastoral care to the integration of pupils with physical and/or sensory disabilities into the mainstream;

3 the extent to which the aims, scope and practice of pastoral care are determined by a school's organisation of its special education department (sometimes still known as the remedial department).

Evaluation

Research should not set out merely to evaluate different pastoral care systems. It should also provide approaches and evaluative tools to enable teachers to carry out their own school-based evaluation of their practices and attitudes.

Training for pastoral care

Research is required into the provision, practice and effectiveness of training aimed to help pastoral care staff to develop their principles and practice.

Research should seek to:

1 identify more closely the tasks and skills which enable teachers and others to carry out successfully their various pastoral roles, including those of teachers as tutors, as subject specialists, as pastoral team leaders and as senior pastoral managers;
2 encourage evaluations of the various ways in which training is delivered — initial, induction, and in-service.

Following the NAPCE pilot study on training, policies towards the provision of training should be examined in detail. Research should analyse practice at school, local authority and national level. NAPCE should aim to influence policy on training and should do so in the context of considering the wider staff development processes. The pastoral care of staff themselves is an issue which requires greater recognition.

Research across sectors and age-groups

Discussion and research about pastoral care tend to focus on the secondary sector of education. The structures and ways of working of care systems in all sectors of education should be investigated with a view to developing a cross-fertilisation of appropriate ideas and methods and a more coherent continuum of care through education. The differences between general pastoral care and specific counselling should be analysed.

The establishment of new schools and colleges offer opportunities for case-studies that can follow through the development of a pastoral care structure from its beginning.

National and LEA policy on pastoral care

It is essential that the Department of Education and Science and local education authorities take on a greater responsibility for the development of pastoral care, and provide appropriate and agreed forms of support. Local education authorities should be studied to see how they currently arrive at policies for pastoral care. Such work should also focus on authority-based projects which provide care through welfare services, voluntary services and self-help agencies, whether or not they involve schools.

Support for small-scale research

There has been a growth in the number of small-scale research projects into pastoral care. This development should now be supported in a formal and systematic way. NAPCE should set up a research committee to monitor and advise on research issues. It should also take on a clearing house function, providing an information bank for researchers and practitioners. A detailed annotated bibliography of pastoral care research and expertise should be established.

Research methodology

Researchers should take account of the diverse range of research methodologies: quantitative and qualitative. Research methodology should be discussed and evaluated in relation to the character of the research problems being considered.

Defining good practice in pastoral care

In all research into pastoral care, a positive approach should be taken to what is happening in the education system. While the notions of 'good practice' and the 'good school' raise as many questions as they seek to answer, this should not preclude the documenting of initiatives and the locating and disseminating of what is considered to be 'good practice'.

Conclusion

Peter Lang

In the introduction it was stressed that this book was more concerned with the identification of approaches and directions, than with pre-specified destinations. Indeed if precise destinations had been indicated, this would have contradicted much of what the book intends to promote. What, then, is it hoped might be the outcomes of the use of the book by schools, teachers and others involved in education?

Firstly, that it will encourage the development of new attitudes and approaches to innovation and practice in schools and elsewhere, and second, that the arguments and analyses presented in the papers will stimulate an active response by teachers to research and evaluation in pastoral care. Finally, that a combination of these two points will mean that further problems and questions can be identified and tackled in appropriate ways. This conclusion will be mainly concerned with a brief consideration of these three areas.

Attitude and approach

The book's introduction emphasised the importance of rigorous analysis and systematic evaluation as necessary accompaniments to innovation, and suggested that research was the most effective way of incorporating these elements in practice.

The papers have been selected in order to illustrate the value of this approach as well as for their focus on a range of important areas relating to pastoral care. Pring's paper, for example, illustrates clearly the importance of analysis in his discussion of the relationship between education and personal development. The importance of rigour or, more to the point, the serious implications of its absence are underlined by the discussion and argument in the papers by Broadfoot and Hargreaves on profiling. These raise important questions about the contradictory hopes and expectations carried by profiling, and expose the rapid and unexamined ways in which its use has spread. They reveal a number of areas of practice in the use of profiles, about which there is very little knowledge or understanding. The papers emphasise both the problems which can result from a lack of rigour and the need for a careful analysis of future implementations. The papers by Best and Maher, and by Lang, demonstrate the value of and need for systematic evaluation. The topic of Lang's paper 'researching pupil perspectives' has considerable implications for evaluation. He illustrates how and why the consideration of pupils' views has been neglected in the past and shows how such investigations could be valuable in future. The research described in Best and Maher's paper, albeit of fairly limited scope, shows clearly the need for a systematic evaluation of the training that teachers receive for their pastoral roles.

Finally, Ribbins and Best's paper which opens the book is in fact an example of all three qualities and is in itself a piece of research (something the writers draw attention to on their first page). Thus, a major aim of the book has been to persuade its readers of the value of research, both to our present understanding and knowledge of pastoral care, and also as an approach for future evaluation and analysis of its developing practice.

Response to the papers

Although the papers included in this book can be seen to illustrate the value of its central theme, i.e. research, this is by no means their only value. Each of the papers can stand on its own as a significant comment on some contemporary aspect of pastoral care. All have implications both in terms of a critique of current practice, and as a basis for future research and policy. As well as this the analysis can operate at different levels. For example, some of Macbeth's suggestions about how schools might endeavour to encourage parental involvement are extremely practical, as are some of the ways Lang proposes that schools might discover what pupils think. Many of the suggestions made by Marland are also at a very practical level and of a sort that will have immediate relevance and appeal to schools. His clear and accessible presentation could lead to immediate practical responses in schools.

It is hoped that every paper included in this book has some significance for schools. We believe that none deal with an area that teachers can really afford to neglect. However, it is also recognised that the nature and settings of particular institution and the interests of individual teachers will mean that some specific papers will have greater impact than others. Certainly the editors would like to think that each paper in the book will provoke a number of responses which go beyond passive agreement into positive action.

In the first instance this book is directed at teachers and schools but, as has been said in the introduction, it is also directed at a much wider audience. This is perhaps most clearly illustrated by the section which immediately precedes this conclusion. Included in this are the results of discussions between the wide range of participants at the Warwick seminar. These proposals and suggestions outline a number of future developments seen as priorities by a group which included a very broad spread of interest, perspective and expertise. Clearly many of the future research needs which are included in the editors' outline of the group's final discussion could not be taken up by schools and their teachers alone. Some are too broad in conception, and some would require a range of expertise, not all of which is available in school. The nature of these proposals, and the book's overall contents and theme generally underline another approach which needs to be promoted. This is something already touched on by Burgess in his paper on collaborative research. If this book is to succeed in its aims it will need more than simply individual responses from teachers, schools, LEAs, training institutions, academics, researchers and HMIs. The response must, at least in part, be collaborative. If the aims of the approach are not shared and understood widely then the level of success is almost certain to be considerably reduced.

Recognising problems

The papers in this book and the overall approach it promotes have drawn attention to a range of problems and unanswered questions which permeate the theory and practice of pastoral care. It is suggested here that unless the attitudes and approaches associated with research are adopted, many of these issues might go unnoticed. However a further point needs making. Although these problems and questions seem to be central now, this may not always be the case. Indeed in the period between the Warwick seminar and the production of this book, a number of relatively new problems and questions have been gaining in significance. Many of these of course are not new: it is the increasing awareness of them that is new.

There are, for example, a whole range of problems for pastoral care and personal and social education which relate to what have been described as the 'new vocationalism'. In addition to the range of schemes which take place during and after the pupil's school career, there are the problems of the 16–19 age group, particularly in the light of an ever-contracting youth employment market. What, for example, is the correct stance for those involved in counselling on TVEI schemes in areas where youth unemployment is virtually the norm? Can those involved ignore the political dimension of 'preparation for life' and 'life skills' programmes? How can the inherent tension between autonomous individual and conforming employees or training scheme attender be resolved within the pastoral curriculum?

The increasing popularity of study skills poses similar questions. Are we simply dealing with a set of techniques and strategies designed to help pupils cope more efficiently with the curricula diet they are currently offered? Or are we concerned with wider questions, for example, what constitutes an 'educated person' in an information society, where work may be home-based and be related more closely to service and processing rather than manufacturing industry? Or again, what constitutes an 'educated person' in the liberal arts/aesthetic sense of human culture? It is becoming increasingly clear that there are a number of uneasy relationships which must be addressed. One of these is the relationship between pastoral care and personal and social education. Another is the one between the pastoral curriculum and moral education.

The recent dramatic uptake by LEAs of programmes of activity-based tutorial work has made the researching of the effects of such programmes a priority. This is particularly important because although the programmes and techniques themselves can make a valuable contribution to tutorial work, whether or not they in fact do so varies very significantly between schools. The reasons for this need to be clearly understood.

Finally, an awareness of the need for a more systematic approach to both pastoral care and personal and social education in the primary school is just beginning to emerge. The training and curricula implications of this are very significant. Moreover such developments will, of course, ultimately effect what goes on in secondary schools. Certainly it is hoped that the themes of this book will be seen to be as significant for the primary area as for the secondary.

The above are presented as examples of relatively new questions and problems currently emerging. It is not suggested that there are not others. Equally, it is clear that in the next few years new ones will emerge. However, even when such changes of emphasis have taken place, it is hoped that this book will still have a significant contribution to make, because it is the approach to problems and questions, especially through the research dimension which has been our most central concern. Although the nature of educational issues will change, hopefully the attitude and approach embodied in this book will remain relevant.

Notes on contributors

David Armstrong trained as a psychologist and worked at the Tavistock Institute of Human Relation and the Centre for Science Education, Chelsea College, before joining The Grubb Institute as a consultant in 1979. Since then he has worked on a number of applied research projects at The Grubb Institute on the transition of young people into working life. These have included work with the young unemployed, those on MSC schemes, school and college students. He has also been involved in management training with heads and deputy heads and in advisory work with schools, the probation service, the prison department, voluntary organisations and industry.

Ron Best is Head of the Educational Research Centre at the Chelmer Institute of Higher Education. He has a continuing interest in pastoral care in education, based on an SSRC-funded project from 1978 to 1981. He is currently researching remedial provision in the comprehensive school, and just beginning research into aspects of school library provision (British Library-funded). He co-authored *Perspectives on Pastoral Care* (1980) and *Education and Care* (1983). He co-ordinates and teaches the 'Care and counselling' option in the in-service B.Ed. at the Chelmer Institute and is interested in researching the adequacy of teacher-training for pastoral roles.

Patricia Broadfoot is Lecturer in Education at Bristol University. She has a long-standing interest in profiles, dating from *Pupils in Profile* (1977). She is particularly interested in pupil self-assessment/negotiation and in the experience of 'profiling' in other countries, e.g. France with a strong guidance/pastoral orientation. She co-authored *Keeping Track of Teaching* (1982) (about assessment for diagnosis and guidance). Most recently she has edited a collection of papers on social issues in assessment: *Selection, Certification and Control* (1984), in which her own and several other papers focus on the potential control function of 'profile assessment'.

Dr Robert Burgess is a Senior Lecturer in Sociology at the University of Warwick. His teaching and research interests include the sociology of education and social research methodology; especially field research.

210

He is particularly interested in ethnography and its use in educational settings. He is the author of *Experiencing Comprehensive Education: A Study of Bishop McGregor School* (1983), *In the Field: An Introduction to Field Research* (1984), *Education, Schools and Schooling* (1985) and the editor of *Teaching Research Methodology to Postgraduates: A Survey of Courses in the UK* (1979), *Field Research: A Sourcebook and Field Manual* (1982), *Exploring Society* (1982), *The Research Process in Educational Settings: Ten Case Studies* (1984) and *Field Methods in the Study of Education* (1984). He was Honorary General Secretary of the British Sociological Association, 1982–4.

Andy Hargreaves has taught in a school, a college of education, the Open University and the University of Oxford. He is now Lecturer in Education at the University of Warwick. He has published widely in the areas of classroom research, curriculum decision-making and education policy. He is co-editor with Martyn Hammersley of *Curriculum Practice: Some sociological case studies* (1983) and with Peter Woods of *Classrooms and Staffrooms* (1984). He is currently involved in developing the 'p' (personal record) component of the Oxford Certificate of Education Achievement and his current research interests are in the broad area of Records of Achievement/pupil profiles.

Daphne Johnson is Senior Research Fellow in the Department of Government, Brunel University. She recently completed a three-year research study of 'School governing bodies', funded by DES, 1980–1983, and is now engaged in a two-year study of 'Patterns of co-existence in the public and private sectors of education', funded by Leverhulme Trust, 1983–1985. She has co-written *Secondary Schools and the Welfare Network* (1980), *Family and School* (1983), and *School Governing Bodies* (forthcoming). She co-edited *Disaffected Pupils* (1981).

Peter Lang is Lecturer in Education at the University of Warwick. He is conducting on-going research into pupil perspectives on various aspects of school and inter-personal relationships, with particular emphasis on pastoral care. He is about to embark on research in the development and practice of personal and social education in schools. He wrote 'It's easier to punish us in small groups' for the *Times Educational Supplement* in 1977, and contributed to *Helping the Low Achiever in the Secondary School*, Educational Review Occasional Papers 7 (1980). Recently he wrote 'How Pupils See It: Looking at pupil perceptions' in the NAPCE journal *Pastoral Care in Education*, 1, 3 (1982). He co-authored with Peter Ribbins the entry 'Pastoral care' in the new Pergamon International Encyclopedia of Education Research and Studies (1985) and is editing a series of books on pastoral care with him.

Dr Bill Law is Senior Fellow and Co-ordinator of the Training and Development Unit (Schools) at NICEC. For several years he was a careers teacher and school counsellor, and later a Lecturer in Education in the Guidance Unit at the University of Reading. He is author of *Decide for Yourself* and *The Uses and Abuses of Profiling* (1984), he is co-author (with Tony Watts) of *Schools, Careers and Community* (1977), and has written many articles on career development and on guidance and counselling. He has planning, development and administrative responsibility within NICEC for training, consultancy and project work designed to improve guidance provision in schools. He also edits the *NICEC Training and Development Bulletin*.

Dr Alastair Macbeth is Senior Lecturer in Education in the Department of Education at the University of Glasgow. A former schoolteacher and headteacher, he specialises in educational administration and is particularly concerned with relations between schools and homes. He directed the EEC School and Family Project, the report of which (entitled 'The Child Between') was published by the EEC in 1984. He has carried out several research studies for the Scottish Education Department, including official investigations of Scottish School Councils and the implementation of statutory requirements about parental choice of school. He is educational adviser to various organisations including the European Parents' Association and the Scottish Parent Teacher Council.

Peter Maher is Deputy Headteacher (Head of Upper School) at Langdon School, East Ham, London. He is involved in research into 'Training and support for pastoral care' on behalf of NAPCE, and 'Leadership effectiveness in a secondary education setting', as part of a post-graduate Diploma in Management.

Michael Marland is Headmaster at North Westminster Community School and Honorary Professor of Education at Warwick University. He is a co-founder of NAPCE and is its first chairman. His publications include *Pastoral Care* (1974), (Ed.) *Sexual Differentiation in Schooling* (1983), and *Information Skills in the Secondary Curriculum* (1981).

Richard Pring is Professor of Education at the University of Exeter. Previously he was in the Curriculum Studies Department at the Institute of Education, University of London. He has taught in two London comprehensive schools, and has continued to teach in schools since his arrival at Exeter University. He has recently been appointed Editor of the *British Journal of Educational Studies*. His academic background (undergraduate studies and doctorate) is in philosophy. Books published are *Knowledge and Schooling* (1976) and *Personal and Social Education* *in the Curriculum* (1984). Current interests lie in social philosophy, particularly in the social ideas that are underpinning developments in secondary education.

Peter Ribbins is Lecturer in Educational Administration at the University of Birmingham. He is interested in various aspects of pastoral care in the secondary school, particularly the role of the subject department in the secondary school. He was the co-author of *Education and Care* (1983), and co-editor of *Perspectives on Pastoral Care* (1980). He is particularly interested in educational administration and contributed to *Educational Administration and Management* (BEMAS). He is the Executive Editor of the NAPCE journal, *Pastoral Care in Education*, and chairman of BEMAS Research Committee. He co-authored with Peter Lang the entry 'Pastoral care' in the new Pergamon International Encyclopedia of Education Research and Studies (1985) and is editing a series of books on pastoral care with him.

Rick Rogers is a journalist and editor. He regularly contributes to the *Guardian*, the *TES* and the *New Statesman* and is the Education Researcher for Thames Television's News Unit. He wrote the article on NAPCE in *The Times Educational Supplement*, 25 February 1983. 'The Caring Bit'. In 1980 his first book was published: *Crowther to Warnock: How 14 Reports Tried to Change Children's Lives* (1980).

Tony Watts is Director of the National Institute for Careers Education and Counselling (NICEC), which is jointly sponsored by the Careers Research and Advisory Centre (CRAC) and Hatfield Polytechnic. He holds degrees in history (Cambridge) and in sociology (York), and was a joint-founder of CRAC. He is Executive Editor of the *British Journal of Guidance and Counselling*, and his recent books include *Work Experience and Schools* (1983a) and *Education, Unemployment and the Future of Work* (1983b). He has carried out a number of research projects for various bodies including the Manpower Services Commission and the Further Education Unit, and has acted as a consultant to various international organisations including OECD and UNESCO.

Appendix: Discussion of papers

This appendix comprises edited reports of a selection of the discussions on the papers presented to the NAPCE seminar. The selection has been made on the grounds that a discussion added valuable evidence about the issues raised, offered further cogent arguments for or against the paper's conclusions, and highlighted omissions or controversial points in the paper presented.

Session two: How do we help children learn from their experience in the school organisation? An important area for pastoral research
David Armstrong and John Bazalgette

The notion of a child taking up a pupil role raises considerable difficulties for pastoral care staff. Some reject the idea; others disagree as to the nature and function of such a role. But the main problem seems to be the lack of focus in schools as to the role of pastoral care itself well before they begin to consider defining a pupil role in school. There are apparent contradictions and unanswered questions in the current formulation of pupils taking up roles in school. For example, while the function of welfare concern and the pastoral curriculum is seen to be to keep a child socialised within the school, it is also acknowledged that the proper exercising of pastoral care may well make it more difficult for a child to stay in such a passive pupil role.

Secondly, there is doubt as to whether a school should confront head-on children's distress over, for example, what may be happening at home, or seek to contain that distress and enable them to get through the school day. In effect, how far can or should the school move in and out of sustaining the defined pupil role? Is the pupil in a different role while being the recipient of pastoral care which is not in the role of being a pupil?

David Armstrong assumes in his paper that the pastoral function of a school is to deal with the problems created because pupils cannot take up their defined role. Thus a variety of feelings and anxieties are thrown up which have their origins in the actual experience of school rather than outside it. These are then dealt with as if they are problems to do with a child's individual circumstances. Indeed, school sometimes reinforces the anxieties brought in from home rather than helping the child to work effectively within school and to manage what might seem unmanageable problems. Rather, the experience of school should be able to give a child some sense of esteem or purpose.

Whether a school does confront or set aside pupil distress depends on the implicit theory of school being put forward by the institution. Schools have several theories to choose from. There is the notion of school as an island where pupils can leave their problems outside. Another model is the school as a clinic, which generally finds favour with many involved in pastoral care partly on the grounds that if the school does not provide such a service it will not be done elsewhere. A third model is the school as a training ground which takes pupils through to some finished product.

Some schools see themselves as both island and clinic for different sorts of pupil. Rather than having to make a choice, it may be easier for pupils to cope with a single dominant theory which the staff adopts. Unfortunately many schools do not know which theory they implicitly convey to their pupils. It would therefore be a useful starting point for schools to work out which model they do favour.

Pupils vary greatly in the extent to which they understand the pastoral system of the school. But when such understanding does exist, schools tend to assume that the pupil is autonomous and able to make choices. The school sees itself as an institution in which everyone can participate. But this is often a fallacy. Pupils are not always in a position to make choices without restraint. They can only make a choice in response to the system as it is, and the dynamic relationship between teacher and pupil involves a struggle for power and becomes an issue of conflict.

Schools can assume too readily that pupils will take responsibility for their own learning and actions. Also that the school is willing to give that responsibility. But the curriculum, for example, is becoming less and less negotiable and pupils' roles are being determined much more for them with little responsibility given to themselves. One danger of this is that the pastoral care system may be seen to underpin a school system which is failing to give greater autonomy to its pupils.

It may well be difficult for a pupil to take up at all the role as defined by the school since that role may just be to do as you are told. Thus it is unlikely many pupils, especially in their older years, will be able to engage actively with such a role. What should happen is for school and pupils together to negotiate the pupil role. The more that pupils are involved in such an exercise the more able will they be to manage the finally defined role than be imprisoned by it.

In turn, schools can start to try to understand how pupils perceive school and what it is about. This can lead teachers to ask questions about themselves and the nature of the aims and tasks of the school and the sort of opportunities they are providing. While the majority of teachers want to understand what is going on in pupils' minds, they do not have the skills required for that task. A basic issue, therefore, is how to develop in-service training programmes which can provide such skills.

One specific problem to be faced by teachers is that the purposes in which they are engaged can be deeply ambiguous. In one sense schools are about getting children to learn the role of pupil and then progressively to unlearn it. Teachers should be helping pupils to become less dependent on teachers and the school. While some children may know the pupil role instinctively, that is by no means the general rule. A body of research is needed to help teachers understand why some children seem able to fall easily into the pupil role and others do not, and also what schools do which enable some children to succeed with that role and not others. Similarly, teachers need to know how schools can best help them fulfil the teacher role.

Researchers should also examine the range of experiences that pupils have in different learning environments, including the transfer of experience between the school and the wider community. One problem is how far the teachers have sufficiently broad-based experience outside school to avoid developing too narrow a pattern of behaviour, which is then reinforced within the tight structure of the school as an organisation. Some see this as central to the dilemma schools face when they set about defining what they mean by pastoral care.

The notion, though, that school is simply about relationships between people fails to appreciate the nature of school as an institution. The cult of personal relationships in a school can be extremely misleading in the exercise of pastoral care. Knowing a child well is a worthless attribute unless the teacher knows what to do with such knowledge to the benefit of the pupil concerned. Second, it can so lock a child into the world of school that it becomes a liberal version of control. Certainly, pastoral care can often be seen by those outside the school as a way that school persuades those pupils for whom it has little to offer simply to toe the line.

Perhaps the most common way of defining roles in school is to regard teachers as teachers and pupils as learners, teachers as controllers and pupils as controlled, teachers as carers and pupils as cared for. But one dimension rarely considered is that of teachers and pupils as equal moral agents.

In terms of research needs, schools should first define the roles which they expect to be useful for pupils to take on, and then research into the effect of those roles on behaviour. In this way the roles, negotiated with the pupils, can be more effectively defined and made use of, and the teachers with the pupils can monitor the effectiveness of these roles. Schools could also see what effects such roles have on pupil participation in the curriculum compared with other schools, which have yet to define such roles, in order to see if there is any difference in learning between the two. Some research already shows that pupils who take on and understand new roles do gain in competence and confidence.

Session three: Parents, schools and pastoral care
Alastair Macbeth

What can be done about home background is probably one of the most problematic and intractable elements of pastoral care. There is now a massive body of evidence on the importance of home background and parental attitudes, and their impact on how children attain at school. From birth to the age of 16, only 14 per cent of the waking life of a child is spent in school. So home unavoidably influences, for better or worse, what happens at school.

The family can claim to be a pastoral care unit operating in parallel with the school's pastoral provision. There are, of course, important differences between home and school – the range of information available to each; the kinds of experience and expertise; the degree of psychological impact; and the ability of each to devote time and energy to the needs of a particular child. But both have the same caring objectives and some impact on educational outcomes, and each affects the other's provision. While pastoral care in school often has to deal with the problems created by the home, the home frequently must cope with the problems created by the school. Thus home/school relations – and what pastoral care practitioners can do with them – could become a most significant element in future pastoral care research.

Key questions to investigate include whether home/school relations are considered to be important to pastoral care staff; whether research can help in the transition from knowing about the problems involved to doing something about them; and whether pastoral care staff are the right people to be improving such relations.

Two phenomena constantly emerge in the literature of pastoral care: first, that pastoral care is trying to re-create in the school a home-like element – so there would seem to be something going on at home that pastoral care practice wishes to latch on to; second, such literature is looking inwards to the school and not outwards to the community and, in particular, the home. None the less, it is questionable just how far parenting can be seen as coming within the arena of pastoral care at school. Ron Best and Peter Ribbins define pastoral care as something which happens between teachers and pupils or students, interacting in the context of an institution which has four basic inter-relating dimensions or functions – disciplinary/order, academic/curricular, welfare/pastoral, and administrative/organisational – and which is itself located in the wider social, historical and cultural milieu. On this definition, it seems hard to build in the parental element.

For parenting has to do with activities that go on in the home between parent and child: the maintenance of order and discipline, educating the child, caring for the welfare of the child, and the administrative arrangements in the home that make these things possible. But these do not go on in relation to the school and parenting should thus not be seen as a legitimate function linked with school.

Best and Ribbins argue that while both the family and the school are properly concerned with the good of the individual child, to add – as Alastair Macbeth does – parenting or even upbringing to the realm of pastoral care is to confuse two different concepts. Parenting as a concept is more like teaching than it is like disciplining, instructing or helping. Thus the family and the school are engaged in the same endeavour and do so in terms of the contribution each makes to the education, welfare and discipline of children. School and family are agencies through which these kinds of activity can take place, and not activities in their own right.

Teachers and parents need to agree on the pastoral messages or priorities of the school. Their partnership is two-fold – first to do with the personal development of the child, which can be sub-divided into trouble-shooting, preventing trouble arising, and helping pupils to develop their capacity for actively dealing with the situations they encounter; second, the educational progress of the child. The parental contract with the school has to be brought in on one or other of these areas. The research implications are that we should look at the different ways in which, and the extent to which school and family can engage in activities designed to support, educate and socialise children, and what part children themselves can and should play in all this.

However, before bringing teachers and parents together via pastoral care, the problems specifically created by school and those created by the home have to be identified, along with an agreement about patterns of accountability. For example, how far are schools accountable to parents for the pastoral care of pupils under 16, and how far to the pupils themselves?

The relationship between the home and pastoral care in school is seen to have three dimensions:

1   concepts: a clarification of the terms used and their implications;
2   values: decisions to be made about what schools should be doing;
3   the bureaucratic: what can be done in practical terms.

Of the three, 'values' is probably the most intriguing and most problematic. For example, parents are considered to have certain legal rights and duties. However it remains unclear how far they have the right to transmit their own values, attitudes and beliefs to their children – and, indeed, how far teachers have a right to block the transmission of parents' values. A liberal educator has the opportunity to present a child with a range of values and ways of looking at life. But does the pastoral care system of a school have the right to cut across parental wishes?

A prime area of research, therefore, would be an evaluative exercise into what rights parent, child and teacher do have in inculcating a particular set of values; what should be the professional mandate of the pastoral carer in school; and which parts of a child's life do carers have the right to interfere with.

The idea of a mutual contract between parents and teachers agreeing specific courses of action implies there ought to be research into teacher attitudes on what the parental role is. What research there is shows that parents think teachers should be allowed to get on with their professional job. It would be valuable to have similar research done into what parents think schools should be doing in terms of pastoral care provision.

Parents, however, are no more an homogeneous group than teachers or pupils. So it is doubtful if research will discover what parents in general do want from school, except at the very basic level – that of caring for the individual pupil. Anything more didactic raises questions of values. Moreover, there is some research on what teachers want from school and a little on what teacher think of parents. But none on why teachers find it so difficult to engage with parents. This problem goes well beyond the area of pastoral care and there are social class issues involved. But there should be research into what does go wrong with this professional relationship which does not occur with other professional relationships. A parent/teacher contract also suggests a degree of flexibility by schools which currently they do not have. It also raises problems about how far schools are capable of meeting and being responsive to parental needs and their different demands.

There are currently two key developments that may help to improve home/school links. First, the effects of falling rolls on schools, which are forcing many schools to become more competitive in attracting parents and seeking to meet their specific needs; and, secondly, the new articulacy of black parents who take the line that it is up to the school to adjust to family needs and concerns and not the other way around.

One problem is that teachers tend to distance themselves from the whole world of home education. There exists an extensive black market in education with children at all social levels being coached, cajoled and coerced by parents, paid tutors, siblings and so on. But for many teachers such activity counts for nothing. Very specific help is given to parents in other professional areas and it is accepted that some kinds of acute maladjustment or handicap can be better cured by parents using specific programmes negotiated between parent and professional. While this help occurs in education through the development of home reading schemes, it has penetrated little further. Research on this in some quasi-medical fields therefore has immense lessons for teachers.

There are frequent calls for research into parental attitudes, assumptions and demands about school. But it may not be a campaign to change parents' attitudes that is required. Research by Daphne Johnson has found that parents know very well what they want. Since they are already made to feel guilty about not being in touch with the school, such a campaign could only increase such feelings. Rather it is the teachers who have to be worked on in order for them to value the parental contribution.

But are campaigns successful? For example, the Health Education Council has decided to spend less on campaigns on smoking and family planning since they have not proved sufficiently effective. Work is now done in a general setting for the media and with a substantial back-up of support groups at a local level with professionals. There is also the danger in campaign work of devaluing the effectiveness of learning of the more intimate, fine-grained variety. Against that, campaigns can have the function of legitimising an activity or way of behaving so that it becomes the conventional wisdom.

Parenting is a large field, especially with the growth of the education for parenthood movement. So a further campaign for parenting may only add to what is already going on. Many agencies are helping parents in their parenting role by organising and evaluating a range of schemes. There is an array of other professionals, services and points of view involved in the area of home/school liaison, such as health visitors, nurses, school social workers, and so on. Indeed, the school should perhaps not be regarded as central but as merely one of several agencies helping the family, and as always supplementary to what the family does.

What we do not seem to know much about is how schools and parents can be led to engage more effectively. It is debatable whether the more urgent problem is getting parents to understand schools better or getting schools to appreciate what parents have to offer. It has to work both ways with the key word always partnership.

How much more research though is actually necessary? We know clearly that parents who listen to their children reading and who receive some straightforward guidance from teachers can be more effective than much remedial teaching. The number of schools which do not encourage this is very small. But we have also known for over 20 years – since Jackson and Marsden's classic study – how many schools subtly and unintentionally discourage contact with parents. The problem is not needing more research to demonstrate what we already know well, it is how to get such ideas across and how to overcome the very real obstacles in order to apply the results of research. Certainly research is not the answer to everything. After years of exhortation there is still no action research to translate exhortation into specific practices for ordinary, hard-pressed, good-enough schools to adopt.

Difficulties also arise through regarding parents either as individuals or as an amorphous group. There is no crystallisation of what are parental expectations of school. Society's usual responses to what parents see as shortcomings in school have been in line with the convention of school – more of the same, but better. Yet when whole communities form critiques of the system which pose as alternatives such as supplementary schools and separate Muslim schools, then more serious research has to be carried out in these areas.

There has, nevertheless, been an increasing amount of professional practice involving parents in children's education. Action research might help individuals to reflect on their own practice in a way which would help them to analyse those factors which distinguish rhetoric from reality, both from the parents' perspective and in what schools say they want and what in fact they are doing. A further stage is to look at the changing legislation and how that is being interpreted in practice by those schools which are taking on the recommendations for closer involvement of parents in their children's schooling at the early stages. One should analyse the features and dynamics of those early stages of development and parental involvement to see how the secondary school can make use of that resource.

How far can the school itself be self-critical and adjust accordingly? Many of the pastoral problems arise from situations that schools can do nothing about. For example, it is very hard for pastoral systems to cope with the problem of failure because schools are not in charge of the structures in society which identify certain pupils as failures. All teachers can do is help pupils and their parents come to terms with reality. It would therefore be quite wrong to suggest that all the problems would go away if schools were prepared to be more responsive to outside concerns.

There is, though, a major educational task to be done in making teachers more ready to meet and engage in a more effective dialogue with parents. Schools should be clear about what they can and cannot do – the limits of their responsiveness to what parents want of schools. In effect, while schools can do something about the processes and not much about the structures, that does not excuse them from trying to do what they can do.

Session four (i): Helping pupils – the needs of schools
Michael Marland

This wide-ranging paper attempts to set down recommendations for the whole area of research needed into pastoral care. Nine of the paper's recommendations are procedural issues, such as needing to know more about learning skills, library use, option choices and so on. Three are partly procedural in that they call for further elucidation of particular areas, such as parenting styles, and the role of the child as a pupil. Only two recommendations are fundamental: the need for research into the knowledge needed for choice of occupation; and for research into what young people need to learn for their personal and social development.

There are though other fundamental issues on the needs of schools that should be a part of the general proposal. For example, what pastoral care is supposed to be in schools and how staff can reach a consensus on its functions and purposes; and how that consensus on pastoral care can be related to the overall enterprise of the school. The latter is covered, in part, in the paper with the reference to how the pastoral curriculum would relate to the other tasks of the school, but pastoral care itself needs to be linked into these tasks.

This is perhaps the basic question of schooling: what are schools hoping children will learn? This can be turned about to ask: how are schools intending to teach? While schools have the autonomy to be able to answer such questions, they do not have the procedures to arrive at that point. The problem lies in the current static structure of schools with little or no room for development, and with the autonomy of head and teacher. Schools should be willing to relinquish some of their autonomy in order to produce a consensus with all the parties to the educational convenant.

The current difficulty is the lack of conceptual clarification about pastoral care, with little or no consensus about what it should be doing. This is perhaps one of the most important areas for research in the future. More information should be collected through research and surveys on attitudes to and conceptions of pastoral care. Teachers should be asked to set pastoral care in order of priority in a list of other educational issues. They should also be presented with typical problems as a way of promoting discussion on how they would handle specific pastoral care issues and incidents. Such details would have implications for training policies.

Teachers themselves maintain that it is important to have curriculum research into what young people need to learn for their personal and social development. Such research they say could meet their own needs, for example, through developing tutorial work schemes, and help to give them confidence to know what they are doing right and what wrong.

An analysis of team leadership of tutors can give schools a set of criteria for divisions of responsibility and for points of audit, particularly at a time when so many schools are having to cope with falling rolls. What is of concern is that as schools shrink, pastoral care responsibility posts are being cut back with very little discussion. Moreover, moves to avoid the dichotomy in school between the pastoral and the academic are being used to undermine the whole concept of leadership in pastoral care.

Research is needed for linking parenting styles with pastoral care teaching styles to ensure some kind of match with what is happening in school. This adds a new dimension to Alastair Macbeth's paper in that parenting style is here seen to have nothing necessarily to do with socio-economic factors. Many children who come from very difficult family backgrounds can cope well with school. Research should seek to discover what goes on at home that enables some children to succeed whilst others do not.

Action research into pupils' perceptions of the requirements and purposes of learning methods is not enough. Research should also continue into how children learn, since there is a mismatch between how teachers think children conceptualise and how children actually do. It is not just a question of finding out how children pick up bodies of knowledge, but how they learn in the context of pastoral care; and having learned, how that learning transfers to other areas of schooling and of life since much pastoral care work is dependent on such a transfer.

There are two learning models taken on by schools. One is the skills model – how you learn a particular skill. This is seen as a one-off process: once you have learnt how to be a pupil, you know how to do it. The skills model assumes any child at any age can learn particular skills. It is considered to be a matter of excellent teaching, good internal relations in school and receptive children to ensure skills are transmitted from adult to child. The other is the developmental model which assumes a continually changing process as the child progresses through the school and develops the capacity for greater comprehension. The knowledge and understanding acquired about a skill at the age of 12 is different from that at 15 or 18.

Each model makes different demands on those concerned with pastoral care and carry a different set of implications. However, schools tend to focus more on the skills model rather than the developmental one. Many tutorial programmes are heavily age-layered – for example; in year one, pupils learn about the school; in year three, about options; and in year five, about the outside world. It allows for little flexibility.

There should be research into innovation in the pastoral care area and how innovations emerge. For example, a recent development has been small group developmental work which seems to have occurred without reference to research or to initiatives from senior management. Rather it has emerged from grassroots level. It is therefore important to find out why and how such developments get taken up nationally in schools.

Session four (ii): Report on preliminary finding of NAPCE pilot survey on initial and in-service training provision, and LEA support for pastoral care
Peter Maher

Many teachers feel inadequately trained for their pastoral care role. They cite insufficient training facilities and in-service opportunities, and little or no support at local authority level for pastoral care and the people working in that field.

The aim of the NAPCE survey was to produce as quickly as possible some supportive evidence on provision and to pave the way for a broader and specially-funded survey of pastoral care provision, support and training. It is therefore accepted as a hurriedly-produced document with clear inadequacies and areas not covered. For example, the schools' survey is exclusively a secondary schools' survey; the sample itself is very small – 119 teachers, 18 schools and 12 local authorities. However, it stands as a useful confirmatory excercise of impressions that had been largely anecdotal and of other pieces of data, which raises a whole variety of questions.

The finding that initial training is seen as minimal by teachers confirms the 1982 HMI survey that 56 per cent of new teachers felt unprepared to undertake pastoral duties. Induction on pastoral themes is low.

Some interesting parallels can be drawn here between the induction of staff in schools and the induction of children into schools – the induction of first-year pupils into schools turns out to be administrative and not person-centred and the same thing might well be happening for teachers.

When teachers were asked what they would need to improve matters, most focussed on resources – the physical setting in which people work; the amount of time they have in which to do their work; the budget for pastoral care, and money for materials. The same applies in colleges where initial training is minimal and in some cases even optional. This links in with the implicit messages in schools where being a tutor is often optional.

Moving beyond initial training, the situation does change for the better. The INSET picture, while still patchy, is healthier. Research at higher degree level is developing, although work remains at a disappointingly low level. Pastoral care is still regarded as not a decent area of study in some academic quarters. Many training institutions have no long-term commitment to pastoral care and courses have been rationalised and even dropped. LEAs are seen to have differing perceptions of pastoral care and INSET provision is non-systematic, based mainly on specific enthusiasms in individual LEAs. Advisers seem particularly hard-pressed.

On some of these issues, a wider sample for research is required. But with others, only case studies are needed, such as Martin Weeks' paper on pastoral care in Clwyd. There are, though, more contentious points in the survey. For example, there is an assumption that training will solve the problems that currently affect pastoral care. But some basic questions have to be tackled first:

1 Does training work?
2 Does it place too much onus on individuals rather than the systems they work in?
3 How far are teachers who go on training courses helped to integrate back into their schools with their new expertise – in effect, are they being trained as good change-agents and able to understand the complex processes about their own organisations?
4 What is training in pastoral care expected to achieve?

The first question – whether training works – can be narrowed down to a more diagnostic question: what sort of training is most useful for what role-holders at what time? The current view of in-service training is that we need to service teachers within their pyramid of roles – trainee teachers, probationary teachers, form tutors, middle management, senior management and advisers. Therefore we need a pyramid of training which includes initial training, induction, in-school and teachers' centre training, with short courses, diplomas and higher degrees. The under-lying thinking of this conventional training model is that the trainers at the top feed training into the next level down.

But there is a growing uneasiness about this kind of training. It is too neat, and may well fail to meet the specific needs of pastoral care. The training available is too patchy and what theories underlie the various training approaches are unclear.

In addition, schools often remain unsure whether training or expertise actually benefits, or fits the needs of, their teachers. This is borne out, in part, by the statistics on secondments. In the university and public sectors, the number of secondments went up from 3096 to 3248 between 1981 and 1982 (DES statistics). However, the number of secondments related in some way to pastoral care declined from 68 to 55. Thus, pastoral care is not sufficiently competitive in winning secondments. The reasons for this go back to issues of staffing in the schools themselves, teachers' perceptions of such courses and their lack of clarity about what they will get out of them, and academic snobbery about pastoral care.

There are omissions from the survey. More data is required on what teachers want from their training; more examples of good practice obtained from case study research; more examples of methods of working and assessment.

A policy for training has to be further developed. The survey paper makes three specific points on this – pastoral care must be a compulsory component of all initial courses; the length of the PGCE must be extended to allow for this without cutting anything else out; and better use must be made of teaching practice opportunities such as attaching student-teachers to a tutor group. But there are two crucial and largely unanswered questions: How, in the present climate, can current provision be developed and extended? And, where there is room for improvement, what are the issues to be faced when setting out to expand and develop training through initial courses, INSET courses, DES short courses, and LEA-sponsored workshops?

All this can encourage the accusation of special pleading – and risk its attendant dangers – in that every specialism can maintain that more training is needed in its own area. One danger of special pleading is that it produces an inflation of content in training courses with no discussion about what ought to be taken out to accommodate the new content. In order to reach a proper balance, breadth and coherence in training, it might be better to carry out a survey of the overall provision generally on offer through the PGCE and to assess where pastoral care – along with other specialisms such as special needs and disruptive pupils – can best be fitted in. Such a survey should be located, especially with regard to the policy-making implications, within a line of thought of crossing the boundaries between pastoral and academic, school and home, school and welfare network, and school and society generally.

Yet the statistics on training strongly suggest that pressing for better pastoral care training is not special pleading at all. For example, every head of a maths department would have attended a course on how to teach maths; few if any heads of year would have been on more than a half-day course. In the ILEA, 30 per cent of deputy heads in charge of the curriculum would have been on at least a three-day training course on timetabling and the curriculum; only 8 per cent of deputy heads in charge of pastoral care would have been on at least a three-day course.

On initial training, only 9 per cent of new teachers say they have not been sufficiently trained for their own subject; only 21 per cent say they have not been trained to manage the classroom. But as many as 56 per cent say they have not had training for pastoral care. In addition, there are no advisers with specific expertise in pastoral care to which teachers can turn for criteria in helping to reach decisions on care issues.

In every secondary school there are five pastoral care responsibility posts plus a deputy headship. But almost none of the postholders will have been trained, whereas at least a third of the academic heads of department will have been. The facts then show that the nation is wasting thousands of millions of pounds on responsibility posts for which it has not invested one penny in training. This does not seem special pleading. While almost all teachers will spend part of their time with some pastoral responsibility, training for that responsibility is always an option. It cannot be right that what a teacher does every day should be an option which is set against much more minor aspects of teaching.

Session five: Pastoral care and welfare networks
Daphne Johnson

There is always a danger that a new specialism increases the social division of welfare. Each profession tends to develop its own knowledge base which makes it more difficults to view clients as a whole and to relate effectively with other professions in the care field. So there exists a problem of disintegration rather than integration through greater specialisation. However, this fear of 'ghettoisation' has to be set against concern that other parts of the education service and external agencies do not take pastoral care sufficiently seriously.

A new conceptual framework is required which links care in schools with care in other places provided by other agencies, which betters that defined by Maurice Craft:

Care framework

Normal	Crisis
Universalistic	Particularistic/residual
No stigma	Stigma
School	School
	Medical, psychological and social services

School operates on both sides of this framework, whereas the medical, psychological, social and education welfare services relate to children in a different way, and are more crisis-orientated. This new framework raises a series of questions: what the relationships of the various agencies are to children; what the differences are and what effect this has on the way children relate together; and how care in school relates to other forms of care.

The Central Policy Review Staff document on a joint framework for social policy points out that it does not help to focus on services or on the boundaries between services. The focus has to be on the children and their needs. So it is essential to move away from thinking in terms of social work care or school-based care and to focus on the child. What is needed is an understanding of what makes people cross boundaries in order to help meet children's needs.

Three sorts of agency exist: school-based, with the focus on the child and the child in the home; school-attached, such as education welfare officers and educational psychologists, who meet their clients through the school but are not seen as part of the school; and community-based, who have clients of school age but do not approach them through the school, and who have as a focus the child in the family.

Research should look at:

1 how each profession relates to children, and how the differences in this relationship make it hard for the welfare network to operate;
2 how the professions and their services relate to each other from national down to local and even street level;
3 how far the administrative structures of each profession affect their ability to co-operate and share information;
4 how the multi-professional groups in the welfare network behave, and what happens when those who join different services for different reasons have to work together.

The 1981 Education Act means that professions are much more obliged to work together and to share information. The role of parents has also been altered by both the 1980 and the 1981 Education Acts. Their access to the multi-professional framework and to schools themselves has been enhanced. Research should explore the implications of these changes. The extent to which schools are able to cope with such changes should also be considered, especially how far pastoral care systems have to adapt to cope with the two Acts' implications, particularly the mainstreaming of children with handicaps, in a positive, caring and controlling way. The agenda for research should be opened out to see school-based care in the context of wider social welfare policy, otherwise the professionalisation of pastoral care could merely enlarge the social divisions in welfare.

However, the problems of co-operation between the professionals could be seen to be of minor consequence when compared with some of the perceptions that some communities have of welfare agencies. For example, there is great suspicion among black communities of the school psychological service and its ways of working. Ethnocentricity can prevent an awareness of key areas for research which are critical to an understanding of society. For example, there is a notable absence of references to the supplementary school system and mother-tongue schools which do not work with the support services or with ordinary school. Many of these projects set up by community groups are attempts to circumvent the ethnocentricity they encounter in the various official welfare agencies. Research, to be relevant and applicable to the whole community, has to take on such issues.

The network of overlapping agencies, familiar to those who work in education, sometimes do need pulling together in the interests of particular pupils. It is the schools, though, which tend to see it as their function to take the lead in this, perhaps because the arm's-length professionalism of the schoolteacher is less highly developed, and especially because pastoral care teachers are less jealously protective of their professional position.

However, pastoral care staff may often find themselves out of touch with external agencies because of school protocol that there has to be a specific person who must liaise with these agencies. In effect, tutors cannot get near to the relevant welfare agency themselves. This issue of status and hierarchy of professionals within schools and in outside agencies has to be seriously addressed. It can be a major area of resentment. For example, tutors are frequently seen to be in the frontline of pastoral care, but when it comes to case conferences it is usually the middle manager, with less knowledge of the child concerned, who attends them.

The differing ideologies of the professions have to be recognised and understood – and social worker and teacher encouraged to make better contact. There is often a reluctance among professionals to share information and knowledge, partly on the grounds that holding knowledge enhances status. Case-study research can be very useful in highlighting examples of innovation and good practice and in seeking developing new ways of working together. Examples include:

1 A DHSS-funded project led by Dr Martin Bax on the work of district handicap teams, which shows that, at district level, the concept of co-operation revolves largely around case conferences. Any planning framework is conspicuous by its absence. Professionals only came together on a case but failed to develop more permanent links.

2 Another DHSS-funded project is working with children and their families in South Glamorgan. This is a major attempt to carry out organisational and staff development with all the agencies involved, and offers an excellent model for this kind of work. Staff workshops are held over 18 months to discuss and resolve issues of organisation.

3 A jointly-funded project by the Inner London Education Authority and the Inner City Partnership in Lambeth is establishing health and social education programmes in four secondary schools. This was with the involvement of the local health authority, which has now taken on the project to develop it further.

4 The Sickle Cell Centre at Willesden Hospital in Brent – a joint initiative by the NHS and the local Sickle Cell Society – has developed a concerted approach to mobilising information and counselling,

informing local health professionals and schools, and encouraging policy changes. It is an example of working from the outside in a community base and pressuring NHS and local education authorities to act.

Such innovative cross-boundary ways of working should be identified, properly written up and disseminated.

Finally, the idea of the family as the central focus of caring for children should be sustained. There is not enough consideration of the parental place in the network of professionals passing around confidential information. Research should therefore look at three areas:

1 parental and senior pupil access to school records;
2 a requirement for parents to divulge information to the school, particularly when they as parents have made contact with the welfare services rather than the school making that contact;
3 the ways in which the school does or does not use confidential information outside the school without parental knowledge.

List of participants

It was at the seminar, jointly run by NAPCE and the University of Warwick, that many of the papers in this book were first presented. The Appendix (p. 214) contains examples of some of the discussions which took place.

Armstrong, David
The Grubb Institute, London

Beattie, Alan
Institute of Education, University of London
Best, Ron
Chelmer Institute of Higher Education, Brentwood
Blackburn, Keith
St George's School, Gravesend
Broadfoot, Patricia
School of Education, University of Bristol
Burgess, Dr Robert
Department of Sociology, University of Warwick

Dare, Dr Jonathan
Department of Child and Family Psychiatry, Belgrave Hospital, London

Galloway, Dr David
University College, Cardiff

Hargreaves, Andy
Department of Education, University of Warwick
Harwood, Douglas
Department of Science Education, University of Warwick
Howle, David
National Youth Bureau, Leicester
Hussey, Mike
Advisor, ILEA

Irving, Ann
Loughborough University of Technology

James, Miss A.
Langley School, Solihull
Johnson, Daphne
Department of Government, Brunel University
Jones, Elizabeth
HMI

Lang, Peter
Department of Education, University of Warwick

Maher, Peter
Langdon School, London
Marland, Michael
North Westminster Community School, London
Macbeth, Dr Alistair
Department of Education, University of Glasgow
McLaughlin, Terry
Department of Education, Cambridge University
Medlock, Peter
Alderman Smith School, Nuneaton

Nuttall, Elizabeth
Blake Comprehensive School, Staffordshire

Pound, Vivienne
Alperton High School, Middlesex

Ribbins, Peter
Faculty of Education, University of Birmingham
Robertson, Irene
Rock Hill School, Bromley
Rogers, Rick
Journalist, London

Sisterson, Dorothy
Department of Education Studies, Newcastle upon Tyne Polytechnic
Smith, Andy
St Martin's College, Lancaster
Snow, Ruth
Advisor, Coventry

Terry, David
Halesowen College, Halesowen
Thompson, Elizabeth
Advisor, Warwickshire

Watkins, Chris
Institute of Education, University of London
Welton, Dr John
Institute of Education, University of London
Whittaker, Roy
School of Education, University of East Anglia
Wienrich-Haste, Helen
Department of Psychology, University of Bath
Wright, Professor Derek
Department of Education, University of Leicester

Bibliography

Abel, B. 1978: *The place of careers education within the secondary school curriculum: a study of pupils in their transition from school to employment.* M. A. Thesis (unpublished). University of London, Institute of Education.

Adams, J. 1982: *Parent/school relations: a case study.* M. Ed. Dissertation (unpublished). University of Birmingham.

Adelman, E. (ed.) 1981: *Uttering Muttering.* Grant McIntyre.

Agee, J. and Evans, W. 1969: *Let Us Now Praise Famous Men.* Panther.

Allport, G.W. 1942: The use of personal documents in psychological science. *Social Science Research Council Bulletin,* 49.

American Anthropological Association 1971: Statements on ethics: principles of professional responsibility. In Weaver, T. (ed.), *To See Ourselves: anthropology of modern social issues.* Scott Foresman, Chicago, pp. 46–8.

APU 1981: *Personal and Social Development.* DES.

Arminger, B. 1975: *Systems of pastoral care in schools.* B. Phil (Ed.) Dissertation (unpublished). University of Birmingham.

Atherton, G. 1982: *The book of the school: a study of Scottish handbooks issued to pupils and their parents.* Scottish Consumer Council.

Auld, W.H. and Stein, H.L. 1965: *The Guidance Worker.* Gage.

Avent, C. (forthcoming): *Careers Across the Curriculum.* Heinemann Educational Books.

Avery, J. 1978: *An examination of truancy and its implications for educational administration.* M. A. Thesis (unpublished). University of London.

Ayre, S. 1982: *Pastoral care in an inner city comprehensive school.* M. A. Dissertation (unpublished). University of London, Institute of Education.

Baldwin, J. and Smith, A. 1983a: Uncertain futures: an approach to tutorial work with 16–19 year olds in the 1980s. *Pastoral Care in Education,* 1 (1), pp. 40–5.

Baldwin, J. and Smith, A. 1983b: *Active Tutorial Work Sixteen to Nineteen.* Basil Blackwell.

Baldwin, J. and Wells, H. 1979, 1980, 1981: *Active Tutorial Work,* Books 1–5. Basil Blackwell.

Ball, C. 1983: *Challenges faced on transfer to sixth-form college: implications for the guidance system.* Diploma in Guidance and Counselling Dissertation (unpublished). University of Manchester.

Ball, C. and Pumfrey, P. 1984: Challenges perceived by students on transfer to a sixth-form college: implications for the guidance system. *Pastoral Care in Education,* 2 (1), pp. 24–31.

Ball, S.J. 1981: *Beachside Comprehensive*. Cambridge University Press.

Balogh, J. 1982: *Profile Reports for School Leavers*. Schools Council/Longman.

Banks, O. and Finlayson, D. 1973: *Success and Failure in the Secondary School*. Methuen.

Bardell, G. (project co-ordinator) 1982: *Options for the Fourth*. Schools Council.

Barnes, J.A. 1979: *Who Should Know What?* Penguin.

Basini, A. 1980: *The establishment of school support units for disruptive pupils* M. A. Thesis (unpublished). University of London.

Bastiani, J. 1978: *Written communication between home and school*. University of Nottingham School of Education.

Batchelor, R. 1976: *Educational guidance in the comprehensive school*. M. A. Thesis (unpublished). University of London, Institute of Education.

Bazalgette, J. 1983: Taking up the pupil role. In *Pastoral Care in Education*, 1 (3).

Becher, T. and Maclure, S. 1978: *Accountability in Education*. NFER-Nelson.

Beck, J. 1972: *Transition and continuity: a study of an educational status passage*. M. A. Thesis (unpublished), University of London Library.

Bell, C. and Encel, S. (eds), 1978: *Inside the Whale*. Pergamon.

Bell, C. and Newby, H. 1977: *Doing Sociological Research*. Allen and Unwin.

Bennett, N. 1976: *Teaching Styles and Pupil Progress*. Open Books.

Bennett, S. 1974: *The School: an organisational analysis*. Blackie.

Berger, J. and Mohr, J. 1967: *A Fortunate Man: the story of a country doctor*. Allan Lane.

Berger, J. and Mohr, J. 1975: *A Seventh Man: a book of images and words about the experience of migrant workers in Europe*. Penguin.

Berger, M. and Taylor, E. 1984: Editorial. In *Journal of Child Psychology and Psychiatry*, 25 (1).

Bernstein, B. 1976: Class and pedagogies: visible and invisible. In *Class, Codes and Control*, 3. Routledge and Kegan Paul.

Bertaux, D. (ed.), 1981: *Biography and Society*. Sage, California.

Best, R. 1980: Review of Johnson *et al* 1980: *Secondary Schools and the Welfare Network*. Unwin Educational. In *British Educational Research Journal*, 6 (2), pp. 215–8.

Best, R., Jarvis, C. and Ribbins, P.M. 1977: Pastoral care concept and process. In *British Journal of Education Studies*, 25 (2).

Best, R., Jarvis, C. and Ribbins, P.M. 1979: Researching pastoral care. In Hughes, M. and Ribbins, P.M. 1979: *Research and Educational Administration*. BEMAS.

Best, R., Jarvis C. and Ribbins, P.M. (eds), 1980: *Perspectives on Pastoral Care*. Heinemann Educational Books.

Best, R., Jarvis, C., Ribbins, P.M. and Oddy, D. 1981: Teacher attitudes to the school counsellor: a reappraisal. *British Journal of Guidance and Counselling*, 9 (2), pp. 159–72.

Best, R., Ribbins, P.M. and Jarvis C., with Oddy, D. 1983: *Education and Care*. Heinemann Educational Books.

Best, R. and Ribbins, P.M. 1983: Rethinking the pastoral–academic split. *Pastoral Care in Education*, 1 (1) pp. 11–18.

Best, R., Ribbins, P. and Ribbins, P.M. 1984: Careers education and the welfare curriculum. *Pastoral Care in Education*, 2 (1), pp. 66–77.

Best, R. and Ribbins, P.M. 1985: Researching the secondary school: the case of pastoral care. BEMAS research paper at Sheffield Polytechnic (forthcoming).

Bird, C., Chessum, R., Furlong, J. and Johnson, D. (eds), 1981: *Disaffected Pupils*. Brunel University.

Blackburn, K. 1975: *The Tutor*. Heinemann Educational Books.

Blackburn, K. 1983a: *Head of House, Head of Year*. Heinemann Educational Books.

Blackburn, K. 1983b: The pastoral head: a developing role. *Pastoral care in Education*, 1 (1), pp. 18–24.

Bland, M. 1981: *Educational guidance and curricular consideration*. M. A. Thesis (unpublished). University of London, Institute of Education.

Bolak, A.C., Bolak, H., Bagerstos, N.T. and Mikel, E.R. 1975: Teaching and learning in English primary schools. *School Review*, 83 (2), pp. 215–43.

Bolger, A.W. 1975: *Child Study and Guidance in Schools*. Constable.

Bond, C. 1981: *Partnership in practice: a study of the pastoral care system and its interaction with a school social worker in a Haringey comprehensive school*. Survey Research Unit, Polytechnic of North London.

Bonser, K. 1985: *Disruptive pupils in schools and the related sanctions of exclusion and suspension*. M. Ed. Dissertation (unpublished). University of Birmingham.

Breivik, P.S. 1977: Resources: the fourth R. In *Community College Forum*, USA, Winter, 1977, 49.

British Sociological Association 1973: Statement of ethical principles and their application to sociological practice. (Mimeograph, revised and updated 1982) BSA.

Broadfoot, P. 1982: Alternatives to public examinations. *Educational Analysis*, 4 (3).

Brown, J. and Armstrong, R. 1982: The structure of pupil worries during the transition from junior to secondary school. *British Educational Research Journal*, 8 (2).

Buckle, K. 1984: *The great divide: a study of the relationship between the pastoral and the academic in secondary schools*. M. Ed. Thesis (unpublished). University of Durham.

Buist, M. 1980: Truants talking. *Scottish Educational Review*, 12 (1), pp. 40–51.

Bulman, L. 1984: The relationship between the pastoral curriculum, the academic curriculum, and the pastoral programme. In *Pastoral Care*, 2, (2), June 1984.

Bulman, L. and Jenkins, D. (forthcoming): *The Pastoral Curriculum*, Basil Blackwell.

Bulmer, M. (ed.) 1982: *Social Research Ethics*. Macmillan.

Burgess, H. *An appraisal of some methods of teaching primary school mathematics*. M. A. Dissertation (unpublished). University of London, Institute of Education.

Burgess, H. 1985: Case study and curriculum research: some issues for teacher-researchers. In Burgess, R.G. (ed.), *Issues in Educational Research: qualitative methods*. Falmer Press.

Burgess, R.G. 1980: Some fieldwork problems in teacher-based research. *British Educational Research Journal*, 6 (2), pp. 165–73.

Burgess, R.G. 1981: Keeping a research diary. *Cambridge Journal of Education*, 2 (1), pp. 75–83.

Burgess, R.G. (ed.) 1982: *Field Research: a sourcebook and field manual*. Allen and Unwin.

Burgess, R.G. 1983a: *Experiencing Comprehensive Education: a study of Bishop McGregor School*. Methuen.

Burgess, R.G. 1983b: Teacher-based research and pastoral care. *Pastoral Care in Education*, 1 (1), pp. 52–61.

Burgess R.G. 1984a: Teachers, research and pastoral care: a reply. *Pastoral Care in Education*, 2 (3) pp. 214–8.

Burgess, R.G. 1984b: *In the Field: an introduction to field research*. Allen and Unwin.

Burgess, R.G. (ed.) 1984c: *The Research Process in Educational Settings: Ten Case Studies*. Falmer.

Burgess, R.G. 1985: The whole truth? Some ethical problems of research in a comprehensive school. In Burgess, R.G. (ed.), *Field Methods in the Study of Education*. Falmer Press, pp. 139–62.

Burgess, T. and Adams, B. 1980: *Outcomes of Education*. Macmillan.

Burgess, T. and Adams, B. 1984: Records of achievement for school leavers: an institutional framework. *Working Papers on Institutions*, 57, North East London Polytechnic.

Burke, T. 1979: *Careers education in the curriculum: approaches to the planning of careers education in the secondary school*. M. A. Thesis (unpublished). University of London, Institute of Education.

Bushin, R. 1978: *The development of careers education with reference to a particular London borough*. M. A. Thesis (unpublished). University of London, Institute of Education.

Button, L. 1981: *Group Tutoring for the Form Teacher*. Hodder and Stoughton.

Button, L. 1983: The pastoral curriculum. *Pastoral Care in Education*, 1 (2), pp. 74–83.

Buzzard, T. 1983: Option choice: no choice. *Pastoral Care in Education*, 1 (1), pp. 36–40.

CSV 1982: *Health*. A school and community kit, (updated version of 1978 kit).

Calvert, B. 1976: *The Role of the Pupil*. Routledge and Kegan Paul.

Carroll, H. (ed.) 1977: *Absenteeism in South Wales*. University of Swansea.

Chambers, B. 1982: *A philosophical appraisal of 'pastoral care'*. M. Ed. Dissertation (unpublished). University of Birmingham.

Clark, J. 1983: Pastoral care: shared concept or catch-all phrase? *Pastoral Care in Education*, 1 (3), pp. 199–200.

Clarke, B. 1984: Introducing social and personal education in a large upper school. *Pastoral Care in Education*, 2 (3), pp. 197–202.

Clarke, L. 1980: *The Practice of Vocational Guidance: a critical review of research in the United Kingdom*. HMSO.

Cogan, M.L. 1953: Towards a definition of profession. *Harvard Educational Review*, 23, pp. 33–50.

Cohen, L. and Manion, L. 1980: Research Methods in Education.

Cohen, L. and Manion, L. 1981: *Perspectives on Classroom and Schools*, Holt, Rinehart and Winston.

Cole, H. 1982: *The development of the teacher's role with regard to the personal and social development of pupils.* B. Phil. (Ed.) Dissertation (unpublished). University of Birmingham.

Collier, J. 1967: *Visual Anthropology: photography as a research method.* Holt, Rinehart and Winston.

Committee of Inquiry into the Education of Children from Ethnic Minority Groups, 1985, *Education For All* (the Swann Report), HMSO, Cmnd. 9453.

Coomber, L. and Whitfield, R. 1979: *Action on Indiscipline.* NAS/UWT.

Corrigan, P. 1979: *Schooling and Smash Street Kids.* Macmillan.

Coulter, F. 1979: Homework: a neglected research area. In *British Educational Research Journal*, 5 (1), pp. 21–33.

Craft, M. 1980: School welfare roles and networks. In Best R., Jarvis, C. and Ribbins, P.M. (eds), *Perspectives on Pastoral Care.* Heinemann Educational Books.

Craft, M. 1980: School welfare roles and networks. In Craft *et al* (eds) *Linking Home and School* (third edition). Harper and Row.

Craft, M. *et al* 1981: *Linking Home and School.* Harper and Row.

David, K. 1982: *Personal and Social Education in Secondary Schools.* Longman, for the Schools Council.

David, K. and Cowley, J. 1980: *Pastoral Care in Schools and Colleges.* Edward Arnold.

Davies, B. 1976: Relations between social workers and teachers. *Social Work Today*, 8 (8).

Davies, J. 1981: *Disruption in Schools.* M. A. Dissertation (unpublished). University of London.

Davis, L. 1985: Teacher-parent cooperation: one school's planned practice, *Pastoral Care in Education*, 3 (1), pp. 45–53.

Daws, P. 1976: *Early Days.* CRAC/Hobsons.

Dawson, P. 1981: *Making a Comprehensive Work.* Basil Blackwell.

Deem, R. 1978: *Women and Schooling*, Routledge and Kegan Paul.

Delves, R. 1980: *Work: a proper focus for the curriculum.* M. A. Thesis (unpublished). University of London, Institute of Education.

Denzin, N. 1970: *The Research Act.* Aldine, Chicago.

Department of Education and Science 1973: *Careers Education in Secondary Schools*, Education Survey 18. HMSO.

Department of Education and Science 1975: *Survey of Absence from Secondary and Middle Schools.* DES.

Department of Education and Science 1983a: *Current Educational Research Projects Supported by the DES List 1.* DES.

Department of Education and Science, and Welsh Office 1983b: *Records of Achievement for School Leavers: a draft policy statement.* HMSO.

Department of Education and Science, and Welsh Office 1983c: *Teaching Quality.* HMSO.

Department of Health and Social Security 1976: *Report of the Committee of Inquiry into the care and supervision provided in relation to Maria Colwell.* HMSO.

Derrick, D. and Watkins, R. 1977: *Co-operative care: practice and information profiles.* Centre for Information and Advice on Educational Disadvantage.

Dicks, S. 1983: *Communication and confidentiality in pastoral care.* M. A. Thesis (unpublished). University of London, Institute of Education.

Dooley, S.K. 1980: The relationship between the concepts 'pastoral care' and 'authority'. In Best, R., Jarvis, C. and Ribbins, P.(eds), *Perspectives on Pastoral Care.* Heinemann Educational Books.

Dweck, C.S. 1977: Learned helplessness and negative education. In Keisler, E.R. (ed.), *The Education,* 19 (2).

Dweck, C.S., and Bush, E. 1976: Sex differences in learned helplessness with peer and adult evaluators. In *Development Psychology,* 12 (2), pp. 147–56.

Dweck, C.S. and Coetz, T.E. 1978: Attributions and learned helplessness. In Harvey, J., Ickes, W. and Kidd, R. (eds), *New Directions in Attribution Research,* 2, pp. 159–79, Halsted, New York.

Dweck, C.S., Davidson, W., Nelson, S., and Enna, B. 1978: Sex differences in learned helplessness: 11 the contingencies of evaluative feedback in the classroom. In *Developmental Psychology,* 14, pp. 268–76.

Dweck, C.S., Elliott, E.S. 1981: Achievement Motivation. In Mussem, P. (general ed.) and Hetherington, E.M. (volume ed.), *Carmichael's Manual of Child Psychology: Social and Personality Development.* J. Wiley, New York.

Eastgate, C. 1982: *Curricular guidance at 14+: teacher and pupil perspectives.* M. A. Thesis (unpublished). University of London, Institute of Education.

Ellis, R. and Whittington, D. 1981: *A Guide to Social Skills Training.* Croom Helm.

Eden, G. 1978: *School-parent communication: a study of parents' perceptions.* M. A. Thesis (unpublished). University of London, Institute of Education.

Education Resource Unit for YOP 1982: *Assessment in Youth Training: made-to-measure?* Jordanhill College of Education, Glasgow.

Eldridge, G. 1978: *A survey of changes in content and method of health education among young children in the UK since 1931.* M. Phil. Thesis (unpublished). University of London, Institute of Education.

Elliott, J. 1982: The idea of a pastoral curriculum: a reply to T. McLaughlin. *Cambridge Journal of Education,* 12 (1).

Elliott, J., Bridges, D., Ebbutt, D., Gibson, R. and Nias, J. 1981: *School Accountability.* SSRC/Grant McIntyre.

Evans, K. and Law, B. 1984: *Careers Guidance Integration Project: final report* (3 volumes). National Institute for Careers Education and Counselling.

Farrell, M. 1984: *Parental involvement with children's problems in school.* M. Ed. Thesis (in process). University of Durham.

FEU 1979: *A Basis for Choice.* DES.

FEU 1980: *Beyond Coping.* DES.

FEU 1981: *Towards a Guidance Base.* DES.

FEU 1982: *Skills for Living.* DES.

Fidge, E. 1978: *A study of parent attitudes towards sex education in the junior school.* M. A. Thesis (unpublished). University of London, Institute of Education.

Fitzgerald, K. and Bodiley, J. 1984: *Work Experience: a study of a school operated scheme.* Longman.

Fitzherbert, K. 1977 *Child Care Services and the Teacher.* Temple Smith.

Ford, J. 1969: *Social Class and the Comprehensive School.* Routledge and Kegan Paul.

Fraser, E. 1959: *Home Environment and the School.* University of London.

Freeman, M.D.A. 1983: *The Rights and Wrongs of Children.* Pinter.

French, R. 1982: *The concept of care: a complete process.* M. Ed. Thesis (unpublished). University of Warwick.

Friday, P. 1983: Pastoral care and the academic child. *Pastoral Care in Education,* 2 (1), pp. 15–23.

Fuller, M. 1980: Black girls in a London comprehensive. In Deem, R. (ed.), *Schooling for Women's Work.* Routledge and Kegan Paul.

Furlong, V. 1976: Interaction sets in the classroom towards a study of pupil knowledge. In Stubbs, M. and Delamont, S. (eds), *Explorations in Classroom Observation.* Wiley.

Galloway, D. 1981: *Teaching and Counselling: pastoral care in primary and secondary schools.* Longman.

Galloway, D. 1983: Disruptive pupils and effective care. In *School Organisation,* 3 (3), pp. 245–54.

Gath, D. *et al* 1977: *Child Guidance and Delinquency in a London Borough.* Oxford University Press.

Gibbs, G. 1981: *Teaching Students to Learn.* Open University Press.

Ginifer, H. 1972: *The role of the teacher in the organisation of pupil guidance in large urban schools.* M. Ed. Dissertation (unpublished). University of Newcastle-upon-Tyne.

Goacher, B. 1983: *Recording Achievement at 16+.* Schools Council/Longman.

Goodall, C. 1982: *School to work: a study of a pilot project.* M. A. Thesis (unpublished). University of London, Institute of Education.

Goodson, I.F. 1983: The use of life histories in the study of teaching. In Hammersley, M. (ed.), *The Ethnography of Schooling.* Nafferton Books.

Goodson, I.F. 1985: History, context and qualitative methods in the study of curriculum. In Burgess, R.G. (ed.), *Strategies of Educational Research: qualitative methods.* Falmer Press.

Grace, A. 1982: *Views of pastoral care by subject and pastoral heads of department.* B. Phil. (Ed.) Dissertation (unpublished). University of Birmingham.

Graef, R. 1980: The case study of Pandora's box. In Simons, H. (ed.), *Towards a Science of the Singular.* Norwich Centre for Applied Research in Education. Occasional publication no. 10, pp. 162–78.

Grafton, T., Miller, H., Smith L., Vegoda, M. and Whitfield, R. 1983: Gender and curriculum choice: a case study. In Hammersley, M. and Hargreaves, A. *Curriculum Practice: some sociological case sudies.* Falmer Press.

Grant, M. 1983: *The needs of teachers of disruptive and disturbed pupils in the ordinary (comprehensive) school.* M. Ed. Dissertation (unpublished). University of Birmingham.

Grant, P. 1982: *Moral objectivity: the presuppositions of pastoral care.* M. A. Thesis (unpublished). University of London, Institute of Education.

Gray, J., McPherson, A.F. and Raffe, D. 1983: *Reconstructions of Secondary Education.* Routledge and Kegan Paul.

Green, F. 1980: *Becoming a truant.* M. Sc. Thesis (unpublished). Cranfield Institute of Technology.

Griffiths, G. 1985: Doubts, dilemmas and diary keeping: some reflections on teacher-based research. In Burgess, R.G. (ed.), *Issues in Educational Research: qualitative methods.* Falmer Press.

Haigh, G. 1975: *Pastoral Care.* Pitman.

Halsall, E. 1971: *The Comprehensive School.*

Halsey, A.H. (ed.) 1972: *EPA: problems and policies.* HMSO.

Hamblin, D.H. 1978: *The Teacher and Pastoral Care.* Basil Blackwell.

Hamblin, D.H. (ed.) 1981a: *Problems and Practice of Pastoral Care.* Basil Blackwell.

Hamblin, D.H. 1981b: *Teaching Study Skills.* Basil Blackwell.

Hamblin, D.H. 1983: Counselling and pastoral care. In Cohen, L. and Manion, L. (eds): *Educational Research and Development in Britain 1970–1980.* NFER-Nelson.

Hamblin, D.H. 1984: *Pastoral Care – a training manual,* Basil Blackwell.

Hampshire Education Authority 1975: *Pastoral Care Arrangements in Secondary Schools.* Hampshire Education Authority.

Hargreaves, A. 1977: Progressivism and pupil autonomy. *Sociological Review,* 25 (3).

Hargreaves, D.H. 1967: *Social Relations in a Secondary School.* Routledge and Kegan Paul.

Hargreaves, D.H. 1972: *Interpersonal Relations and Education.* Routledge and Kegan Paul.

Hargreaves, D.H. 1982: *The Challenge for the Comprehensive School.* Routledge and Kegan Paul.

Harris, J. 1976: *Home/school and parent/teacher relations: a case study.* M. Ed. Dissertation (unpublished). University of Birmingham.

Harris, J. 1983: Teachers and social workers. *Pastoral Care in Education,* 1 (2).

Hattersley, R. 1983: *A Yorkshire Boyhood.* Chatto and Windus/The Hogarth Press.

Hayes, J. and Hopson, B. 1972: *Careers Guidance: the role of the school in vocational development.* Heinemann Educational Books.

Hayes, S. 1974: *16–19: pastoral care and authority.* M. Ed. Dissertation (unpublished). University of Birmingham.

Healy, M. and Goodhand, L. 1983. *Effective Learning Skills. a pupil guide.* ILEA.

Healy, M. 1984: Developing a social education programme: a case study. *Pastoral Care in Education,* 2 (2), pp. 93–98.

Henstock, E. 1982: *Aspects of pastoral care in two comprehensive schools: reflected in pupils' views of transfer from primary to secondary level.* M. Ed. Dissertation (unpublished). University of Birmingham.

HMI 1968: *Guidance in Scottish Secondary Schools.* HMSO.

HMI 1976: *Guidance in Scottish Secondary Schools.* HMSO.

HMI 1977: *Ten Good Schools.* HMSO.

HMI 1979: *Aspects of Secondary Education in England.* HMSO.

HMI 1980: *A View of the Curriculum.* HMI Services: Matters for Discussion 11. HMSO.

HMI 1982: *Pastoral Care in the Comprehensive Schools of Wales.* HMSO.

HMI 1982: *The New Teacher in School.* HMSO.

HMI 1983: *Records of Achievement at 16: some examples of current practice.* HMSO.

Hibberd, F. 1984a: The pastoral curriculum. *Pastoral Care in Education,* 2 (2).

Hibberd, F. 1984b: Does pastoral care need a theory of self? *Pastoral Care in Education,* 2 (3), pp. 174–8.

Hill, M. and Lloyd-Jones, M. 1970: *Sex Education: The Erroneous Zone.* National Secular Society.

Hilsum, S. and Cane, B.S. 1971: *The Teacher's Day.* NFER-Nelson.

Hilsum, S. and Strong, C. 1978: *The Secondary Teacher's Day.* NFER-Nelson.

Hitchcock, G. 1983: Profiles: A report arising from secondment to University of Bristol (unpublished). University of Bristol.

Hopson, B. and Hough, P. 1979: *Exercises in Personal and Career Development.* CRAC/Hobsons Press.

Hopson, B. and Scully, M. 1981: *Lifeskills Teaching.* McGraw-Hill.

Hopson, B. and Scully, M. 1982: *Lifeskills Teaching Programmes,* nos. 1 and 2. Lifeskills Associates.

Horsfield, J. and Shaw, J. 1984: Interview, intake and induction. *Pastoral Care in Education,* 2 (1), pp. 36–43.

Howard, A. 1958: Some methods of organising a comprehensive school. In NUT 1958: *Inside the Comprehensive School.* Schoolmaster Publishing.

Hoyle, E. 1974: Professionality, professionalism and control in teaching. In *London Educational Review,* 3 (2), pp. 13–19.

Hughes, M. and Ribbins, P.M. 1979: *Research and Educational Administration.* BEMAS.

Hughes, P.M. 1971: *Guidance and Counselling in Schools: a response to change.* Pergamon.

Hughes, P.M. 1980: Pastoral care: the historical context. In Best, R., Jarvis, C. and Ribbins, P.M. (eds), *Perspectives on Pastoral Care.* Heinemann Educational Books.

Hull, C. and Ruddock, J. 1981: The Effects of Systematic Induction Courses for Pupils' Perceptions of an Innovation. Final report of project HR 6848/1 to SSRC, (available from British Library).

Hurman, A. 1978: *A Charter for Choice.* NFER-Nelson.

Hutchinson, M. 1979: *Attitudes of three ethnic groups of children towards school and discipline.* B. Phil. (Ed.) Dissertation (unpublished). University of Birmingham.

ILEA 1960: *Non-attendance at school: some research findings*. ILEA.

ILEA 1980: *Consultation Paper on Curriculum in Schools*. ILEA.

ILEA, Division 2 1984: Transfer to secondary school. Internal DO2 circulation.

ILEA 1984: *Improving Secondary Schools*, Report on the curriculum and organisation of secondary schools. ILEA.

Irving, A. 1983: *Educating Information-Users*, British Library Research and Development Department.

Irving, A. 1985: *Study and Information Skills Across the Curriculum*. Heinemann Educational Books.

Irving, A. and Snape, W. 1979: *Educating Library Users in British Secondary Schools*. British Library Research and Development Report no. 5467, British Library, R and D Dept.

Jackson, D. 1978: *A comparative study of the perceptions of school pupils who are frequent absentees, and regular attenders*. M. Ed. Dissertation (unpublished). University of Sheffield.

Jackson, S. 1978: How to make babies: sexism in sex education. In *Women's Studies International Quarterly*, 1 (4) pp. 342–52.

Jackson, S. 1982: *Sexuality and Childhood*. Basil Blackwell.

Jamieson, I. and Lightfoot, M. 1982: *Schools and Industry*. Methuen.

Jayne, E. 1974: *Management Training for Senior Staff*. ILEA.

Jennings, A. 1979: *Discipline in Primary and Secondary Schools Today*. Ward Lock Educational.

John D. 1981: *Leadership in Schools*. Heinemann Educational Books.

Johnson, D. 1980: Secondary schools and neighbourhood welfare agencies. In Craft *et al* (eds) *Linking Home and School* (third edition). Harper and Row.

Johnson, D., Ransom, E., Packwood, T., Bowden, K. and Kogan, M. 1980: *Secondary Schools and the Welfare Network*. Allen and Unwin.

Johnson, D. 1982: Research into home/school relations, 1970/80. In Cohen, L. *et al* (eds), *Educational Research and Development in Britain 1979–1980*. NFER-Nelson.

Johnson, D. 1982: Families and Educational Institutions. In Rapoport, R.N. *et al* (eds), *Families in Britain*. Routledge and Kegan Paul.

Johnson, D. and Ransom, E. 1983: *Family and School*. Croom Helm.

Johnson, S. 1977: *School-based social workers in Haringey*. Centre for Information and Advice on Educational Disadvantage.

Joint Board for Pre-Vocational Education 1984: *The Certificate of Pre-Vocational Education*. B/TEC and CGLI.

Jones, A. 1979: *Counsellors in Practice*. Kogan Page.

Jones, A. and Forrest, R. 1977: *A Continuing Approach: Fairfax House and Group 4 at Sidney Stringer School*. Sidney Stringer School.

Jones, J. 1983: *The use employers make of examination results and other tests, for selection and employment*. An interim report for employers. University of Reading, School of Education.

Joy, M. 1981: *An exploration of the relationship between pastoral care and the curriculum: a study of two schools*. M. A. Thesis (unpublished). University of London, Institute of Education.

Kahn, J., Nursten, J. and Carroll, H. 1981: *Unwilling to School*. Pergamon.

Keys, W. and Ormerod, M.B. 1976: A comparison of the pattern of science subject choices for boys and girls in the light of the pupils' own expressed subject preferences. In *School Science Review*, 58 (203), pp. 348–50.

Khun, T. 1962: *The Structure of Scientific Revolutions*. Chicago University Press.

Killeen, J. and Watts, A.G. 1983: The place of research in careers guidance. *Careers Bulletin*, Spring 1983.

King, R. 1978: *All Things Bright and Beautiful*. Sage, California.

Kingston, W. and Rowbottom, R. 1983: *The new NHS districts and their units*. Working Paper HSOR, BIOSS, Brunel University.

Kitwood, T. 1980: *Disclosures to a Stranger*. Routledge and Kegan Paul.

Kohlberg, L. 1981 and 1983: The philosophy of moral development . In *Essays on moral development* (1); The psychology of moral development. In *Essays on moral development* (2). Harper and Row, USA.

Kyte, J. 1979: *Perspectives of pastoral care in a sixth form college*. B. Phil. (Ed.) Dissertation (unpublished). University of Birmingham.

Lacey, C. 1970: *Hightown Grammar: the school as a social system*. Manchester University Press.

Lago, C. and Ball, R. 1983: The almost impossible task: helping in a multi-racial context. In *Multi-racial Education*, 11 (2).

Lambert, K. 1984: Communication between home and school. *Pastoral Care in Education*, 2 (3) pp. 98–107.

Lang, P. 1977: 'It's easier to punish us in small groups.' In *Times Educational Supplement*, 6.5.77.

Lang, P. 1980: Pastoral care: problems and choices. In Raybould *et al* 1980: Helping the low achiever in the secondary school. *Educational Review* occasional publication no. 7.

Lang, P. 1981: Pastoral Care; the pupils' view. *Journal of West Midlands Association of Pastoral Care*, 2.

Lang, P. 1982a: *Pastoral care: concern or contradiction?* M. A. Thesis (unpublished). University of Warwick.

Lang, P. 1982b: How pupils see it: looking at how pupils perceive pastoral care. In *Pastoral Care in Education*, 1 (3).

Lang, P. 1983a: Review of *Perspectives in Pastoral Care* (Best, R., Jarvis, C. and Ribbins, P. (eds). In *Pastoral Care in Education*, 1, (1).

Lang, P. 1983b: Pastoral care: some reflections on possible influences, in *Pastoral Care in Education*, 2 (2). In Ribbins, P.M., Lang, P. and Healy, M. 1984: Editorial to *Pastoral Care in Education*, 2 (1).

Lang, P. 1984a: Pupils, problems and pastoral care. NAPCE seminar paper.

Lang, P. 1984b: Pastoral care and educational research. *Research Intelligence*, 15. BERA.

Lang, P. and Ribbins, P.M. 1983: *Pastoral Care in Action in 1983*. National Book League.

Lang, P. and Ribbins, P.M. 1985: Pastoral care in education. In Husen, T. and Postlethwaite, N. (eds), *International Encyclopaedia of Education*. Pergamon Press.

Langford, G. 1978: *Teaching as a Profession: an essay in the philosophy of education*. Manchester University Press.

Laslett, R. 1977: Disruptive and violent pupils: the facts and the fallacies. *Educational Review*, 29 (3).

Law, B. 1978: The concomitants of system orientation in secondary school counsellors. *British Journal of Guidance and Counselling*, 6 (2).

Law, B. 1981: Community interaction: a mid-range focus for theories of career development in young people. *British Journal of Guidance and Counselling*, 9 (2).

Law, B. 1982: *Beyond Schooling*. National Institute for Careers Education and Counselling.

Law, B. 1984: *The Uses and Abuses of Profiling*. Harper and Row.

Law, B. and Roberts, C. 1983: On leading horses to water. *NICEC Training and Development Bulletin*, 24.

Law, B. and Watts, A.G. 1977: *Schools, Careers and Community*. Church Information Office.

Lawrence, J. *et al* 1981: *Dialogue on Disruptive Behaviour: a study of a secondary school*. P.J.D. Press.

Leavold, J. 1977: *Care, control, and the urban school: a study of Downtown Sanctuary*. M. A. Dissertation (unpublished). University of London.

Lee, V. and Zeldin, D. (eds) 1982: *Challenge and Change in the Curriculum* and *Planning in the Curriculum*. Hodder and Stoughton, for the Open University.

Licht, B.G. and Dweck, C.S. 1983: Sex differences in achievement orientation: consequences for academic choice and attainments. In Marland, M. (ed.), *Sex Differentiation and Schooling*. Heinemann Educational Books.

Ling, R. 1983: A suspended sentence: the role of the LEA in the removal of disruptive pupils from school. *Pastoral Care in Education*, 1 (3).

Linguistic Minorities Project, 1985: *The Other Languages of England*, Routledge and Kegan Paul.

Llewelyn-Davies *et al* 1977: Birmingham home–school liaison officers. In *Educational Action Projects*, 1. Department of the Environment.

Lloyd, I. 1984: Does pastoral care need a theory of self? A reply to F. N. Hibberd. *Pastoral Care in Education*, 2 (3), pp. 178–182.

Lord, E. 1983: Pastoral care in education: principles and practice. *Pastoral Care in Education*, 1 (1), pp. 6–11.

Lunzer, E. and Gardner, K. 1979: *The Effective Use of Reading*. Heinemann Educational Books, for the Schools Council.

Lynch, J. (ed.) 1981: *Teaching in the Multi-Cultural School*. Ward Lock Educational.

Lyons, K. 1973: *Social Work and the School*. HMSO.

Lyons, K. 1980: School social work. In Craft, M. *et al* (eds), *Linking Home and School* (third edition). Harper and Row, pp. 233–43.

Macbeth, A.M. 1982: School politics in Europe: exchange bargaining or professional partnership? In *Educational Management and Administration*, 10 (2).

Macbeth, A.M. 1985: Parents, schools and pastoral care: some research priorities. In Lang, P. and Marland M. (eds) 1985: *New Directions in Pastoral Care*. Basil Blackwell.

Macbeth, A.M., Corner, T., Nisbet, N. and A., Ryan, D. and Strachan, D. 1984: *The child between: A report on school-family relations in the countries of the European Community*. Commission of the European Communities, Brussels, Education Series, No 13.

Macbeth, A.M., MacKenzie, M.L. and Breckenridge, I. 1980: *Scottish School Councils: policy-making, participation or irrelevance?* HMSO.

McGeeney, P. 1974: Reaching home. In Marland, M. *Pastoral Care*. Heinemann Educational Books.

McGuiness, J. 1982: *Planned Pastoral Care*. McGraw-Hill.

McKay, A. 1983: *Books 'N' Things*. National Association of Young People's Counselling and Advisory Services.

McLaughlin, T.H. 1982: The idea of a pastoral curriculum. *Cambridge Journal of Education*, 12 (1).

McLaughlin, T.H. 1983a: The pastoral curriculum: concept and principles. *Educational Analysis*, 5 (1).

McLaughlin, T.H. 1983b: The pastoral curriculum: concept and principle. *Educational Analysis* 5 (3).

Macmillan, K. 1977: *Education Welfare: strategy and structure*. Longman.

McPhail, P. *et al* 1972: *Moral Education in the Secondary School*. Longman.

Mace, R. 1980: *Teacher attitudes to pastoral care in two secondary schools*. B. Phil. (Ed.) Dissertation (unpublished). University of Birmingham.

Maher, P. and Best, R. 1984: *Training and Support for Pastoral Care*. NAPCE.

Manpower Services Commission 1984: *TVEI Review 1984*. Manpower Services Commission.

Marjoribanks, K. 1979: *Families and their Learning Environments: an empirical analysis*. Routledge and Kegan Paul.

Marjoribanks, K. 1983: Family Learning Environments: an overview. Advance paper for the EEC School and Family Conference, Luxembourg, 1983.

Marland, M. (ed.) 1973: *The Experience of Work: an anthology of prose*. NAPCE.

Marland, M. 1974: *Pastoral Care*. Heinemann Educational Books.

Marland, M. 1980a: The New Fourth-Year Curriculum. North Westminster Community School.

Marland, M. 1980b: The Pastoral Curriculum. In Best, R., Jarvis, C. and Ribbins, P. (eds) *Perspectives in Pastoral Care*. Heinemann Educational Books.

Marland, M. (ed.) 1981: *Information Skills in the Secondary Curriculum*, Schools Council Curriculum no. 9. Methuen Educational.

Marland, M. 1982: Preparing for promotion in pastoral care. In *Pastoral Care*, 1 (1). Basil Blackwell.

Marland, M. 1983: Parenting, schooling and mutual learning: a teacher's viewpoint. Paper for EEC School and Family Conference, Luxembourg, 1983.

Marland, M. (ed.) 1983: *Sex Differentiation and Schooling*. Heinemann Educational Books.

Marsden, D. and Duff, E. 1975: *Workless: some unemployed men and their families*. Penguin.

Marshall, T. 1980: Ethical and political aspects of counselling and social work. In Craft *et al* (eds) *Linking Home and School* (third edition). Harper and Row.

Maynard, A. 1975: *Experiment with choice in education*. Hobart Paper, Institute of Economic Affairs.

Meigham, R. 1981: *A Sociology of Education*. Holt, Rinehart and Winston.

Metcalf, T. *et al* 1982: *The Rowlinson School Pastoral System: a study in delegation*. Sheffield Papers in Educational Management.

Midwinter, E. 1973: *Patterns of Community Education*. Ward Lock.

Miller, G.W. 1971: *Educational Opportunity and the Home*. Longman.

Millerson, G. 1973: Education in the professions. In *Education and the Professions*, History of Educ. Soc., Methuen.

Milner, D. 1983: *Children and Race*. Ward Lock Educational.

Milner, P. 1980: Guidance and counselling: changing patterns of care in schools. In Best, R., Jarvis, C. and Ribbins, P. (eds), *Perspectives on Pastoral Care*. Heinemann Educational Books.

Moore, B.M. 1970: *Guidance in Comprehensive Schools*. NFER-Nelson.

Moore, W.E. 1973: *In Loco Parentis*. Centre for Research in Measurement and Evaluation, Sydney, Australia.

Morgan, J. 1984: *Pastoral care in the sixth form: a phenomenological analysis of actors' accounts in an upper school*. M. Ed. Dissertation (unpublished). University of Birmingham.

Mortimore, J. and Blackstone, T. 1982: *Disadvantage and Education*. Heinemann Educational Books.

Mortimore, P. and J. 1981: How to get the most out of the school night-shift. In *The Guardian*, 7 April 1981.

Mowforth, J. 1979: *A discussion of the balance and breadth of knowledge in the curriculum for fourth and fifth year pupils*. M. A. Thesis (unpublished). University of London, Institute of Education.

Murgatroyd, S. and Wolfe, R. 1982: *Coping with Crisis: understanding and helping people in need*. Harper and Row.

Murphy, S. 1984: *Moral dissonance in secondary schools*. M. Phil. Thesis (unpublished). University of Exeter.

Mwale, J. 1979: *Transition and continuity: a survey of pupils' attitudes and their perceptions of the school following transfer from primary to secondary education*. M. A. Thesis (unpublished). University of London, Institute of Education.

Myres, K. 1980: *Sex stereotyped at option choice: an attempt at intervention*. M. A. Thesis (unpublished). University of London, Institute of Education.

NACRO Working Group 1984: *School Reports in the Juvenile Court*. NACRO.

Nagra, J. and Ribbins, P.M. 1984: Counselling in a multi racial educational setting. *The Counsellor*, 4 (1), pp. 39–51.

Nash, R. 1973: *Classrooms Observed*. Routledge and Kegan Paul.

Nixon, J. (ed.) 1981: *A Teacher's Guide to Action Research*. Grant McIntyre.

247

Nordling, J.A. 1978: The high school library and the classroom: closing the gap. In Lubans, J. jnr (ed.), 1978: *Progress in Educating the Library User*. Bowker.

O'Connor, D.J. 1957: *An Introductin to the Philosophy of Education*. Routledge and Kegan Paul.

Ormerod, M.B. *et al* 1979: Girls and physics education. In *Physics Education*, 14, pp. 271–7.

Ormerod, M.B. with Duckworth, D. 1975: *Pupils' Attitudes to Science: a review of the research*. NFER-Nelson.

Oxford Certificate of Educational Achievement 1984: *The Personal Record Component: a draft handbook for schools*. OCEA.

Parkes, K. 1983: *The education welfare service: a study of the service in Warwickshire*. M. Ed. Dissertation (unpublished). University of Birmingham.

Pashley, B. and Shepherd, A. 1975: Student welfare and guidance: the pastoral role of the academic. *British Journal of Guidance and Counselling*, 3 (1).

Pashley, B. and Shepherd, A. 1978: How university members see the pastoral role of the academic. *British Journal of Guidance and Counselling*, 6 (1).

Paul, C. 1983: Consistency of aim not treatment. *Pastoral Care in Education*, 1 (2), pp. 129–132.

Peers, I. 1981: *Dealing with Solvent Misuse*. TACADE.

Peterson, L.J., Rossmiller, R.A. and Volz, M.M. 1978: *The Law on Public School Operation*. Harper and Row.

Plowden, B. 1971: Foreword. In Miller, G.W. *Educational Opportunity and the Home*. Longman.

Plummer, K. 1983: *Documents of Life*. Allen and Unwin.

Pollard, A. 1985: Opportunities and difficulties of a teacher-ethnographer: a personal account. In Burgess, R.G. (ed.), *Field Methods in the Study of Education*. Falmer Press, pp. 216–33.

Power, M. 1967: *Delinquent schools*. New Society, 10 (264).

Preedy, M. 1981: Pastoral Care and Guidance. Block 5 of E323 *Management and the School*. Open University Press.

Pring, R.A. 1981: Behavior modification: some reservations. In *Perspectives 5*. University of Exeter School of Education.

Pring, R.A. 1984: *Personal and Social Education in the Curriculum*. Hodder and Stoughton.

Pulbrook, R. 1962: Teachers as pastors. *Learning for Living*, 1 (4).

Purnell, C. 1983: Towards a personal and social development programme for an open access sixth form. *Pastoral Care in Education*, 1 (3), pp. 180–9.

Pyke, J. 1984: *The development and evaluation of a life skills programme*. M. Ed. Dissertation (unpublished). University of Durham.

Raven, J. 1982: Educational home visiting and the growth of competence and confidence in adults and children. In *Curriculum Inquiry*, 12 (1), pp. 87–104.

Reed, B.D. and Bazalgette, J. 1983: TWL network and schools. In Watts, A.G. (ed.), *Work Experience and Schools*. Heinemann Educational Books.

Reid, K. 1980: *Persistent school absenteeism*. Ph. D. Thesis (unpublished). University of Wales.

Reid, M.I., Barnett, B.R. and Rosenberg, H.A. 1974: *A Matter of Choice*, NFER-Nelson.

Reynolds, D. 1976: The delinquent school. In Hammersley, M. and Woods, P. (eds), *The Process of Schooling*. Routledge and Kegan Paul.

Reynolds, D. and Murgatroyd, S. 1977: The sociology of schooling and the absent pupil. In Carroll, H. (ed.), *Absenteeism in South Wales: studies of pupils, their homes and their secondary schools*. University College of Swansea.

Ribbins, P.A. 1983: *Towards an evaluation of a pastoral care and social education programme in the fourth year of a developing comprehensive school*. B. Ed. Dissertation (unpublished). College of St Marks and St Johns.

Ribbins, P.M. (ed.) 1985: *Schooling and Welfare*, Falmer Press.

Ribbins, P.M. 1985: The welfare curriculum and the work of the school. In Ribbins, P.M. (ed.) 1985: *Schooling and Welfare*, Falmer Press.

Ribbins, P.M., Best, R. and Jarvis, C. 1977: A phenomenological critique of some pastoral care concepts. *Educational Adminstration*, 5 (2).

Ribbins, P.M., Best, R. and Jarvis, C. 1982: *Teacher attitudes to pastoral care*. Unpublished research report of part of an SSRC–funded study.

Ribbins, P.M., Best, R., Jarvis, C. and Oddy, D. 1981: Meanings and contexts: the problem of interpretation in the study of a school. In Ribbins, P.M. and Thomas, H. (eds), *Research in Educational Management and Administration*. BEMAS.

Ribbins, P.M. and Nagra, J. 1981: Counselling in a multi-racial setting: some reflections on the activities of an Indian school councillor. *The Counsellor*, 3 (3).

Ribbins, P.M. and Ribbins, P.A. 1983: The conversation of care. *Educational Review*, 35. (1).

Roberts, B. 1977: Treating children in secondary schooling. *Educational Review*, 29 (3).

Robinson, E. 1978: *Drugs and Young People*. University of Aston.

Robinson, M. 1978: *Schools and Social Work*. Routledge and Kegan Paul.

Rogers, C. 1982: *A Social Psychology of Schooling*. Routledge and Kegan Paul.

Rose, G. and Marshall, T. 1975: *Counselling and School Social Work*. John Wiley and Son.

Rossborough, P. 1982: *Towards the practice of positive pastoral care*. M. Ed. Dissertation (unpublished). University of Warwick.

Roth, J.A. 1970: Comments on 'secret observation'. In Filstead, W.J. (ed.), *Qualitative Methodology: firsthand involvement with the social world*. Markham, Chicago, pp. 278–80.

Ruddock, J. and Hull, C. 1981: Pupils' group of classroom process. Paper to Educational Research Association.

Rutherford, R. and Edgar, E. 1979: *Teachers and Parents: a guide to interaction and co-operation*. Allyn and Bacon. Quoted in Wolfendale, S. 1983: *Parental Participation in Children's Development and Education*. Gordon and Breach.

Rutter, M. 1975: *Helping Troubled Children*. Penguin.

Rutter, M., Maughan, B., Mortimore, P., Ouster, J. and Smith A. 1979: *Fifteen Thousand Hours: Secondary schools and their effects on pupils*. Open Books.

Schools Council/Health Education Project 1983: *Health Education 13–18*. Forbes Publications/Holmes McDougall.

Schostak, J.F. and Logan T. (eds) 1984: *Pupil Experience*. Croom Helm.

Schostak, J.F. 1984: The revelation of the world of pupils. In Schostak, J.F. and Logan, T. (eds), *Pupil Experience*. Croom Helm

Schostak, J.F. 1984: A day in the life . . . a study of pastoral care. Paper presented at The Effective Curriculum Conference, St Hilda's College, Oxford, September 1984.

Scott, L. 1979: *A critical review of changing concepts of health in selected aspects of the curriculum*. M. A. Thesis (unpublished). University of London, Institute of Education.

Scottish Council for Research in Education 1977: *Pupils in Profile*. Hodder and Stoughton, for Scottish Council for Research in Education.

Scottish Education Department 1968: *Guidance in Scottish Secondary Schools*. HMSO.

Sharp, R. and Green, A. 1975: *Education and Social Control*. Routledge and Kegan Paul.

Sharpe, A. 1981: The significance of classroom dissent. *Scottish Educational Review*, 13 (2).

Shaw, J. 1980: *Sex education as an example of curricular integration*. M. A. Thesis (unpublished). University of London, Institute of Education.

Shayer, M. and Adey, P. 1981: *Towards a Science of Science Teaching*. Heinemann Educational Books.

Sherman, H. and Wood, J. 1979: *Sociology: traditional and radical perspectives*. Harper and Row.

Shoesmith, C. 1982: *The suspension of children from comprehensive school in two authorities*. M. Ed. Dissertation (unpublished). University of Birmingham.

Simon, B. 1984: To whom do schools belong? *Forum* 27 (10).

Simpson, P. 1983: The role of the home–school liaison teacher in the Birmingham Education Authority: a personal viewpoint. Advance paper for the EEC School and Family Conference, Luxembourg, 1983.

Skinner, A. with Platts, H. and Hill, B. 1983: *Disaffection From School: issues and interagency responses*. National Youth Bureau.

Smith, E. 1981: *A study of home/school relations in five primary schools*. M. Ed. Dissertation (unpublished). University of Birmingham.

Smith, I.R.H. 1984: Curriculum Guidance and Differentiation at 14+. End-of-grant report to SSRC on Grant c/00/23/0039/1.

Social Work Services Group 1980: *Working Together for Children in Trouble*. Scottish Education Project.

Sockett, H., Bailey, C., Bridges, D., Elliott, J., Gibson, R., Scrimshaw, P. and White, J. 1980: *Accountability in the English Educational System*. Hodder and Stoughton.

Southgate, V., Arnold, H. and Johnson, S. 1981: *Extending Beginning Reading*. Heinemann Educational Books, for the Schools Council.

Speight, E. 1981: *Sex Education: a guide to resources.* Sheffield Central Library.

Squires, A. 1982: *Pastoral care in the urban school.* M. A. Dissertation (unpublished). University of London, Institute of Education.

Stakes, J. 1984: *Life and social skills in a comprehensive school with special reference to pupils with special educational needs.* M. Ed. Dissertation (unpublished). University of Durham.

Stenhouse, L. 1975: *An Introduction to Curriculum Research and Development.* Heinemann Educational Books.

Stenhouse, L. 1979: Using research means doing research. In Dahl, H. *et al* (eds), *Pedagogikkens Skelys.* Universitets Forlaget, Oslo.

Stenhouse, L. 1981: Using case study in library research. *Social Science Information Studies*, 1, pp. 221–30.

Stenhouse, L. 1984: Library access, library use and user education in academic sixth forms: an autobiographical account. In Burgess, R.G. (ed.), *The Research Process in Educational Settings: ten case studies.* Falmer Press, pp. 211–33.

Stenhouse, L., Verma, G.K., Wild, R.D. and Nixon, J. 1982: *Teaching about Race Relations.* Routledge and Kegan Paul.

Stephenson, M. 1982: the development of schools as pastoral centres. *West Midlands Journal of Pastoral Care in Education*, 3.

Stephenson, M. 1983: *Secondary schools as pastoral centres.* M. Ed. Dissertation (unpublished). University of Birmingham.

Swales, T. 1980: *Record of Personal Achievement: an independent evaluation of the Swindon RAP Scheme.* Schools Council.

Tattum, D. 1982: *Disruptive Pupils in Schools and Units.* John Wiley and Son.

Taylor, D. and Harris, P.L. 1981: Knowledge of strategies for the expression of emotion among normal and maladjusted boys. In *Journal of Child Psychology and Psychiatry*, 24, 1, pp. 141–5.

Taylor, M. 1980: The language of pastoral care. In Best *et al* 1980: *Perspectives on Pastoral Care.* Heinemann Educational Books.

Taylor, P. 1984: Pastoral care and in-service training. *Pastoral Care in Education*, 2 (3), pp. 218–23.

Thompson, B. 1975: Secondary school pupils: attitudes to schools and teachers. *Educational Research*, 18 (1).

Thorp, J. 1980: *From primary school to secondary school.* B. Phil. (Ed.) Dissertation (unpublished). University of Birmingham.

Thorp, J. 1983: Evaluating practice: pupils' views of transfer. *Pastoral Care in Education* 1 (1), pp. 45–52.

Turner, G. 1983: *The Social World of the Comprehensive School.* Croom Helm.

United Nations 1959: *United Nations Declaration of the Rights of the Child.* Quoted in total as an appendix in Freeman, M.D.A. 1983: *The Rights and the Wrongs of Children.* Pinter, pp. 283–5.

Vaughan, T. 1975: *Education and the Aims of Counselling.* Basil Blackwell.

Vousden, B. 1983: *A view of a whole school pastoral curriculum.* M. Ed. Dissertation (unpublished). University of Warwick.

Wakeman, B. 1984: *Personal, Social and Moral Education*, Lion Books.

Walker, R. and Wiedel, J. 1984: Using photographs in a discipline of words. In Burgess, R.G. (ed.), *Field Methods in the Study of Education*. Falmer Press, pp. 191–216.

Wasserman, E. and Garrod, A. 1983: Application of Kohlberg's theory to curricula and democratic schools. *Education Analysis* 5 (1).

Watkins, C. 1985: A NAPCE policy statement on the initial training of teachers. *Pastoral Care in Education*, 3 (1), pp. 71–8.

Watson, P. 1979: *A survival kit: a study of teachers' attitudes towards careers education for girls*. M. A. Thesis (unpublished). University of London, Institute of Education.

Watts, A.G. and Kidd, J.M. 1978: Evaluating effectiveness of careers guidance: a review of the British research, *Journal of Occupational Psychology*, 51 (3).

Watts, A.G. 1983a: *Work Experience and Schools*. Heinemann Educational Books.

Watts, A.G. 1983b: *Education, Unemployment and the Future of Work*. Open University Press.

Watts, A.G. and Ballantine, M. 1983: Computers in careers guidance: the British experience. *The Counselling Psychologist*, 2 (4).

Watts, A.G., Super, D.E. and Kidd, J.M. (eds), *Career Development in Britain*. CRAC Hobsons Press.

Wax, M.L. and Wax, R. 1971: Great tradition, little tradition and formal education. In Wax, M.L., Diamond, S. and Gearing, F.O. (eds), *Anthropological Perspectives on Education*. Basic Books, New York, pp. 3–18.

Weddon, M. 1979: Some implications for education of the concept of the person. Ph. D. Thesis (unpublished). University of London, Institute of Education.

Weeks, M.S. 1984: *A Brief Description of the Growth and Progress of the Clywd Pastoral Care Professional Development Programme*. NAPCE.

Welton, J. 1983: Pastoral care in the social division of welfare. *Pastoral Care in Education*, 1 (2).

Welton J. and Dwyer, S. 1982: Schools in the welfare network: a report of the home–school links project. Unpublished report to the Department of Education for Northern Ireland and the Department of Health and Social Services.

Went, D. 1984: *Sex Education: some guidelines for teachers*. Bell and Hyman.

West Sussex County Council 1983: *Handbook for Pastoral Heads*. West Sussex Education Department.

White, J. 1982: *The Aims of Education Restated*. Routledge and Kegan Paul.

White, R. and Brockington, D. 1983: *Tales out of School*. Routledge and Kegan Paul.

Whitmore, K., Bax, M., Watt, C. and Hall, K. 1984: *Health and Psychological Services in Inner City Primary Schools*. North Westminster Community School.

Wilcox, B. and Lavercombe, S. 1984: Preparation for life: curriculum and issues. In Varlaam, C. (ed.), *Rethinking Transition: educational innovation and the transition to adult life*. Falmer Press.

Williamson, D. 1980: Pastoral care: or pastoralization. In Best, R., Jarvis, C., Ribbins, P. (eds), *Perspectives on Pastoral Care*. Heinemann Educational Books.

Willis, P. 1977: *Learning to Labour: how working class kids get working class jobs.* Saxon House.

Wilson, H. 1980: Parental supervision: a neglected aspect of delinquency. In *The British Journal of Criminology*, 20 (3), pp. 203–35.

Wilson, H. and Herbert, G.W. 1978: *Parents and Children in the Inner City.* Routledge and Kegan Paul.

Wilson, J. and Cowell, B. 1983: First steps in pastoral care. *Pastoral Care in Education*, 1 (2).

Winter, R. 1983: The politics of reality construction: action research and pastoral care. *Pastoral Care in Education*, 1 (3), pp. 210–13.

Wolfendale, S. 1983: *Parental Participation in Children's Development and Education.* Gordon and Breach.

Woods, N.E. 1983: The structure and practice of pastoral care at Oakfield School. M. Ed. Dissertation (unpublished). University of Birmingham.

Woods. P. 1976: The myth of subject choice. In *British Journal of Sociology*, 27 (2), pp. 130–49.

Woods, P. 1978: Negotiating demands of schoolwork. In *Curriculum Studies*, 10 (4), pp. 309–27.

Woods, P. 1979: *The Divided School.* Routledge and Kegan Paul.

Woods, P. 1983: *Sociology and the School: an interactionist viewpoint.* Routledge and Kegan Paul.

Working Party into the Education of Bilingual Learners in Division Two of the ILEA, chaired by Marland, M. and Goodhand, L. 1985: *The Education of Bilingual Learners, Towards a Coherent Policy*, ILEA, Division Two.

Wright, H. and Payne, T. 1979: *An Evaluation of a School Psychological Service: the Portsmouth Pattern.* Hampshire Education Department.

Young, P. 1979: *Pastoral care: a critique of its organisation in two secondary schools.* B. Phil. (Ed.) Dissertation (unpublished). University of Birmingham.

Zeldin, D. 1983: *Strategies in Curriculum Planning.* Open University.